THE EXTENDED FAMILY
Women and Political Participation in India and Pakistan

By the Same Author

THE KHILAFAT MOVEMENT : Religious Symbolism and Political Mobilization in India

The Extended Family
Women and Political Participation in India and Pakistan

Edited By
Gail Minault

South Asia Books

HQ 1743
. E95x

Copyright © Gail Minault 1981

South Asia Books, Columbia, Missouri.

ISBN : 0-8364-0765-2

First Edition : 1981

Printed in India at Kay Kay Printers,
150 D Kamla Nagar, Delhi-110007

To
LAILA
My little Indian woman

PREFACE

The nucleus of this volume was a panel at the fifth Berkshire Conference on the History of Women held at Mt. Holyoke College, in August, 1978. Barbara Ramusack had organized the panel around the question of women's participation in the Indian nationalist movement and its contribution to the attainment of women's rights. Geraldine Forbes, Ramusack, and I presented papers examining various aspects of that question based on our recent research, and we agreed to try and publish our papers as a group. A number of other scholars doing research on Indian women had also written about women's political participation, whether before or after independence, and thus it seemed to me that a volume incorporating new work on this theme would be a useful addition to the history of South Asian Women.

Encouraged by Gerald Barrier of South Asia Books, I agreed to edit the volume and wrote to a number of scholars with whose work I was familiar. Several people contributed revised versions of papers previously presented at conferences, others wrote articles specifically for this volume, and still others suggested names of scholars working in the field. The volume as it now stands therefore represents an informal network of scholarly contacts and is by no means exhaustive. There are doubtless many others working on various aspects of this theme, just as there are a number of issues I had hoped to see addressed here which are not. Research in the field of women's history in South Asia is just beginning, and many of the conclusions reached in these articles may be revised. Beyond asking the contributors to address the general theme of women's political participation, and exercizing a reasonably firm editorial hand, I made no attempt to control the content of these articles. There is certainly no attempt at ideological or methodological uniformity. The contributors are historians, sociologists, political scientists. The sources are many and varied, so too are the questions raised. These articles, and the research on which they are based, represent a small proportion of current work on the history of South Asian Women. We hope that these contributions will arouse further interest in and investigation of this history.

The articles by Karen and John Leonard and by Mary Katzenstein were originally presented, in somewhat different form at the Wellesley Conference on Women and National Development in June, 1976. Mary Katzenstein's article, "Toward Equality? Cause and Consequence of the Political Prominence of Women in India," was subsequently published in *Asian Survey* in May, 1978 and is reprinted here by permission of the Regents of the University of California. The articles by Geraldine Forbes, Barbara Ramusack, and Gail Minault are considerably revised versions of papers presented at the Berkshire Conference on the History of Women in August, 1978. Sylvia Chipp-Kraushaar's article was originally presented in an earlier form at the South-West Conference of Asian Studies, Houston, Texas in October, 1975. The articles by David Gilmartin, Gail Pearson, Shahida Lateef, and Amrita Basu were written for this volume, as was the introduction.

Acknowledgements are due to Gerald Barrier for encouraging this enterprise, to David Lelyveld, Geraldine Forbes, and Annette Weiner for critical comments on my articles, and to Robert Crunden, colleague, sounding board, and mate, for providing a summer of reasonable peace and quiet while the editorial work proceeded. The American Institute of Indian Studies has provided research grants at one time or another to the Leonards, Forbes, Minault, Ramusack, Basu, and Katzenstein, and it is safe to say that without that beneficient institution this volume could not exist. David Gilmartin's research in Pakistan and India was carried out under a Fulbright grant. Gail Pearson's work in India was supported by an Australian Commonwealth scholarship. The University of Texas Research Institute provided a small grant to aid in preparing the manuscript for the press. To all these funding organizations, my fellow contributors and I express thanks. Bharat Bhatt was kind enough to contact Sandra Hannum, who produced the maps for Amrita Basu's article. Finally my special thanks go to Sandra Martin and Connie Averyt, both of the staff of the Center for Asian Studies at the University of Texas, who typed the final manuscript, often from heavily edited copy.

The volume is dedicated to my daughter, Laila Minault, who may not yet understand the concept of freedom, but who will doubtless grow to appreciate it.

Austin, Texas and GAIL MINAULT
Port Lorne, Nova Scotia
1980

LIST OF CONTRIBUTORS

AMRITA BASU is a PhD candidate in Political science at Columbia University, from which she also holds an MA. Her dissertation research deals with economic marginalization and political protest among rural women in India. She has published several articles on Indian women and is currently a Research Assistant at the Center for the Social Sciences, Columbia University.

SYLVIA CHIPP-KRAUSHAAR received a PhD in social sciences from Syracuse University in 1970 with a dissertation entitled "The Role of Women Elites in a Modernizing Country: The All-Pakistan Women's Association." She is the editor, with Justin J. Green, of *Asian Women in Transition* (Pennsylvania State University Press, 1980). She was Associate Professor of Political Science at Northeastern State University, Tahlequah, Oklahoma until June, 1980.

GERALDINE FORBES received a PhD in history from the University of Illinois at Urbana in 1972 and is Associate Professor of History at the State University of New York, College at Oswego. She is the author of *Positivism in Bengal* (Calcutta: Minerva, 1975), winner of the Rabindranath Tagore Memorial Prize in 1979, and of numerous articles. She edited *A Pattern of Life*: *The memoirs of an Indian Woman* by Shudha Mazumdar (New Delhi: Manohar, 1977), and is currently writing a history of the Indian Women's movement.

DAVID GILMARTIN received a PhD in history from the University of California, Berkeley in 1979. His dissertation was entitled "Tribe, Land, and Religion in the Punjab: Muslim Politics and the making of Pakistan." His article, "Religious Leadership and the Pakistan Movement in the Punjab," appeared in *Modern Asian Studies* (July, 1979). He was a visiting Assistant Professor at the University of Arizona in 1979-80, and a Lecturer in History at the University of California, Berkeley in winter 1981.

MARY FAINSOD KATZSENSTEIN holds an MSc from School of Oriental and African Studies, University of London, and a PhD in political science from the Massachusetts Institute of Technology. She is Associate Professor of Political Science at Cornell University. Her publications include *Ethnicity and Equality: The Shiv Sena Party and Preferential Policies in Bombay* (Cornell University Press, 1979) and *India's Preferential Policies: Migrants, the Middle Classes and Ethnic Equality*, co-authored with Myron Weiner (Chicago, 1981), and numerous articles.

SHAHIDA LATEEF holds an MA from Delhi School of Economics and is a candidate for a D. Phil at the Institute for Development Studies, Sussex University. She served on one of the committees which contributed to *Towards Equality: Report of the Committee on the Status of Women in India* (1974), and is a fellow of the Indian Council for Social Science Research.

JOHN G. LEONARD received a PhD in history from the University of Wisconsin in 1970 with a dissertation entitled "Viresalingam and Modern Andhra; A Biography of an Indian Social Reformer." His articles have appeared in *Modern Asian Studies* and the *Journal of Commonwealth Political Studies*. He was a member of the History Department at the University of California, San Diego, and is currently a Senior Financial Analyst in the Finance Office, University of California, Los Angeles.

KAREN I. LEONARD holds MA and PhD degrees from the University of Wisconsin and is Associate Professor of Social Relations at the University of California Irvine. She is the author of *Social History of an Indian Caste : The Kayasths of Hyderabad* (University of California Press, 1978) and numerous articles, including "The 'Great Firm' Theory of Mughal Decline," *Comparative Studies in Society and History* (April, 1979).

GAIL MINAULT holds MA and PhD degrees in South Asian Studies from the University of Pennsylvania, and is Associate Professor of History at the University of Texas,

LIST OF CONTRIBUTORS

Austin. Her publications include *The Khilafat Movement: Religious Symbolism and Political Mobilization in India* (Columbia University Press, 1981), and several articles. In addition to editing the current volume, she is working on a history of women's education among Indian Muslims.

GAIL PEARSON received a PhD from Jawaharlal Nehru University in 1979 with a thesis entitled "Women in Public Life in Bombay City with Special Reference to the Civil Disobedience Movement." She is currently a tutor in the School of History, University of New South Wales.

BARBARA N. RAMUSACK received a PhD in history from the University of Michigan in 1969. She is the author of *The Princes of India in the Twilight of Empire: Dissolution of a Patron-Client System, 1914-1939* (Ohio State University Press, 1978), and several articles. She is Professor of History and Director of Graduate Studies in History at the University of Cincinnati.

CONTENTS

Preface vii

List of Contributors xi

PART I: EXTENDING WOMEN'S REALM BEYOND THE FAMILY   1

1. Introduction: The Extended Family as Metaphor and the Expansion of Women's Realm—*Gail Minault*   3

2. Social Reform and Women's Participation in Political Culture: Andhra and Madras—*Karen I. Leonard and John G. Leonard*   19

PART II: WOMEN'S RIGHTS AND POLITICAL INDEPENDENCE IN SOUTH ASIA   47

3. The Indian Women's Movement: A Struggle for Women's Rights or National Liberation?—*Geraldine Forbes*   49

4. Sisterhood or Separation? The All-India Muslim Ladies' Conference and the Nationalist Movement—*Gail Minault*   83

5. **Catalysts or Helpers?** British Feminists, Indian Women's Rights, and Indian Independence—*Barbara N. Ramusack* — 109

6. **Kinship, Women, and Politics in Twentieth-Century Punjab**—*David Gilmartin* — 151

7. **Nationalism, Universalization, and the Extended Female Space in Bombay City**—*Gail Pearson* — 174

PART III: WOMEN'S RIGHTS AND POLITICAL PARTICIPATION IN CONTEMPORARY INDIA AND PAKISTAN — 193

8. **The Indian Women's Movement and National Development : An Overview**—*Shahida Lateef* — 195

9. **Two Faces of Protest** : Alternative Forms of Women's Mobilization in West Bengal and Maharashtra—*Amrita Basu* — 217

10. **The All-Pakistan Women's Association and the 1961 Muslim Family Laws Ordinance**—*Sylvia Chipp-Kraushaar* — 263

11. **Towards Equality?** Cause and Consequence of the Political Prominence of Women in India—*Mary Fainsod Katzenstein* — 286

INDEX — 304

PART I

EXTENDING WOMEN'S REALM BEYOND THE FAMILY

1
Introduction:
The Extended Family as Metaphor and the Expansion of Women's Realm

GAIL MINAULT

The extended family in India is the subject of much study and controversy. Anthropologists and sociologists have analyzed its cyclical development and predicted its demise, prematurely. Novelists and diarists have portrayed extended family life, extolled it for providing the resiliency and continuity of the culture, and deplored it as a brake on individual development and expression. The extended family is not, and may never have been, the predominant living pattern in India, and yet, it is still regarded as the norm. The reason for this is that the extended family, whether living under the same roof or not, provides the individual with essential points of reference. One's identity depends upon membership in a kin group, so does access to property, and the choice of a marriage partner. In fact, a whole variety of life choices depend less on individual preference than on the family: what sort of education to pursue, the choice of a profession, the number of children to have, whether the wife should work, and whether to make certain major purchases. If group solidarity limits individual choices, however, it also holds a number of advantages: Affective bonds can be strong; reciprocal obligations are respected, and support is usually available in times of trouble. A widowed daughter can return to her natal family; the aged can live out their lives among kin; a distant cousin can find a place to stay when arriving from his native village or even from overseas. The extended family provides a variety of social services and does so more humanly, and usually more humanely, than public institutions.

The extended family, in its many forms and through its manifold services, thus assumes importance, not only as a social norm, but also in the Indian imagination. The family can be an incubus, but it can also be a metaphor for broader social concerns. A social reformer might regard those whom he seeks to help as his family (and if they are his caste fellows, they could well be). The disciples of a Sufi *pir* or the inhabitants of an ashram may regard themselves as an extended family, with similar lines of authority and division of duties and property. The students of a college, especially one with a residential tradition, look upon themselves as the sons and daughters of their *alma mater,* with an obligation to support her even after they have left the hearth.[1] National leaders regard the nation as their family writ large, and are referred to in return affectionately as "Bapuji" or "Chachaji." The Indian extended family, with its ability to expand virtually indefinitely through the device of fictive kin—the bevy of aunties, uncles, brothers, and sisters adopted through friendship, and thereby granted mutual rights and obligations—provides a model for extending one's concerns beyond the kin group.

Familial terms of reference used metaphorically in public discourse are not unique to the Indian subcontinent, of course, but the variety and persistence of such references in India are remarkable. There is a good historical explanation for this phenomenon, resting upon the kin-like structures of traditional social and political life. The Mughal system of administration was based on local lineages, which exchanged goods and services among themselves according to hierarchical relationships. Locally prominent lineage groups were then tied to the imperial system through similar patron-client relationships, ceremonially affirmed. The system tended to discourage broad-based social solidarity in favor of vertical and personalized relationships, both locally, and between local notables and the ruler. Other social relationships mirrored these personalized or kin-like ties: Patron-client relationships also existed in urban *muhallas*, and the relationship of religious teacher to his network of disciples was personalized and ritually confirmed. Such kin-like networks undoubtedly preceded Mughal rule in Hindu as well as Muslim states, though the Mughals were particularly capable, for a time, of using them for their dynastic purposes.[2]

Women were an important component of this traditional structure of authority, if not as individuals, then as links between lineage groups. Brides were items of exchange in marriage networks, and by cementing alliances between important lineages, they could be of considerable political importance. But wives were not simply commodities of exchange, they were also the mothers of the next generation, and as such were the media for the transmission of inheritance, even when they did not inherit property themselves. It follows that a woman gained prestige and influence within her conjugal family to the degree that she produced heirs, that is, sons. A woman's traditional role was thus two-fold and normatively ambiguous. As a wife, she was under the control of her conjugal family, ideally self-effacing and obedient. As a mother, she was nurturing but also punishing. She could be fearful, and increasingly with age, powerful and self-sufficient. An older woman would have some say in the matter of her sons' and daughters' marriages, further cementing alliances with other influential and landed lineages, decisions which had political ramifications. In her supervisory capacity at home, the older woman also helped manage the property, dispense food to dependents and servants, husband resources in times of scarcity, carry out important life-cycle rituals and acts of religious patronage (such as gifts to brahmins or *pirs*), and even regulate the sexual contact between her sons and daughters-in-law. A woman therefore had several roles in an extended family, any of which could have political importance. She was a commodity of exchange and a vehicle for propagating the line, but she also developed into an individual whose decisions could influence the career of the lineage, its marital and political alliances, its material prosperity, its moral and ritual status. Women exercized power, both as individuals and as members of the group, to the degree that decisions made in the private sphere—the women's realm—influenced the fortunes of the family in the public sphere, dominated by men.[3]

These generalizations not only apply to pre-British India, but to later periods as well, for the kin-based nature of political authority was slow to yield to more impersonal forms of administration during the period of British rule, and in some areas persists to the present. The British, as successors to the Mughals in North India, sought to incorporate the king-like structures of native authority into their own administrative system, thereby helping to insure their survival. British identification of "tribal" groups in the Punjab and their legislation for such groups in land-holding matters represents one example of this.[4] Other examples of the persistence of the kin-based structures of local politics into the administrative and political life of British India are myriad.[5] Recent scholarship on the Indian national movement has demonstrated the localized and "parochial" nature of many of the emerging public movements and organizations of the late nineteenth and early twentieth centuries.[6] British administrators of the period were inclined to sneer at the idea that an Indian "nation" could ever exist.[7] And yet the nationalist movement succeeded in mobilizing a broad-based constituency, submerging such parochial interests, in favor of the ideals of freedom from British rule, democratic nationhood, and economic and cultural self-determination. Kin-based structures, formal and informal patron-client relationships, and localized interests, while submerged, continued to exist.

The nationalist movement, as it developed in India from its original narrow base among urban, educated, and professional groups, was thus faced with the problem of creating a national identity out of a multiplicity of narrower identities, whether regional, religious, linguistic, or caste or class-based. Disagreements arose over how to accomplish this task. One may distinguish two major nationalist ideologies in the early twentieth century. The first was the liberal or "moderate." Its advocates saw Indian self-determination as the inevitable result of a gradual process in which the British would devolve power as the Indians became trained in operating the institutions of secular, parliamentary democracy, at local, provincial, and then national levels. The other ideology was the radical or "extremist." Its representatives felt that the adoption of British-inspired institutions on a British-imposed timetable was not enough. The nationalist movement should seize the initiative, and it should do so on the basis of Indian symbols, traditions, and institutions. The radicals were cultural nationalists as well as impatient activists.[8]

The division between the liberals and the radicals was not based on class, for both were drawn from the same western-educated, urban groups in Indian society, nor did they disagree over the ultimate goal: Indian independence. Their ideological differences, however, entailed different tactics to achieve that goal. The liberals were not averse to collaborating with the British to achieve gradual and peaceful devolution of power, while the radicals were dedicated to the idea of mass popular mobilization to resist British rule. They also differed over the question of social reform, with the liberals giving it high priority, while the radicals regarded it as a diversion from their major political goal. These two ideological positions were later integrated in the Gandhi-led movement which combined the liberals' faith in ultimate British concessions with the radicals' talent for broad-based public protest to help hasten those concessions.[9] Ideological differences nevertheless persisted in the nationalist movement. Liberal and radical are neither mutually exclusive categories—individuals changed their views over time and according to circumstance, nor do they encompass all possible shades of opinion in the nationalist ideological spectrum.[10]

For purposes of the present analysis, however, the liberals and the radicals had clearly differing views about the place of women in their efforts to secure Indian freedom and national solidarity. For the liberals, heirs to the social reformers of the nineteenth century, the status of women was symbolic of India's preparedness for self-rule. In this view, if Indian men were to claim political rights for themselves, it behooved them to grant greater rights to their women, through increasing their opportunities for education, raising the legal age of marriage, and reforming inheritance laws.[11] Muslims among the liberals regarded lessening the restrictions of purdah, if not its abolition, as a necessary part of social and educational reform for their women.[12] These various reforms would grant women greater dignity and status within the family and would permit them to perform better their traditional roles, and this in turn would benefit the nation. The domestic sphere would be enlightened; men would find greater companionship at home; children would be healthier and better prepared for life. The Indian family, far from being displaced by impersonal political and social institutions, would be revalidated as the most important social influence. Indian liberals sought in their private lives to respond to the ideological pressures of British rule, just as they had sought in their public lives to respond to its economic and political pressures.[13]

For the cultural nationalists, on the other hand, efforts for social and religious reform, by the British or by Indian reformers, were unwarranted foreign and Christian-inspired interference in their culture. In this view, women were symbolic of all that was distinctive and sacred in Indian culture. To many, India herself was a goddess, calling her sons to defend her honor, and thus a fertile source of symbolism binding Hindu religious imagery to the nationalist cause.[14] Individual radicals, like Tilak, educated their daughters and married them off past puberty, but resisted legislative interference in their home lives just as they demanded self-determination in their public lives. Muslims of this ideological bent looked to their own religion for symbols of resistance to foreign rule, and collaborated with the nationalists during the Khilafat movement. To them, purdah was much more a symbol of cultural distinctiveness than of female subordination, and thus its abolition was out of the question.[15] The radicals' response to the pressures of foreign rule was to find inspiration in their own traditions. The reformers often did this as well, in response to the cultural nationalists' accusations of undue Christian inspiration. Both reformers and cultural nationalists reinterpreted traditions to suit their own political purposes. The radicals' ideology concerning the role of women found its source in the traditional structure of Indian political authority in which the private and public spheres, though separate, were closely related, in which marital alliances mirrored political ones, and in which domestic rituals and public rituals reinforced each other.

According to both these ideologies, women act not as individuals but as members of families. In fact, they did not act in the public realm, but served as symbols. Neither the liberals nor the radicals envisaged women as political participants, demanding education and rights for themselves or aiding the nationalist struggle, except from behind the scenes. This was perfectly natural at the time. One should not project current feminist consciousness back too far in seeking to understand the origins of women's political participation in India. Women themselves were slow to seek public roles, and then only did so as extensions of their familial roles, both in deference to male opinion and because they felt more comfortable defining their public ventures in such terms.

For the liberals, a program of reforms to grant women greater dignity and status within the family was sufficient. It suited their gradualist political program; it assured a certain amount of government sympathy in getting reform bills through the legislature; and it was in the interests of the women themselves, for they gained status without having to subject themselves to the slings and arrows of outraged public opinion. This was not undue timidity, but rather pursuing the art of the possible. Liberals knew from experience that to advocate raising the legal age of marriage entailed braving tremendous social and political opposition, even though such a reform did not challenge the basic partriarchal structure of the family. In their own role as the advocates and protectors of women, the liberals could not imagine asking women to come out and fight political battles. On the other hand, women could acceptably be involved in social works which were natural extensions of their nurturing maternal role. Liberals encouraged their women to become involved in social and educational work, and women from prominent reformist families were among the first to found women's organizations in India. These organizations at first concentrated on social service and girls' education and only later became involved in politics.[16] Whether engaged in social service or politics, women who had emerged from a liberal, social reformist background stressed the compatibility of their public and private roles. Such women could easily assert that there was no conflict of interest between nationalist men and women, but rather a common interest in social reform as a prelude and accompaniment to national independence.

The radicals had a different approach. To them, freedom from foreign rule was the top priority. Further, since foreign domination was the chief source of injustice, freedom was the prerequisite for righting a host of wrongs, economic and social as well as political. Cooperating with the British government to secure piecemeal reforms was self-defeating as it merely put off attainment of independence. The need of the hour was for men and women, Hindus and Muslims, peasants and landlords, professionals and untouchables, Madrasis and Marathas, to sink their various differences and to work for independence. Legal reforms imposed by the British government were illegitimate and thus unacceptable, but reforms granted by an independent, truly national government would find easy acceptance, and thus would be enacted with alacrity. Many greeted such reasoning with skepticism, but others responded favorably to this broad-based appeal. Even liberals had to admit that the social legislation they desired would probably never be enacted by a foreign government chary of arousing opposition. The radicals regarded woman's political participation as necessary to the national cause, but here again, it could best be an extension of her household duties. She should urge her husband to support nationalism and imbue her children with patriotism; she should boycott foreign goods and wear only *swadeshi* saris. She could work politically among other women, just as she did among her extended kin, spreading the message of *swadeshi*, spinning *khaddar*, and urging temperance. These were issues with which women identified, but which were also symbolic of resistance to foreign economic domination.[17]

Mahatma Gandhi, as leader of the civil disobedience movements of the 1920s through 1940s, interpreted women's political participation as an extension of traditional roles as well. The Mahatma emphasized Sita as a norm for Indian women to follow. Hindu women were brought up hearing about Sita's self-sacrifice and devotion to Rama, her god-husband, as models for their behavior in their conjugal families.[18] And even though Sita was not a mother goddess, she was nevertheless a symbol of strength, as the chaste one who resisted the blandishments of the demon Ravana. Gandhi frequently characterized the British *raj* as *Ravanraj*. The Mahatma thought that women had a greater capacity to resist the temptations of foreign rule, and to suffer non-violently for their beliefs. Through his *satyagraha* movements, Gandhi sought to instill non-violent courage in all

THE EXTENDED FAMILY AS METAPHOR

Indians. For the Mahatma, therefore, women's participation in the nationalist movement was necessary for ideological reasons as well as for the practical reason that with women involved, the national movement would be linked to every home in India.[19] Some have regarded this use of the Sita model as a clever move by Gandhi to co-opt Indian women into a paternalistic national effort and thus to defuse their efforts for women's rights.[20] This argument has much to recommend it from a feminist point of view, but it ignores the dual nature of the Sita symbol, and of traditional women's roles.[21] In addition, one must bear in mind that Indian women, if they were mobilized at all, were divided ideologically. Gandhi was attempting to mobilize women generally and to overcome ideological divisions among them by using a widely-known symbolic model which supported his own priorities, which were—quite naturally—national and cultural autonomy.

The most active women in the civil disobedience movements also interpreted their activities either as natural extensions of their household roles, or as part of their congruent role as the guardians of India's cultural distinctiveness. Sarojini Naidu, one of the best-known Congress women activists during the non-cooperation movement of 1920-22 and again during the salt *satyagraha* of 1930, emphasized traditional feminine models in a speech championing *swadeshi* before a gathering of women in 1921. They were the custodians of Indian culture, supreme in everyday affairs of life; only they could bring about a renewed pride in India. *Swaraj* had to begin in their homes, not by politics alone. She recalled the sacrifices of Sita, of Savitri, and the strength of Draupadi, and asked the women to give up all foreign clothing, to take up spinning, to wear only homespun saris, and in this way to resist foreign rule.[22] Naidu thus emphasized the dual nature of women's roles, the self-sacrificing wife, the strong, self-sufficient mother.

Another example of a woman who became involved in Indian nationalism as a result of her opposition to foreign cultural domination, but who justified her actions as a natural extension of her household roles, was Abadi Banu Begum, or "Bi Amman," the mother of Muhammad Ali and Shaukat Ali, the Khilafat leaders. She was always known publically by her maternal nickname, "Bi Amman," a term at once affectionate and honorific. A strong-willed widow and the mother of many sons, Bi Amman observed strict purdah all her life, and only became politically active in her old age. Her public activities began in 1913, when she attended meetings for women only organized by the Anjuman-e-Khuddam-e-Ka'aba (Society of Servants of the Ka'aba). This association had been organized by her sons and their religious preceptor, Maulana Abdul Bari of Lucknow. The purpose of the association was to maintain the honor of the Ka'aba and other Muslim holy places, and to defend them against non-Muslim aggression. Their British rulers were clearly among the possible aggressors. At the purdah meetings, Bi Amman urged Muslim women to give money and gold ornaments to help defend the holy places.[23]

These meetings to raise money for a religious and political cause kept to traditional patterns while helping to change women's roles. The women were disciples of Sufi *pir*, Maulana Abdul Bari, and thus were participating in a type of religious gathering for which they could acceptably leave their homes. As gatherings of a network of religious disciples, the meetings could also be regarded as the reunion of a fictive extended family, with Bi Amman assuming the maternal role. The actual fund-raising also followed a traditional pattern. Gold ornaments were the women's personal property, and hence theirs to preserve or to lend for a good cause, usually familial, but in this case for the preservation of their faith.

Bi Amman again appeared on a political stage at the annual meeting of the Muslim League in 1917. Muhammad Ali had been chosen to preside but was not released from internment by the British, so his photograph graced the presidential chair. His mother spoke briefly on his behalf from behind the veil of her *burqa*.[24] This was perhaps the first time that a Muslim woman had spoken to a mixed political gathering, as opposed to a purdah meeting. By so doing, she made attendance at national political meetings acceptable for purdah-observing women. She had not defied purdah, nor expressed opinions in favor of women's emancipation, but her actions contributed to those ends.

Bi Amman surfaced again in 1921, touring India, speaking for the Khilafat cause and non-cooperation. She said that the government had enchained India in the twin fetters of slavery and eternal damnation. The people had to choose whether to wear those chains or to work for national and religious freedom. At a mass meeting in the Punjab, she lifted the veil of her *burqa* to speak to the crowd, saying that all present were her sons and daughters, and thus there was no reason to maintain purdah before them.[25] Bi Amman justified her action by including all nationalists within her family. She had progressed from her early appeals at ostensibly religious meetings for women only, through speaking veiled before the 1917 Muslim League, to a stage where she could speak unveiled before mass meetings. She had also advanced from being the mother of a numerous family, to being mother for an extended fictive family, to the point where the entire nation regarded her as a mother figure *par excellence*. Bi Amman's career illustrates the legitimacy of strength and self-sufficiency within the maternal role for Indian women.

Bi Amman may not be typical of all purdah-observing Muslim women who became involved in nationalist political activity, nor Sarojini Naidu typical of Hindu Congress women, but they provided patterns which many women could emulate. The strong, nurturing mother, the self-sacrificing wife, were familiar images with wide moral and cultural appeal. In working for their national freedom, Gandhi emphasized, Indians had to turn their weakness into strength, to exercize moral force against British governmental power. As an example of how this could be done, Gandhi pointed to the position of women in the patriarchal extended family. Women knew how to turn their subordinate position into one of strength and influence through the exercize of moral suasion.[26] Indian women in the nationalist movement took note. They followed strategies derived from their family roles, not only because they were familiar but also because they were effective, whether in aiding the nationalist effort or in gaining greater acceptance for increased roles and rights for women.

The extended family provided a metaphorical construct for the expansion of women's realm beyond the home into arenas of public activity in the context of the Indian nationalist movement. Men and women both used this metaphor when articulating their thoughts about women's political participation. Liberals regarded women's public concerns as legitimate extensions of their nurturing roles. Radicals accepted women in public roles to the degree that they symbolized resistance to foreign cultural, as well as political, domination. Women identified with these and other ideological persuasions, and used the metaphor of the family to justify their actions to the public and to themselves.[27]

This metaphor was also useful as a common denominator in a women's movement which, like the nationalist movement, had many divisions within it. Like the social feminists in the west and the liberals in India, many Indian women were concerned with reforms to ameliorate the status of women within their separate sphere.[28] Like the radical feminists in the west, other Indian women sought equality of status, and emphasized the fact that all Indians were subordinate to the paternalist authority of the empire.[29] Hence, like the radical nationalists, they wanted freedom first. Both these groups of women found in the terminology of family roles a conceptual framework for expressing their ideas. But it is well to remember that both these groups of Indian women, like the early nationalist leadership, came from the educated, urban middle and upper classes, and from the higher castes as well. As the nationalist movement gradually broadened its base of support, it mobilized members of urban lower castes and the middle peasantry, and women. Women of all social groups could be mobilized for a mass demonstration, but those women who were the most active in the Indian women's movement and in nationalism were still drawn from a narrow social base. Such women had an interest in preserving social authority.

One must refer to the picture of kin-based authority presented above to understand why the Indian women's movement did not do more to challenge women's subordinate position within the patriarchal structure of their society. To women from powerful lineages, their traditional familial roles were as much a source of strength as they were evidence of subordination. The ambiguous nature of those roles, obedient wife and increasingly powerful mother, has been discussed. To the degree that their public roles mirrored their private influence within their families, women activists were willing to play up that influence, and not ask for power for a separate interest group, women, which lacked any kin-based identity. Women traditionally could not act as individuals apart from their families, and that tradition remained strong throughout the nationalist period.

The argument can be made that female socialization within the extended family also had ambiguous results. Female solidarity has a much stronger traditional base in India than in Western society. Since the society is segregated, a girl's socialization takes place mostly among women, and arranged marriages eliminate the sense of competition among women for male attention and favors. On the other hand, the segregation of women and the subordination of younger wives to older mothers-in-law is a situation fraught with conflict. Perhaps it is the conflict in the extended family rather than the female solidarity which provides the skills for public roles.[30]

The structure of the family thus provides a framework for the analysis of changes in women's roles. The extended family as a social norm helped shape Indian women's thinking about their place in society, and also provided a metaphor for the expansion of their social concerns. The extended family is also a useful metaphor for the historian seeking to analyze the many dimensions of Indian women's political participation. An extended family may look harmonious to the casual observer, but it may contain many divisions. Inside the courtyard, there are probably several hearths.

NOTES

[1]David Lelyveld, *Aligarh's First Generation: Muslim Solidarity in British India* (Princeton: Princeton University Press, 1978), ch. VI, "Brothers of the *Akhara*," pp. 253-99.

[2]*Ibid.*, pp. 16-26; Richard G. Fox, *Kin, Clan, Raja, and Rule* (Berkeley: University of California Press, 1971), pp. 14-17, 129ff.

[3]A number of accounts of Indian family life contribute to this assessment, chief among them: Doranne Jacobson, "The Women of North and Central India," and Susan S. Wadley, "Women and the Hindu Tradition," in Doranne Jacobson and Susan S. Wadley, *Women in India: Two Perspectives* (New Delhi: Manohar, 1977), pp. 17-111, 113-139; Hanna Papanek, "Purdah: Separate Worlds and Symbolic Shelter," *Comparative Studies in Society and History* XV, 3 (June, 1973),

pp. 289-325; Manisha Roy, *Bengali Women* (Chicago: University of Chicago Press, 1975).

[4]For this example, see David Gilmartin, "Kinship, Women, and Politics in Twentieth-Century Punjab," below.

[5]Accounts which deal with the continuities between the traditional and British administrative systems are: Robert E. Frykenberg, "Elite Groups in a South Indian District, 1788-1858," *Journal of Asian Studies* XXIV, 2 (February, 1965), pp. 261-281; Bernard S. Cohn, "The Initial British Impact on India: A Case Study of the Benares Region," *Journal of Asian Studies* XIX, 4 (August, 1960), pp. 418-431; and David Lelyveld, *Aligarh's First Generation*, "The *Kacahri* Milieu," pp. 56-68.

[6]For the somewhat doctrinaire approach of the Cambridge school, see the articles in Anil Seal, John Gallagher, and Gordon Johnson, eds., *Locality, Province and Nation* (Cambridge: Cambridge University Press, 1973). More balanced approaches are: C.A. Bayly, *The Local Roots of Indian Politics, Allahabad, 1880-1920* (Oxford: Oxford University Press, 1975); John H. Broomfield, *Elite Conflict in a Plural Society: Twentieth-Century Bengal* (Berkeley: University of California Press, 1968.

[7]Sir John Strachey, *India* (London: Kegan Paul, 1888), pp. 5-8, cited in Ainslie T. Embree, *India's Search for National Identity* (New York: Knopf ,1972), p. 21.

[8]Good accounts of the "moderates" and the "extremists" in Indian nationalism are: Stanley Wolpert, *Tilak and Gokhale: Revolution and Reform in the Making of Modern India* (Berkeley: University of California Press, 1961); B.R. Nanda, *Gokhale: The Indian Moderates and the British Raj* (Princeton: Princeton University Press, 1977); John R. McLane, *Indian Nationalism and the Early Congress* (Princeton: Princeton University Press, 1977). Indian Muslims also divided along ideological lines, see e.g., Gail Minault and David Lelyveld, "The Campaign for a Muslim University, 1898-1920," *Modern Asian Studies* VIII, 2 (April, 1974), pp. 145-189; and Francis Robinson, *Separatism Among Indian Muslims, The Politics of United Provinces' Muslims, 1860-1923* (Cambridge: Cambridge University Press, 1974).

[9]Charles Heimsath, *Indian Nationalism and Hindu Social Reform* (Princeton: Princeton University Press, 1964), pp. 205-229; Wolpert, *Tilak and Gokhale*, pp. 157-212; B.R. Nanda, *Gokhale*, pp. 407-421; Judith M. Brown, *Gandhi's Rise to Power, 1915-1922* (Cambridge: Cambridge University Press, 1972), pp. 16-51.

[10]Kay Boals examines a wide spectrum of ideological responses to colonialism in her article, "The Politics of Cultural Liberation: Male-Female Relations in Algeria," in Berenice A. Carroll, ed.. *Liberating Women's History* (Urbana: University of Illinois Press, 1976), pp. 194-211.

[11]Vina Mazumdar, "The Social Reform Movement in India From Ranade to Nehru," in B.R. Nanda, ed., *Indian Women: From Purdah to Modernity* (New Delhi: Vikas, 1976), pp. 41-66; see also two articles

below: Karen I. Leonard and John G. Leonard, "Social Reform and Women's Participation in Political Culture: Andhra and Madras," and Geraldine Forbes, "The Indian Women's Movement: A Struggle for Women's Rights or National Liberation?"

[12]Jahanara Shah Nawaz, *Father and Daughter* (Lahore: Nigarishat, 1971), p. 59.

[13]For recent studies of Indian reform movements and the adaptation of the Indian educated elite to Western ideological and political pressures, see: Kenneth Jones, *Arya Dharm: Hindu Conciousness in 19th Century Punjab* (Berkeley: University of California Press, 1976); David Kopf, *The Brahmo Samaj and the Shaping of the Modern Indian Mind* (Princeton: Princeton University Press, 1979); Cf. Bruce T. McCully *English Education and the Origins of Indian Nationalism* (Reprint. Gloucester, Mass.: Peter Smith, 1966), pp. 176-237.

[14]Bankim Chandra Chatterjee, "Bande Mataram," in W.T. DeBary ed., *Sources of Indian Tradition* (New York: Columbia University Press, 1958), pp. 709-714; for other Hindu religio-political symbolism, see Richard I. Cashman, *The Myth of the Lokamanya* (Berkeley: University of California Press, 1975), ch. IV, "The Political Recruitment of the God Ganapati," pp. 75-97.

[15]Gail Minault, *The Khilafat Movement: Religious Symbolism and Political Mobilization in India* (New York: Columbia University Press, forthcoming); see also the account of the career of Bi Amman, below. This kind of rationale is also at the base of the movement back to the *chador* in post-revolutionary Iran.

[16]Geraldine Forbes, "From Purdah to Politics: The Social Feminism of the All-India Women's Organizations," forthcoming in Hanna Papanek, ed., *Purdah in South Asia: The Segregation of Women*; see also Geraldine Forbes, "The Indian Women's Movement," below.

[17]*Ibid.*, cf. Gail Minault, "Purdah Politics: The Role of Muslim Women in Indian Nationalism, 1911-1924," forthcoming in Hanna Papanek, ed., *Purdah in South Asia*.

[18]Manisha Roy, *Bengali Women*, pp. 32-33.

[19]Suzanne H. Rudolph, "The New Courage; an Essay on Gandhi's Psychology," *World Politics* XVI, 1 (October, 1963), pp. 98-117; cf. Lloyd and Suzanne Rudolph, *The Modernity of Tradition* (New Delhi: Orient Longmans, 1969), pp. 160-192.

[20]Maria Mies, "Indian Women and Leadership," *Bulletin of Concerned Asian Scholars* VII, 1 (March, 1975), pp. 57-58.

[21]I am grateful to Geraldine Forbes for pointing out the dual nature of the Sita symbol. Cf. Susan S. Wadley, "Women and the Hindu Tradition," in Jacobson and Wadley, *Women in India*, especially pp. 119-125. An earlier version of this article was published in *Signs* III, 1 (Autumn, 1977), pp. 113-125.

[23]*Bombay Chronicle*, April 11 and 25, 1921.

[23]Muhammad Ali, *My Life, A Fragment* (Reprint. Lahore: S.M. Ashraf, 1966), pp. 4-5; Notice of a women's meeting of the Anjuman-e-Khuddam-e-Ka'aba, Delhi, November 6, 1913, Abdul Bari Papers,

Firangi Mahal, Lucknow; cf. Gail Minault, *The Khilafat Movement*, ch. I.

[24]Mazhar Ansari, *Tarikh-e-Muslim League* (Delhi: Maktaba-e-Jamia, 1940), p. 189.

[25]Abdur Razzaq Qureshi, ed., *Nava-e-Azadi* (Bombay: Abadi Publishers, 1957), pp. 199-202; *Independent* (Allahabad), September 28, 1921.

[26]*Young India*, April 10, 1930, in M.K. Gandhi, *The Role of Women*, ed. by A.T. Hingorani (Ahmedabad: Navajivan, 1964), pp. 18-19.

[27]Geraldine Forbes, in a personal communication, points to another possible connection between the extended family and individual women's efforts. That is, many of the women who were most active politically and socially were not members of extended conjugal families. In interviews with Forbes, several stressed loneliness or free time as reasons for seeking new activities. In this sense, the extension of a woman's activities beyond her home may be interpreted as an effort to recapture a fictive extended family.

[28]William L. O'Neill, *The Woman Movement* (Chicago: Quadrangle, 1971), p. 34; cf. Geraldine Forbes, "From Purdah to Politics."

[29]Sheila Rowbotham, *Women, Resistance and Revolution: A History of Women in the Modern World* (New York: Vintage, 1974), pp. 96-97, 200-201, Blanche W. Cook, ed., *Crystal Eastman on Women and Revolution* (Oxford: Oxford University Press, 1978), pp. 31-32.

[30]I am grateful to Annette Weiner for this observation. Cf. Louise Lamphere, "Strategies, Cooperation, and Conflict Among Women in Domestic Groups," in Louise Lamphere and Michelle Z. Rosaldo, eds., *Woman, Culture, and Society* (Stanford: Stanford University Press, 1974), pp. 97-112.

2

Social Reform and Women's Participation in Political Culture: Andhra and Madras

KAREN I. LEONARD AND
JOHN G. LEONARD

I. Introduction

The position of women has often been used as a measure of civilizational progress. This was so in nineteenth-century colonial India, where the status of women was criticized by both Englishmen and Indians. British administrators and missionaries were no less strong in their criticism than were western-educated Indians. The problem was forcefully stated by a Bengali Brahmo Samaj leader, Sivanath Sastri, on his 1890 visit to a small town in South India. "Women are fishbones in our throats. We cannot cough them up, and we dare not swallow them," he said.[1] His phrase suggests both structural and cultural difficulties, though speaking as a Bengali, fish-eating Brahman, he may not have intended the flavor of pollution which his South Indian, predominantly vegetarian, audience must have picked up.

Here, we explore structural and cultural features of two South Indian regional cultures as they developed in the late nineteenth century. More similar to each other than to other regions of India, Andhra and Tamil Nadu (the names for the Telugu- and Tamil-speaking regions respectively) nonetheless differed. We contend that they differed most strikingly in the way the movements for social, religious, and linguistic reform were conducted. The contrasts lay less in the content, the messages, of the movements than in the way the messages were transmitted and implemented. The widow marriage movements, in particular, attacked orthodox concepts of women and the family very differently in the two regions, leading to a stronger emphasis on women's participation in the political culture of Andhra.

The concept of political culture delineated in the early 1960's by Lucien Pye and others provides our analytical framework. We are not interested in the associated concept of political development, worked out with reference to the dichotomous modernity/tradition model of that decade. We arte interested, rather, in the concept of political culture as "he system of empirical beliefs, expressive symbols, and values which defines the situation in which political action takes place."[2] Pye's fuller definition is useful:

> ...in any operating political system there is an ordered subjective realm of politics which gives meaning to the polity, discipline to institutions, and social relevance to individual acts. The concept of political culture thus suggests that the traditions of a society, the spi it of its public institutions, the passions and the collective reasoning of its citizenry, and the style and operating codes of its leaders are not just random products of historical experience but fit together as a part of a meaningful whole and constitute an intelligible web of relations. For the individual the political culture provides controlling guidelines for effective political behavior, and for the collectivity it gives a systematic structure of values and rational considerations which ensures coherence in the performance of institutions and organizations.[3]

Following this, we believe that political socialization involves not only the private processes in family and home, but, just as significantly, an individual's later experiences in schools and public life. Emphasizing the historical development of a culture and the life experiences of individuals within that culture, we will argue that the way in which the widow marriage movement was conducted in the Telugu-speaking region, the way it connected with religious and linguistic reform movements, developed strong positive values concerning women's participation in the political culture of Andhra.

II. Social Reform Movements in Andhra and Madras

Few attempts have been made to measure the results of social reform efforts in India because they were eclipsed by political reform efforts—that is, by the nationalist movement. One historian has described social reform as "an intellectual phenomenon whose behavioral consequences are difficult, if not impossible, to measure..."[4] Most social reforms concentrated on improving the condition of women, but men were the chief advocates of reforms. Historians have not seriously attempted to ascertain if the reform efforts made any real difference for women in particular local or regional contexts; they have simply noted the failure of Indian society to respond immediately and measurably to the specific reforms advocated and turned their attention to the political movement at an all-India level.

Reform movements affecting women and the family occurred in the context of Hindu orthodoxy, the prevailing norm in southern India during the nineteenth century. Indian and foreign observers have attested to the relatively greater strength of Brahmanical Hinduism, its purity and pollution prohibitions, in the South. While the historically weaker political and cultural influence of Muslim rule in the South was undoubtedly an important factor, equally significant was the fact that Brahmans, though a proportionately smaller element in the southern population, were more often major landholders. This was particularly true of the centers of literary and cultural development, such as Rajahmundry in the Telugu-speaking region and Tanjore in the Tamil-speaking region.[5]

There were only two instances of social reform campaigns involving several leaders, organized followers, and the use of political institutions in nineteenth-century South India. Both were widow marriage compaigns; one was centered in Rajahmundry, the other in Madras. The small town of Rajahmundry was in the Telugu-speaking region, several hundred miles north of the city of Madras. Here college teachers and students held meetings in 1879 to advocate widow marriages, and ten widow marriages were celebrated in a three-year period, from 1881 to 1884. Some thirty more widow marriages were performed in Andhra by 1919, making this the most intensive widow marriage campaign in all of India. The second social reform campaign, in Madras city, the capital of the presidency, featured government officials managing an association, sponsoring lectures and debates and promoting widow marriages from 1874 to 1890. These two campaigns occurred almost simultaneously, and there were personal, intellectual, and institutional connections between them.[6] Yet the two campaigns differed strikingly, both at the time they were carried out and in terms of their lasting impact upon the regions. While widow marriage was the most dramatic issue for social reformers in both places, they also worked in girls' education at the same time, and we will look at regional developments in this sphere as well.

These two linguistic regions were similar in many respects. Both were part of the same administrative unit until 1953, first the British Indian Presidency of Madras and then Madras State. The Andhra movement for a separate Telugu-speaking state led to division in 1953, and then other state boundaries within India were realigned to coincide with linguistic ones.[7] Andhra and Madras shared many general characteristics of economic and social structure: each region was centered on a large-scale river and canal irrigation system, with 60-70% of cultivable land under cultivation. In each case, about 40% of the cultivated land was irrigated. Rice was the main crop, and the same cash crops were increasingly cultivated at the end of the nineteenth century.[8] A recent analysis contrasts the "dry" rural districts, (chiefly in the Tamil-speaking region), with the "wet" rural districts (chiefly in the Telugu-speaking region), and it generalizes about different degrees of political and cultural integration in these areas.[9] While the analysis generally supports the points to be made here concerning the twentieth-century involvement of women in political culture, its focus is rural, and late nineteenth century social reform efforts began in urban centers.

In the late nineteenth century, the most important differences between these two regions lay in the size and nature of the urban populations. Rajahmundry was the district headquarters for the Godavari district, with a population of 25,000 in 1881, almost all Hindu and Telugu-speaking. Rajahmundry was the historical center of classical Telugu culture. There were only a few European administrators and missionaries in the town, while there were many in Madras city, the colonial administrative capital of the Presidency.[10] Madras city had a population of 406,000 in 1881. Madras was the third largest city in India and the best-educated; the entire presidency was ahead of the others in literacy. The population of Madras city was 78% Hindu, 12% Muslim, and 10% Christian. While Tamil was spoken by 59% of the urban population Telugu was spoken by 23%, and Marathi, English, Urdu, Kannada, Bengali, and Malayalam were spoken by minorities of importance in the city.[11]

In Madras Presidency as elsewhere, it was the western-educated men, those moving into administrative service and the professions, who led the social reform movements. Members of the Brahman caste predominated, especially in the university-educated elite, and the rate of English literacy was highest among Brahmans.[12] This small but growing educated elite, then, was drawn from the Brahman and other high caste categories, those which held most strongly to orthodox Hindu customs concerning women. The contradictions seen by members of the educated elite led them to instigate efforts for social change.

A few figures will illustrate the difference between these high castes and the rest of the population with respect to girls' age at marriage and the incidence of widows. Marriage was a universal event for girls: 83% of Hindu girls were married before the age of fifteen and 96% before the age of twenty. Census figures for Madras Presidency in 1881 show that 5% of Hindu girls, but 11% of Brahman girls, married before the age of ten.[13] Pre-puberty marriage was considered mandatory for the daughters of 25% of the population, common for 15%, and rare for the remaining 60%, in 1891. Thirty percent of the population prohibited widow remarriage, 40% did not, and for 30% the evidence was not conclusive.[14] The incidence of widows among all Hindus was high in South India: in 1881, 22% of all Hindu women were widowed. But the incidence of widows among Brahmans was 33%, or half again that of the rest.[15] Sometimes

TABLE I

THE CIVIL CONDITION OF (SELECTED) WOMEN IN MADRAS PRESIDENCY, 1911-1921

Category of Women	Age Cohorts (1000 in each)									
	(0-5) Married/ Widowed		(5-12) Married/ Widowed		(12-20) Married/ Widowed		(20-40) Married/ Widowed		(over 40) Married/ Widowed	
Telugu Brahmans	6	1	274	7	878	65	730	257	299	699
Tamil Brahmans	4	—	130	2	863	31	804	180	348	645
	(0-5)		(5-10)		(10-15)		(15-40)		(over 40)	
N. E. Coast [Telugu districts; all Hindus]	15	1	147	4	488	19	820	141	367	625
S. E. Coast [Tamil districts; All Hindus]	2	—	13	1	123	2	802	99	408	585
	(0-5)		(5-12)		(12-20)		(20-40)		(over 40)	
Telugu Brahmans	6	1	193	7	814	93	744	249	307	687
Tamil Brahmans	15	—	69	2	772	46	824	164	357	640

1911 Census (rows 1-4); 1921 Census (rows 5-6)

SOURCES: *Census of India*, 1911. XII. *Madras*. Part I (Madras, 1912), 113, 116; *Census of India, 1921*. XIII. *Madras*. Part I (Madras, 1922), 112.

the Brahman rate of widowhood was three or four times that of the rest of the population, and this was attributable to their earlier age at marriage. In 1891, 3.3% of Brahman girls 10 to 14 were widowed, compared to less than 1% of all girls 10 to 14.[16]

Within Madras Presidency, it is clear that the age at marriage was lower for Telugu girls than for Tamil ones, and that the proportion of widows in the female population under the age of forty was consequently higher in the Telugu districts.[17] We do not try to explain the causes of the different social structures here; we want to simply point out that the problem of child widows was greater in the Telugu-speaking districts. Table I illustrates this.

To understand these patterns and the dilemma they posed for western-educated Indians, we must outline the orthodox Hindu concepts underlying the treatment of women in India, and especially of widows. These concepts were logical and systematic. Hindu society was a caste society; each caste was an endogamous unit, into which individuals were recruited by birth. Caste members were thought to share a physical substance, blood and its products, and they shared a code of conduct (dharma) which was embodied and transmitted in the physical substance. Individuals married within that large pool of relatives sharing the same substance and code, that is, within a caste. All life cycle ceremonies, including marriage, involved a transformation of substance and code. For the man, the transformation at marriage was primarily one of code—he entered the householder stage of life, charged with begetting sons and maintaining his family. For the woman, the transformation was not only one of code—she too entered the householder stage charged with producing sons—but also of physical substance. She was said to become the "half-body" of her husband, sharing his substance and becoming part of his lineage. This transformation of the bride's substance began with the marriage ceremony, traditionally performed before puberty. An early age at marriage for girls facilitated this process of transformation. Therefore parents arranged the marriages of their prepuberty daughters, and physical consummation of the marriage often did not follow for several years.[18]

There are further implications for women of this cultural

concept of substance and code. For a man, proper performance of the householder role could justify a second marriage, should his first wife die without giving him the son necessary for proper performance of his funeral ritual, or should he be unprepared to enter the stage of retirement. But it was not possible to conceive of remarriage for a woman. Her marriage made her a relative by blood as well as law (substance as well as code); it was not just a legal contract which could be dissolved and remade. Her substance, already merged with that of another, could not again be transformed. With the death of her husband, her social role was over, and she became a widow, the undesired last stage of life for a female. For her, the cycle could not be set back or reversed. This stage was in some ways analogous to that of *sanyasi*, the final stage of life in the model for men, and one outside of society. A widow's social death had occurred, brought about by her husband's physical death, and just as a *sanyasi* symbolically celebrated his own ritual cremation, a widow could be literally cremated. Thus some castes had the institution of *sati*, or immolation of a widow on her husband's funeral pyre. This occurred not only because there was no further social role for widows, but because the state of widowhood, in contrast to that of a *sanyasi*, was not auspicious. Both widows and *sanyasis* were dead to society, but widows were polluting and endangered others. Their lowered status was marked in many ways—a shaven head and other physical disfigurements, menial work, enforced physical and ritual distance from family and community events, and so on. The plight of the Hindu, particularly the virgin or child widow, and the logical but rare performance of *sati* were the most horrifying aspects of Hindu society, both to outsiders and to the increasing numbers of western-educated Indians in nineteenth-century colonial India.[19]

Criticism of Hindu society over time consistently focused upon the treatment of widows. The Mughal Emperor Akbar had tried to prohibit *sati* in the sixteenth century. British colonial rulers also issued several proclamations trying to change the status of widows. Ram Mohun Roy, the Bengali social reformer best known as founder of the Brahmo Samaj in 1828, had begun requesting anti-*sati* legislation in 1818, and the British East India Company prohibited it in 1829. That proclamation was followed by the Hindu Widow Remarriage Act of

1856, which permitted the remarriage of Hindu widows.[20]

Under British rule in the nineteenth century, those Indians acquiring western education and entering the colonial service came largely from the highest castes, the very castes whose cultural concepts concerning women were fundamentally challenged by western education and colonial critics. Sensitive to criticism of an early age of marriage, the fate of widows, and lack of education for girls, Indian social reformers throughout India initiated campaigns to change Indian society. Their strategies were diverse. In some cases, they addressed themselves to secular or religious authorities, asking the British government for social legislation or the Hindu sectarian gurus for orthodox sanction of social and religious reforms. In other cases, they addressed their classmates or their relatives, trying to change the customs of existing castes and communities or to create a new class of educated people. Individual social reformers debated textual sanctions for widow marriages, sponsored a few widow marriages, and a very few married widows themselves. Reformers also established schools for widows, hoping that educated widows could serve as teachers for Hindu girls, thereby solving another cultural problem and furthering girls' education.[21]

The contradictions between Hindu orthodox views of women and the ideal presented by western education were focused sharply in the families of the young western-educated men who were moving into government service and the professions. Girl's education gradually won acceptance, with the backing of the British government, missionaries, and the majority of the educated men. But widow marriage, with the same backing from government and missionaries, gained few champions, even among western-educated men. The major features of the widow marriage campaigns shows why they were so controversial, and largely unsuccessful, in both South Indian regions. The regional contrasts in the campaigns helps explain why the campaign in the Telugu-speaking region nonetheless had a major and measurable impact upon Andhra society.

The widow marriage campaign in Andhra was central to, and directly connected with, all other educational, political and social movements in the Telugu-speaking region.[22] The educational system was of fundamental importance to the widow marriage movement there, for most of its leaders were teachers in the first regional boys' college, opened in Rajahmundry in 1873. Many students participated, some as bridegrooms, most as enthusiastic participants in the widow marriage celebrations.

The Government College had started as a high school and become a two-year college in 1873. By 1875, it produced nearly fifty percent of the Matriculation (high school degree) and First Arts (two years of college) candidates from the districts of coastal Andhra. After the college was raised to a four-year institution in 1877 (making it the only school in the Telugu-speaking region to offer the BA), it produced nearly forty percent of BAs awarded to Andhras, making it "... the centre of learning, not only in this district, but in the whole Telugu [speaking] country." The college drew students primarily from its own district, Godavari, where primary schools had increased throughout the district; secondary and collegiate education remained concentrated in Rajahmundry.[23] While many of the first college teachers had been from the Tamil-speaking districts to the south, they were soon replaced with local Telugu-speaking teachers, including the three who became major reform leaders (Viresalingam, Narasimham, and Basavaraju).

For the first generation of Andhra BAs, these campaigns were part of their education experience. As a later faculty member there (an Indian Christian with a Cambridge degree) put it:

> The fact of these marriages having taken place in Rajahmundry has been the means of making boys in the local College take a deep interest in social questions. Year after year young men go out of the College with a firm determination to do their best to improve the wretched condition of the women of India. It is very strange that in the whole of India the Madras Presidency should take the lead in this good movement; and still more strange that in the whole of the Presidency a comparatively obscure town like Rajahmundry should do so much in the way of practical reforms.[24]

Of major significance was the use of the vernacular, Telugu, for speaking and writing on the widow marriage issue. The chief leader of the reform movement, a college teacher named Viresalingam, had his own press and journal. He wrote the Telugu section of this English-Telugu journal; his colleagues Narasimham and Basavaraju wrote the English. Viresalingam was a Brahman trained as a scholar of classical Telugu, and he was instrumental in the modern Telugu movement to promote spoken Telugu for purposes of modern education and communication. Viresalingam and other reform leaders were also early members of the Brahmo Samaj and Prarthana Samaj religious reform associations in Andhra. Thus the widow marriage reform leaders were also central figures in linguistic and religious reform movements. When municipal politics became a major activity after the Ripon reforms in 1880s, the same men participated enthusiastically in that arena too. The reformers used local schools as centers of operation, and they founded institutions and associations in the Andhra towns. They often had the support of local British administrators and missionaries, and they relied upon student support.

Viresalingam added his own indispensable stubbornness to the campaign. It must be said he was unusual even among Indian social reformers in this respect. Not incidentally, Viresalingam's father had died when he was three, he had no elder brother, and he had no children about whose marriages he had to be concerned. (He adopted a son, the child of a "remarried" couple whose marriage did not work out, and tried to make him marry a widow; the boy left him.) He also had his own well, from which he and other reformers drew water after being outcasted.[25]

While a small town like Rajahmundry offered a concentration of resources, leadership and reform activities, it had considerable disadvantages for the reformers as well. Their Widow Marriage Association was initially a secret one, and young reformers faced not only an older, less educated, group of local Indian administrators and politicians, but the orthodox Hindus of Rajahmundry and the social controls of a small town. The dramatic events of the first widow marriage, celebrated in 1881, illustrate this well.[26] The prospective bride, a child widow "kidnapped" from a village by Viresalingam's students, was kept in his custody until the ceremony. Viresalingam, as a Brahman, could perform the marriage himself, but members of other castes were essential participants in the ceremony, and they were bribed by both the 'orthodox' and 'reformers.' They were finally convinced by the higher fees of the reformers. The ceremony was held under the benevolent eyes of a British official and his police, but the town was thrown into conflict. Those who financed and participated in the wedding festivities were immediately outcasted by their sectarian guru, and they were placed under social and economic boycott by Rajahmundry orthodox society. Jobs, services, and potential marriage alliances were cut off. Far from being heroes, the first and subsequent bridegrooms discovered that they were unable to secure jobs and maintain social contacts.

One concrete result of the widow marriages was a community of remarried couples, a growing group directly dependent upon the reformers and their Widow Marriage Association for their housing and livelihood. This development, almost certainly unanticipated, drained the resources of the reformers and involved them in disputes with the bridegrooms and with each other. Many of the reformers underwent penance to re-enter caste; some of the bridegrooms converted to Christianity, deserted their brides, or sued the Association for more support.

Given the problems which resulted, many reformers ceased supporting this drastic reform of widow marriage. Viresalingam went on undeterred, stubbornly performing widow marriages wherever he found willing participants. He was outcasted, an 'untouchable' to the end of his life. He wrote continually about the issue in his journal and other publications, and he linked widow marriage and the condition of women to the oppression of the lower castes and untouchables. He irreversibly linked reform and nationalism (political reform). A biographer has called him the "Founder of Telugu Public Life," and noted that:

> Mr. Viresalingam conveyed to his generation in a multitude of forms the consciousness of the power of these changing causes [contact with Western culture and Christianity] ... And the more closely we study the various movements of our time, the more persistently we are led to conclude that, if he was not the original centre and first cause of them all, he had however, laid the foundation for many of them in a sound and secure manner. He was, as it were, the initial principle of change throughout the whole course of the Telugu advance within the recent times.[27]

The characteristics of the widow marriage campaign in Madras and its results were quite different.[28] It was led by older men, at the peak of their careers in government service or after their retirement from service, and the social reform association was one of many essentially English-medium westernizing societies to which these leaders belonged. Because these leaders were not all Tamil-speakers, they spoke and wrote most often in English and utilized the English language press in the city. There was virtually no connection to the development of modern Tamil language and literature. When they performed marriages (and sometimes it was Viresalingam who brought wedding parties to Madras, to publicize the reform and coordinate activities and leadership), these leaders did not always attend themselves or interdine across caste lines following the ceremony. They, like Viresalingam, were Sanskrit scholars, but they were drawn into the Theosophical Society and the defense of Hinduism by the strong missionary educational establishment in the city. They did not have positions in the educational system, and there was no student following or student participation in the few widow marriages held in Madras.

Western education had expanded in Madras city, but it was characterized by conflict over religious reform, not social reform. Madras city was the educational center of the presidency, enrolling forty percent of all college students. The growth of colleges and schools depended mainly on private initiative, and until 1880, the city had three arts colleges, one government and two missionary ones. The Principal of Christian College had developed his college as a showplace of missionary education. By 1881 Christian College had fifty percent more boys enrolled than the government's Presidency College. The high school attached to Christian College was the largest in the city. The importance of the missionary element in secondary education was obvious: of the twenty high schools open to Hindus in the city, twelve were managed by missionaries, six by Indians, and two by the government. Over half the Hindu students enrolled in primary and secondary schools attended missionary institutions.

The struggle over control of education in Madras was a defensive one for Indians in the late 1870s and increasingly so in the 1880s. The rhetoric and confrontations associated with the conflict between the missionaries and educated Indian leaders prevented social reformers from invoking stereotypes critical of Hinduism. For instance, while the reform leaders in Rajahmundry made use of the image of orthodox, bigoted, ritualistic Brahmans obstructing social change, in Madras this image belonged to the missionary's rhetoric and was used to attack all Hindus. Raghunath Rao, the widow marriage reform leader in Madras, wrote a pamphlet on widow marriage, but refrained from attacking Brahman priests or orthodox Hindus. He described himself as "a loyal follower of the Hindu religion." Meanwhile, in contrast, Viresalingam in Rajahmundry was helping to sue the Sankaracharya (religious head of his Smartha Brahman sect) for his outcasting of those who aided and participated in the widow marriages.[29]

The results of the widow marriage campaigns, in terms of numbers of widows married, were negligible in both Andhra and Madras. Before assessing the ideological impact the campaign had in Andhra, it is useful to compare the development of girls' education in the two regions, which occurred at this same time. It occurred without the conflict and publicity which accompanied the widow marriage campaigns and can more easily be measured.

TABLE II

GIRLS' EDUCATION IN MADRAS PRESIDENCY

Year	Girls in School	Number of Schools		
		Primary	Middle	High
1871	10,185	138	91	1
1881	32,355	500	32	8
1893	104,988	808	196	27

SOURCE: *Indian Education Commission Report of the Madras Provincial Committee* (Calcutta: Government of India, 1884), 20, 41, 133.

The growth of girls' education in South India came in the last three decades of the nineteenth century. Table II shows the number of girls in school tripling from decade to decade. Girls' education was concentrated at the primary level, with at least 98% of the school girls enrolled in the first five grades. The pace of establishing schools lagged behind the enrollment of girls during the 1880s, and many girls joined boys' schools as a result —there was an increase of slightly over fifty percent in the 1880s of girls attending co-educational schools.[30] It is clear that girls' education, while it encountered initially strong opposition from some, was accepted and grew steadily. Its growth was not connected to support for other reforms affecting women.

Girls' education proved ultimately acceptable because it could be developed to support and reinforce cultural norms. The following quotations show the way in which girls' education was regarded. An audience of educated men was asked, "Do you not feel in your daily life, that your wives and mothers are great impediments, sometimes insuperable objects in the way of your own intellectual and moral improvements."[31] Girls' education would benefit men. This is even clearer from the type of education advocated for Indian girls at that time:

> ...[India's] need is to devise such a system of education for Hindu females as will make her an agreeable companion, a good mother, an intelligent and loving wife, and an excellent housewife. We want her to possess those mental accomplishments which enable the wife to serve as a solace to her husband in his bright and dark moments, the mother to undertake , or at least to superintend the early instruction of her child , and the lady of the house to provide those sweet social comforts idealized in the English word—Home.[32]

Unlike widow marriage, girls' education did not challenge the complementary roles of men and women within the family. Education, in fact, would enhance a woman's contribution to her home and family.

Both regions advanced in this area, though the figures were slightly higher for girls' education and literacy in the Tamil-speaking districts. Looking more closely at girls' education in Madras Presidency in 1881, the conditions varied greatly from district to district.[33] The significant difference

TABLE III

GIRLS' EDUCATION BY LEADING DISTRICTS IN MADRAS PRESIDENCY, 1881

District	Hindu girls in school	Govt. No.	%	Girls Primary Schools Christian No.	%	Private No.	%	Total	Male Lit.	Boy/Girl Ratio
Madras	2581	1	1	66	90	7	10	74	26%	4:1
Tinnevelly	1785			144	99	2	1	146	12.1%	13:1
Godavari	1443	13	33	5	12	22	55	40	4.5%	7:1
Krishna	847			25	86	4	14	29	5.5%	10:1
Tanjore	997	7	21	20	61	6	18	33	11.7%	18:1
TOTALS	7653	21	260			41		322		

SOURCE: *Report on Public Instruction in Madras Presidency for 1881-82* (Madras, 1882), 5; Government of India, Madras Financial Proceedings, No. 58, 10 January 1884 (IOL).

between Andhra and Madras, in patterns of education and particularly girls' education, was not the number of institutions and scholars, although Madras city and the Tamil-speaking region have generally been ahead in such quantitative measures. The significant differences lay in the sponsorship and funding of the schools. Table III gives this information for primary schools in the five leading districts in Madras Presidency in 1881. Godavari district, which included Rajahmundry, was the only one where missionary sponsorship was an insignificant factor: 55% its of schools were run by private individuals; 33% were sponsored by the government; and only 12% were missionary schools. In the three Tamil districts cited (Madras, Tinnevelly, and Tanjore), missionary control of girls' education at the primary level ranged from 61 to 99%.

In Rajahmundry's district, there was greater freedom from colonial and missionary criticism, criticism which in Madras determined the issues with which western-educated Indians dealt to a large extent. In the town of Rajahmundry, the center of education and social reform efforts in Andhra, the school system was dominated by Indian educators, funded by private individuals, and by government through the Municipal Council. In Madras, the missionary domination of the educational system shaped educational politics in the 1880s and 1890s, leading to direct conflict between an evangelical Christian condemnation of Hindu beliefs and customs and the western-educated Indians' defense of Hinduism through the Theosophical Society and other Hindu revivalist movements. Both orthodox and reforming Hindus in Madras were engaged in dialogue with missionaries, rather than with each other as was the case in Andhra. This was an additional factor helping to restrict educational and social reform conflicts to English-using publications and audiences.[34]

III. Differential Consequences of the Regional Reform Movements

A comparison of reform activities focused on the position of women in Andhra and Madras emphasizes the importance of ideology and its transmission in the spoken, regional vernacular. In both regions, the widow marriage movement resulted in no quantitatively measurable decrease in the proportion of widows in the population. The steady increase of girls' education at first glance appears far more consequential, with higher rates of girls' education and literacy consistently achieved in the Tamil-speaking region. But by a number of significant indexes, women in Andhra participated more in political culture than in Madras. This trend can be traced directly to the widow marriage movement and the historical developments linked with it from the 1880s.

The widow marriage campaign was the catalyst which initiated the first generation of western-educated Andhras into social, religious and political reform activities. A symbolic effort to change the status of women, it posed a fundamental challenge to orthodox concepts of women and their role in family and society. The campaign had a major ideological impact upon the development of modern Telugu literature and the nationalist movement in Andhra, successfully integrating into them ideas of both social and political reform. It spurred women's literary activities and the formation of strong women's associations. None of these developments were duplicated in Madras, where orthodox views of women were less directly and dramatically challenged and where a lasting legitimacy for change in the social position of women was not firmly established.

The women's movement in coastal Andhra found its origins in the education of girls, the growth of literacy among older women, and the founding of Telugu journals for women.[35] Women gradually became active participants in public life, working with men and other women in voluntary associations. A Bengali speaker in the Rajahmundry Town Hall in 1890 daringly prophesied that within 300 years, women would be attending public meetings with men. Yet this happened in Andhra only seven years later, in 1897, at the Third Godavary [district] Social Conference in Ellore ; twelve Hindu women attended it.[36]

Women writers and editors, associated with women's journals and schools sponsored by Viresalingam and his colleagues, appeared at public gatherings in Andhra by the end of the nineteenth century. K. Sitamma, a Telugu authoress, gave a major speech in 1903 at the Krishna District Social Conference;

Vire-salingam had been one of her first tutors. In 1904, Rajahmundry's annual celebration of the King Emperor's birthday included high caste Hindu women as a special feature and in the same year, two hundred women were present for the opening of a Prarthana Samaj hall for women in Rajahmundry. The featured speaker was the female editor of an Ellore journal.[37]

The content, and sometimes even the style (the so-called 'women's Telugu' used to reach female readers of particular journals), reflected a commitment to changing the status of women in society. In the opinion of one critic, modern Telugu literature has "suffered irretrievably" from the stamp of social reform put upon it by Viresalingam and his followers.[38] Books, journals, and other Telugu publications have consistently shown a strong commitment to social reform, in marked contrast to modern Tamil literature.[39]

The social and religious reform movements, the Brahmo Samaj and its offshoot, the Prarthana Samaj, had a major impact on Telugu literary and political culture, but they did not become part of Tamil Nadu's intellectual history. The Brahmo Samaj strongly advocated women's education and emancipation. One Brahmo hymn contained the line, "men and women are all equals ...."[40] A political scientist recently was unable to find books or pamphlets on the Brahmo Samaj in Madras libraries, Brahmo characters in Tamil novels, or more than one Tamil Brahman in the Madras chapter of the Southern Indian Brahmo Samaj. He concluded that the Brahmo Movement "has been wholly forgotten by the Tamils." In contrast he noted the prominence of Telugus in the Brahmo Samaj, the involvement of Telugu *zamindars* in funding it, and of Telugu school teachers in popularizing "Brahmo and reformist ideals" in Andhra. Citing a 1912 source, he listed six Samajs (associations) in the Tamil region and twenty in the Telugu-speaking region. Finally, he remarked on the appearance of missionaries in Tamil novels in the proselytizing roles given to Brahmos in Bengali (and Telugu) literature of that period, and on the Tamil intelligentsia's commitment to the religious revivalism of the Theosophical movement.[41]

Surveying Madras periodicals of the late nineteenth and early twentieth century to examine the development of Tamil Nadu's political culture, the same author found that the Tamil journals, "remained popularisers of primordial beliefs and of customs," while western ideas and reform issues were discussed only in English-language periodicals. Furthermore, "modernizing" journals never popularized contemporary ideas from the southern regional language materials, in contrast to such journals in Bengal.[42] The contrast is equally strong with Andhra, where the Telugu journals popularized reform ideas from all over India and from diverse vernacular sources.[43]

Madras Presidency as a whole was ahead of most other parts of India in female literacy, but the modern Telugu movement proceeded to change the nature of education in the Telugu-speaking region in ways that necessitate different interpretations of the literacy and education statistics relating to Telugu- and Tamil-speakers. The Tamil language has still not undergone the transformation from a classical to a spoken version in the written form. Tamil still features significant diglossia; it is far less accessible. This means that five years of education in Tamil transmits less knowledge than five years of education in Telugu, since the language itself is far more difficult for students. While Tamil-speaking women and men are somewhat ahead of Telugu-speaking women and men in terms of education and literacy, these statistics are misleading and do not reflect knowledge.[44]

Madras Presidency was also a leader in some indexes of political activity. Madras was the first branch of the Indian National Congress to pass a resolution favoring women's suffrage, in 1921. Madras city appointed the first woman magistrate in India in 1922, and the first woman was nominated to the Legislative Assembly from the Madras Presidency in 1922. But the regional distinction is crucial here. The Indian National Congress in Madras Presidency included both Telugu- and Tamil-speakers, and that first woman legislator (Dr. Mrs. Muthulakshmi Reddi) was married to a Telugu-speaker.[45] In the second decade of the twentieth century, when more than one or two women began attending the annual meeting of the Indian National Congress as delegates, the women from Madras were invariably Europeans or Telugu-speakers. In 1915, when the first group of women attended the Congress in Bombay, 10 of the 11 women were Telugu-speakers.[46] One of the most prominent women nationalist leaders from Madras (Mrs. Durgabai Deshmukh) was an Andhra; she revived the Andhra women's organization in

Madras city in the 1930s.[47] The Congress politician Sarojini Naidu, who had been married to her husband, a Telugu non-Brahman, in an intercaste marriage in 1898 by Viresalingam, toured the Telugu-speaking districts frequently in her early political career.[48] After leading the movement for linguistic states and becoming a separate state in 1953, Andhra became the first, and possibly still the only state to require that at least one member of each village council (*panchayat*) be a woman.[49]

Organizational activity among Indian women, generally higher in southern than in northern India, has been particularly marked in Andhra. Historians have made much of the western-educated male elites and their voluntary associations, seeing the new organizational patterns as a major index of social and political modernization; women's associations have received little attention. Yet women were even more constrained by the hierarchical caste system than men, seldom meeting with women from outside their family or caste. In Andhra, women's literary and religious associations were founded in most of the towns and these associations used the vernacular rather than English. The Andhra Mahila Sabha, the organization for women founded by a female follower of Viresalingam in 1910,[50] grew very powerful throughout the Telugu-speaking region in the late 1930s. It now provides health and educational service to thousands of Andhra women of all castes and classes.[51] The leadership of the organization was and is undoubtedly middle and upper-class, but it serves a very broad clientele and should not be dismissed as a 'women's social service effort.' Andhra is one of two states with a regional women's organization, and the Andhra Mahila Sabha is the only women's organization listed in an all-India directory as publishing its journal in the vernacular language. Andhra also leads the nation in total number of local women's associations.[52] Again, distinctive historical features of a regional vernacular culture help to explain these developments.

We want to suggest that a very recent survey of attitudes towards women's role in the family and society also shows the lasting consequences of Andhra's widow marriage movement. Prepared by the Committee on the Status of Women in India, the survey summarizes its results by state.[53] Andhra and Tamil Nadu contrast strongly in many areas, and Andhra is generally the more "progressive" in attitudes towards women. Table IV shows the response to "It is alright for a widow to remarry" question. Thus, 78% of the Andhra respondents approved or partially approved of widow remarriage, compared to only 59% of the Tamil Nadu respondents; 19% of the Andhras disapproved compared to 37% of the Tamil Nadu respondents. And, while the Tamil Nadu respondents favored education for women more,[54] the Andhra respondents favored women's participation in politics far more than respondents from any other state, with 39% of the responses rated 'modern' here (Tamil Nadu was next with 20% 'modern').[55]

TABLE IV

APPROVAL OF WIDOW MARRIAGE

	Disagree	Partially Agree	Agree
Andhra	19%	11%	67%
Madras	37%	9%	50%

SOURCE: *Towards Equality, Report of the Committee on the Status of Women in India* (New Delhi: Government of India, 1974), 421.

We have looked at the widow marriage compaigns carried out in two South Indian regions with relatively similar economic and social structures, Andhra and Tamil Nadu. Neither campaign produced a measurable increase in the numbers of remarried widows, but one had a far-reaching impact on its regional culture. Girls' education, however, has increased steadily in India and especially southern India. Girls' education found justification in improved family welfare, for its contribution to the home, children, and husband. But widow marriage found no such justification. Indeed, it is still almost totally unacceptable in those castes and communities which prohibited it, despite high educational levels in many of those same castes and communities. Widows' homes, schools for widows, and widows as teachers could be accepted, but a widow could not re-enter the householder stage as a wife.

Though the results of the widow marriage reform were insignificant everywhere in terms of numbers of remarried widows, the campaign in Andhra had a lasting ideological impact because of its integration with linguistic, religious, and political reform movements. The symbolic nature of the widow marriage issue, the dramatic conflict generated by the relatively frequent public performance of widow marriages in Andhra, have helped stimulate active participation on the part of Telugu-speaking women in the political culture of their region.

While we recognize that this essay is suggestive rather that definitive, we hope it will stimulate other work on regional differences in the position of women in India. Quantitative measurements of women's work participation, literacy and educational levels, political office-holding, and voting patterns are not adequate. We need to know more about the qualitative aspects of the regional cultures, their changing ideological content, and the ways in which social movements and educational institutions have transmitted that content to participants in India's political culture.

NOTES

[1] Quoted in a letter from the local Lutheran missionary, H. C. Schmidt, in *The Foreign Missionary*, XII, 2 (February, 1891), p. 14.

[2] Lucien W. Pye and Sidney Verba, eds., *Political Culture and Political Development* (Princeton: Princeton University Press, 1965), p. 513.

[3] Pye and Verba, *Political Culture*, p. 7.

[4] Charles H. Heimsath, *Indian Nationalism and Hindu Social Reform* (Princeton: Princeton University Press, 1964), p. 5.

[5] Anil Seal, *The Emergence of Indian Nationalism* (Cambridge: Cambridge University Press, 1968), p. 97; *The Imperial Gazetteer of India* (Oxford: 26 Vols., new ed., 1908-1931), XII, p. 287; XV, p. 324. See Andre Beteille, *Caste, Class, and Power* (Berkeley: University of California Press, 1965), for Brahmans in a Tanjore village.

[6] Some of the leaders were members of both regional associations, donors gave to both, and written communications were frequent: John G. Leonard, "Social Reforms in Rajahmundry and Madras, 1874-1891," unpublished manuscript.

[7] John G. "Leonard, Politics and Social Change in South India: A Study of the Andhra Movement," *The Journal of Commonwealth Political Studies* V, 1 (March, 1967), pp. 60-77. At India's independence in 1947 there were nine states and assorted "native states" and union territo-

ries; after the linguistic states reorganization in 1956, there were fifteen states, and there are now (1979) twenty-one states. Madras Presidency, on which this article focuses, consisted of twenty-two British districts in four distinct regions: Andhra, Tamil Nadu, Malabar (Malayali-speaking), and South Kanara (Kannada-speaking). We will be concerned with the Telugu-speaking Andhra districts (6 to 7) and the Tamil-speaking districts (10).

[8]N. V. Sovani, *The Population Problem in India: A Regional Approach* (Poona: Gokhale Institute of Politics and Economics, 1942), pp. 46-63.

[9]David Washbrook, "Country politics: Madras 1880 to 1930," in *Modern Asian Studies* VII, 3 (July, 1973), pp. 475-531. He points to the more popular nature of politics, the greater urban-rural integration, and the congruence of Congress nationalist activities with vernacular and religious activities in the Andhra "wet" area. A criticism of Washbrook's analysis by Eugene F. Irschick, "Interpretations of Indian Political Development," appears in *Journal of Asian Studies* XXXIV, 2 (February, 1975), pp. 467-472.

[10]Articles on Rajahmundry and Madras make these comparisons: John G. Leonard, "Urban Government Under the Raj," *Modern Asian Studies* VII, 2 (April, 1973), pp. 227-251 (on Rajahmundry); and Susan J. Lewandowski, "Urban Growth and Municipal Development in the Colonial City of Madras, 1860-1900," *Journal of Asian Studies* XXXIV, 2 (February, 1975), pp. 341-360.

[11]Seal, *Emergence of Indian Nationalism*, pp. 100-103.

[12]*Ibid.*, pp. 103-110; R. Suntharalingam, *Politics and Nationalist Awakening in South India, 1852-1891* (Tucson: University of Arizona Press 1974), pp. 113, 125.

[13]*Imperial Census of 1881 (Presidency of Madras)* (Madras: Government of India, 1883), I, pp. 70-73.

[14]*Census of 1891 (Presidency of Madras)* Madras: Government of India, 1893), XIII, pp. 145-149.

[15]*Census of 1881 (Madras)*, I, pp. 70-72.

[16]*Census of 1891 (Madras)*, XIII, pp. 146-147.

[17]The Census of 1891 commented that the influence of Brahmanical customs was greater in the Telugu country, meaning an earlier age of marriage and stronger prohibitions on divorce and widow marriage, and this conclusion was repeated in 1901: *Census of 1891 (Madras)*, XIII, pp. 151-152; *Census of 1901 (Madras)*, XV, Part I, p. 59.

[18]Ronald Inden and Ralph Nicholas, *Kinship in Bengali Culture* (Chicago: University of Chicago Press, 1977). See also Susan Wadley, "Women and the Hindu Tradition," *Signs* III, 1 (Autumn, 1977), pp. 113-125.

[19]Dorothy Stein, "Women to Burn," *Signs* IV, 2 (Winter, 1978), pp. 253-268, reviews this literature; Vina Mazumdar, in a "Comment on Suttee" following Stein's article (*Ibid.*, pp. 262-273), attributes these controls of women to social stratification and a demographic shortage of women.

[20]Brief accounts appear in *Towards Equality, Report of the Committee on the Status of Women* in *India* (New Delhi: Government of India, 1974;) pp. 50-54, 102-103.

[21]For an overview of social reform efforts, see Heimsath, *Indian Nationalism and Hindu Social Reform.*

[22]This has been shown in detail by John G. Leonard, "Kandukuri Viresalingam, 1848-1919, a biography of an Indian social reformer" (Ph. D. dissertation, University of Wisconsin, 1970), particularly pp. 146-253.

[23]Henry Morris, *A Descriptive and Historical Account of the Godavary District in the Presidency of Madras* (London, 1878), p. 30; Indian Education Commission, *Report of the Madras Provincial Committee* (Calcutta: Government of India, 1884), p. 38; quote from letter of H. C. Schmidt, *The Foreign Missionary* II, 2 (February, 1881), p. 2; *Report on Public Instruction in the Madras Presidency*, 1880-81 (Madras, 1880), pp. 65-67.

[24]*The Madras Mail*, December 30, 1884. The letter's author was Samuel Satthianathan, a distinguished educator and author.

[25]Since Viresalingam wrote in Telugu, he is little known outside Andhra. See his collected works: *Kandukuri Viresalinga Krita Granthamulu* (Rajahmundry: 9 Vols., 1951-1952). For English details (and the sources of the above information), see John G. Leonard, "Kandukuri Viresalingam."

[26]Viresalingam's account is in his collected works, VII, p. 20-22; for an English account, see D. V. Prakasa Rao, "The Widow Marriage Movement in South India," *Kayastha Samachar* (Allahabad: 1901), VII, 6; VIII, 4 and 5. For this event and the following summary see John G. Leonard, "Social Reform."

[27]J. Gurunatham, *Viresalingam ,The Founder of Telugu Public Life* (Rajahmundry, 1911), pp. 165-166.

[28]John G. Leonard, "Social Reform," pp. 44-104, 134-211, provides the details for this summary. In Madras city, the first Widow's Home was that founded by Viresalingam in 1898; it was moved back to Rajahmundry by him in 1904. The second was founded only in 1912 by a Tamil-speaking widow, and its goals were purely educational. Neither she nor her few charges remarried. Monica Felton, *A Child Widow's Story* (New York: Harcourt, Brace and World, 1967).

[29]For the dispute with Sankaracharya, see Leonard, "Kandukuri Viresalingam," ch. 5; *Madras Times*, February 6, 1882; *Indian Law Review* VI, pp. 381-385. The Madras leaders, Raghunath Rao and Centsal Rao, publicly disassociated themselves from this suit: *Madras Mail*, Sept. 12, 1882.

[30]*Report on Public Instruction in the Madras Presidency for 1881-1882* (Madras: Government of Madras, 1882), p. 5; V. Venkat Rao, *A Hundred Years of Local Self-Government and Administration in the Andhra and Madras States, 1850 to 1950* (Bombay, 1960), p. 285. See also Samuel Satthianathan, *History of Education in the Madras Presidency* (Madras, 1894).

[31] Keshub Chandra Sen, *The Improvement of Indian Women* (Calcutta: 1871), p. 15.

[32] V. Krishnamachari, *Madras Mail*, May 18, 1885.

[33] This has been documented for males by Seal, *Emergence of Indian Nationalism*, pp. 104-106.

[34] John G. Leonard, "Social Reform," pp. 134-211.

[35] A. Vivekananda Devi, "Stri Janoddharana," [The Women's Movement], *Yuga Purusudu Viresalingam* (Hyderabad, n. d.), pp. 190-194; T. Ramachandra Rao, "Women's Journals," in K. R. Seshagiri Rao, ed., *Studies in Telugu Journalism* (Delhi: Narla Shashtyabdapurti Celebration Committee, 1968).

[36] Sivanath Sastri was the speaker on the same occasion cited in footnote 1. For the Third Godavary Social Conference, see *The Madras Times*, June 11, 1897.

[37] G. V. Sitapati, *History of Telugu Literature* (New Delhi: Sahitya Akademi, 1968), pp. 228, 278-92; reports of meetings in *Indian Social Reformer* (Madras and Bombay), June 13, 1903; *Ibid.*, Oct. 3, 1904; *Ibid.*, September 5 and 12, 1904.

[38] V. L. Sastri, ed., *Encyclopaedia of the Madras Presidency and Adjacent States* (Cocanada: The Oriental Encyclopaedic Publishing Company, 1921), p. 338.

[39] See the discussion of Tamil Literature in Sastri, *Encyclopaedia of Madras Presidency*: and T. P. Meenakshisundaran, "Tamil Literature," in *Contemporary Indian Literature* (New Delhi: Sahitya Akademi, 1957), pp. 238-249, compared to K. Ramakotiswara Rau, "Telugu Literature," pp. 250-263 of the same volume.

[40] N. S. Bose, *The Indian Awakening and Bengal* (Calcutta: K. L. Mukhopadhyay, 1960), p. 97.

[41] R. Srinivasan, "The Brahmo Samaj in Tamilnadu", *Journal of the University of Bombay*, Arts Numbers, XLIV, and XLV, 80-81 (1975-76), pp. 213-225. The 1911 Census recorded 17,038,000 Tamil-speakers and 15,782,000 Telugu-speakers in Madras Presidency: *Census of 1911 (Madras)*, XII, pt. II, p. 140.

[42] R. Srinivasan, "Madras Periodicals and Modernization of Values," *Journal of the University of Bombay*, Arts Number, XL, 76 (October, 1971), pp. 154-155.

[43] Sitapati, *Telugu Literature*; Rau, "Telugu Literature;" Leonard, "Social Reform," pp. 382-87.

[44] David McAlpin, personal communication, March, 1980.

[45] A. Appadorai, ed., *The Status of Women in South Asia* (Bombay: Orient Longmans, 1954), p. 86. A Tamil Brahman career woman, she chose a "social reform" marriage: S. Muthulakshmi Reddi, *Autobiography* (Privately printed. Madras: MLJ Press, 1964).

[46] A. M. Zaidi, ed., *The Encylopedia of Indian National Congress*, 7 Vols. (New Delhi: S. Chand, 1979),VI, pp. 710-714. Annie Besant was the eleventh woman that year.

[47] Freda Bedi, "Voluntary Social Service," in Tara Ali Baig, ed., *Women of India* (Delhi: Government of India, 1958), p. 227. Despite

these leadership factors the proportion of female voters in the southern states and of female candidates for state and national office has not been higher than elsewhere, disappointing those who thought female literacy rates would correlate with political participation. (Appadorai, ed., *Status of Women*, pp. 102-103, 112-113; Bose, "A Demographic Profile," in Devaki Jain, ed., *Indian Women* (New Delhi: Government of India, 1973), p. 183.

[48] Padmini Sengupta, *Sarojini Naidu* (New York: Asia Publishing House, 1966). pp. 34, 90-97, *et Passim*.

[49] Padmini Sengupta, *Women Workers of India* (London: Asia Publishing House, 1960), p. 217.

[50] First Andhra Mahila Sabha, *Upanyasa Manjari* [collected speeches] (Kakinada, 1910).

[51] Andhra Mahila Sabha, *Silver Jubilee Souvenir* (Madras: 1962); Bedi, "Voluntary Social Service," in Tara Ali Baig, ed., *Women of India*, p. 227; and Sitapati, *Telugu Literature*, pp. 278-292.

[52] *Towards Equality, Report of the Committee on the Status of Women in India* (New Delhi: Government of India, 1974), p. 465; Durgabai Deshmukh and M. S. Gore, eds,, *Encyclopaedia of Social Work in India*, 3 Vols. (New Delhi: Government of India, 1968), II, p. 646.

[53] Their survey was administered to 5603 respondents, and it is not clear from the information published whether the sample from each state conformed to their general guidelines to secure 75% female and 25% male respondents, 60% rural and 40% urban respondents, and a cross-section of communities and classes. There were 336 respondents from Andhra and 784 from Tamil Nadu. *Towards Equality*, pp. 393-395.

[54] *Towards Equality*, p. 444.

[55] *Ibid.*, p. 450.

PART II
WOMEN'S RIGHTS AND POLITICAL INDEPENDENCE IN INDIA

The Indian Women's Movement: A Struggle for Women's Rights or National Liberation?

GERALDINE FORBES

I. Introduction

"By their participation in [the] political movement, Indian women helped their own struggle for liberation. In India, feminism and nationalism were closely interlinked."[1] If this statement, characteristic of much contemporary writing on the Indian women's movement of the inter-war years, is true, then the nationalist movement in India is unique. It is unique, not in the sense that the women who fought for political rights in other countries were not also deeply concerned with women's rights, but rather in terms of the compatibility of women's and nationalist aims. One of the ways of testing this assertion about the congruence of feminism and nationalism in India is to focus on the women's movement[2] as it mediated between women's rights and nationalist activities in relation to three key issues affecting Indian women's emancipation: child marriage, purdah, and legal reform.

To do so, it will be necessary first to examine the statements and activities of Indian women's organizations during this period. Unfortunately, purely political groups of women were either unable to keep records of their membership and activities,[3] had their records destroyed in riots,[4] or were *ad hoc* in nature and somewhat careless about record-keeping.[5] By contrast, information about women's social service organizations is detailed and accessible. In addition, the members of these women's service organizations saw their work as patriotic. For example, the Women's Indian Association and the All-India Women's Conference were national in orientation, sought to include women of all castes, religions, and classes, and clearly stated that their efforts to help women were hampered by the colonial situation. In examining the response of women's associations to the three issues mentioned above: child marriage, purdah, and legal rights, specific questions can be asked about how these particular issues fit with the demands of the nationalist movement, and what choices the women committed to both movements had to face.

II. Review of the Literature

If one looks at studies of women's rights issues in the context of nationalist movements, some sharp contrasts appear between other countries and India. Examining the lives of Muslim women who participated in the Turkish war of independence (1920-23), the Algerian war of independence (1955-62), and the contemporary Palestinian movement, Sandra Danforth concludes that these women experienced significant personal change and national gratitude, but no transformation of their status. Further, even when social change is a goal of the new regime, independence is usually accompanied by a drive to reestablish stability, meaning that major transformation in women's status is unlikely.[6]

In a survey of the history of Japanese women, Joy Paulson traces the development of a women's rights movement from its genesis in the general civil rights movement of the 1870s and 1880s, through the founding of the Blue Stocking Society of 1911, to the championship of equal rights, birth control, better women's labor conditions, and the franchise. Then came the Manchurian incident and the Japanese feminist movement was overwhelmed by the rising tide of militarism and mobilization to support the war effort.[7]

Leith's study of the early Chinese Communist movement makes the point that issues affecting peasant women were incompatible with the peasant unity desirable for the political struggle. Women workers, whose concerns were the same as those of working men: better pay, working conditions, and the freedom to organize, could work harmoniously within Communist strategy. Peasant women, however, were concerned about marriage and divorce rights, issues which divided them from men and made the goals of women's peasant unions dysfunctional to the overall rural movement.[3]

There is general agreement in the historical literature that a women's rights movement does not easily fit with a nationalist movement, although women are desirable comrades in a nationalist struggle. The need to redress women's grievances can be an important component of nationalism, but when women insist that redress for their grievances be given higher priority than the national struggle, they will be considered subversive. In times of crisis, feminism appears to be an expensive luxury.

India seems to be an exception to this rough model. Most authors agree that the connection between women's rights and nationalism in India was of long standing. Nineteenth-century reformers focused on the status of women before they tackled the problems associated with colonial status. The reformers were concerned with sati, child marriage, polygamy, child widowhood, and they sought to change these customs by urging the British to pass laws, by forming organizations to promote such causes as widow remarriage and female education, and by writing and speaking about social reform. These efforts were directed toward increasing public awareness of the problems, and tolerance of the new practices they espoused. The reformers' aims were "dignity and status" for women within the family; no one urged women to become economically and legally independent.[9] The same Western-educated, urban middle class that produced the social reformers provided the impetus for the Indian National Congress.

Indian reformers who focused on women's issues fully accepted that favorite nineteenth-century refrain that women's position was an excellent indicator of a society's advancement.[10] Missionaries were overly fond of explaining Indian backwardness prior to British rule as due to the low status of women. Reverend E. Storrow, a missionary who arrived in India in 1848, argued that in historically powerful countries, such as ancient Rome and contemporary Britain, much of the strength, courage and virtue of the race was due to the position and respect granted to women.[11] In his comments on caste and marriage, Sir Herbert Hope Risley wrote that while education had produced a class of Indians interested in political advancement, it was unlikely that they could attain it, for:

> A society which accepts intellectual inanition and moral stagnation as the natural condition of its womankind cannot hope to develop the higher qualities of courage, devotion and self-sacrifice which go to the making of nations.[12]

With such messages emanating from their rulers and inculcated by their imported education, it was not surprising that the early Indian nationalists sought to improve the position of their women.

The concern of politically and socially advanced Indians for women's status continued into the twentieth century. M. K. Gandhi was not only committed to improving women's lot, but he developed a mass movement that sought the support of women, as housewives who could support the family while men participated in the freedom struggle, and as active participants in that struggle.[13] That women responded positively to his call has been ceaselessly reiterated. Eye-witnesses were stunned by the sudden emergence of Indian women into the streets as they joined processions and began picketing foreign cloth and liquor shops. According to Gail Omvedt, Gandhi recruited women to channel the energies of an emerging women's movement into the political movement he controlled.[14] Maria Mies develops this idea further. Gandhi, she claims, created a new myth of Indian womanhood, Sita-like in her devotion to service and self-sacrifice, whether in her family or to her nation. As a consequence, Gandhi attracted women from the well-to-do classes, "with a good education, well-placed husbands, and servants." For these women, family came first, and concern with socio-political issues second. Their social status and economic reliance on their husbands meant that they could approach political involvement as a hobby. Their partial involvement meant they did not "frontally attack the official ideology of women," and thus were unable to promote the essential issues related to women's emancipation.[15]

Other writers, most of them Indian women, have been far

more generous to Gandhi. Women joined the movement because his message "offered the women of India an opportunity to break from the past with all its frustrations."[16] Vina Mazumdar stresses that Gandhi was concerned with women's personal dignity.[17] Gandhi encouraged women to join the political movement, according to Aparna Basu, by emphasizing their importance and by giving them specific tasks which appealed to them. He felt that women were the true satyagrahis, embodying the talents which were needed for nonviolent struggle: courage, tolerance, and self-suffering. Gandhi saw women as one of the most oppressed groups in Indian society, who consequently had developed an ability to endure suffering which could lead to the deliverance, not only of women, but of the entire nation.[18]

Two quite different interpretations of Gandhi's role in relation to the women's movement emerge from the literature. He has been seen as directing a movement that had barely gone beyond the drawing rooms, and alternatively as pre-empting a movement on the brink of becoming radical. It is significant that the different interpretations of Gandhi come from people holding different views of the essential goals of a women's rights movement. Omvedt's criteria for liberation are "equal participation in the productive and political affairs of society, and freedom from sole responsibility for home and child care."[19] These, however, were not the goals of the Indian women's movement. Since the nineteenth century, the basic message of the reform movement had been that "women must not be ill-treated and must be given some dignity and status, because they are the custodians of the family."[20] The women's movement in India, therefore, was two-pronged. It aimed, first, at removing those customs which were detrimental to women's gaining "dignity and status" (child marriage, purdah, legal disabilities), and secondly, at promoting measures which would allow for "recognition of the distinctive features of womanhood," particularly those related to the family.[21] While the first of Omvedt's criteria would have been acceptable, the second would not.

According to the various Indian writers cited above, Gandhi gave women new dimensions for their concerns, charted a role that both won them the respect of Indian males and involved them in activities which facilitated their movement from home to world. In short, "by their participation in the political movement, Indian women helped their own struggle for liberation."[22] From this perspective, it would appear that feminism and nationalism are compatible.[23]

III. The Women's Organizations

Two women's organizations, the Women's Indian Association (WIA) formed in 1917, and the All-India Women's Conference (AIWC), formed in 1927, sought to bring women together to advance their status through education, social reform, and politics. They wanted to educate women by opening schools and to influence government policy concerning women's education. They founded ameliorative institutions and encouraged social reform legislation. They demanded women's suffrage, lobbied for women's issues, and promoted candidates for election to the councils and appointment to government commissions. Their work included political petitioning, voluntary social work, and local organization.[24] They developed branches all over India and by the mid-1930s claimed jointly a membership of over 10,000 women.

These organizations were for women only, although they did not confine themselves to women's issues. The earliest associations for women were begun by men in the nineteenth century. They trained the first generation of women leaders, but at the same time, the men dominated their issues and activities. In the early twentieth century, organizations for women only were begun and justified in terms of providing an environment in which women raised in a sex-segregated society could speak and act with some degree of autonomy.[25] Women explained the need for their own separate organizations in terms of the special "nature" of women and the inability of men to understand them. By the 1920s, it was taken for granted that women would form organizations to deal with women's problems. In their speeches, Indian women often referred to the "golden age" when women moved freely and took part in all activities, and to the goddesses and heroines from whom they were descended. In the present circumstances, they said, women outside the home could complement the work of men, but not compete with it, by contributing their special talents for nurturing and housekeeping. They explicitly denied any similarity between their movement and the movements of

Western "feminists" with their implied sexual antagonism.[26]

With such an ideology, the women's associations were unlikely to encounter much male criticism. The WIA and AIWC began with women's issues: education, social and legal reform, and graduated, naturally and quickly, to some of the larger social problems affecting the country. Such issues as the problems of children, or the plight of untouchables, ear-marked by Gandhi as among India's most serious problems, could easily be interpreted as extensions of their nurturing role. The women's organizations discussed these problems at their annual meetings, passed resolutions, and set up committees to deal with them, but their major interest remained women's issues.

While they remained primarily interested in women's rights, these organizations were nevertheless affected by the nationalist movement. As Charles Heimsath and others have pointed out, the connection between social reform activities and early nationalism was close. The leaders of these women's organizations almost all came from reformist families. The women had been educated, a result usually of their fathers' interests in female education and improving the status of women. As the men became increasingly absorbed by political activities, their female relatives became active in social service organizations. While the women formed "women only" groups that were formally unattached to political parties, informal family networks supplied close ties to the political arena. Through fathers, husbands, sons, and in-laws, the women leaders had contact with prominent male nationalists.

In addition, many of the women leaders were also nationalists. The WIA was begun by Margaret Cousins, a Theosophist, suffragette, and Irish and Indian nationalist, and by Dorothy Jinarajadasa, another Theosophist and suffragette. The organization's first president was Annie Besant, founder of the Home Rule League, first woman president of the Indian National Congress, and one of the foremost champions of Indian nationalism before 1920. In 1917, Annie Besant was interned for her political activities and the WIA protested. In the same year, they sent a delegation to meet Edwin Montagu, the Secretary of State for India, to ask that women be given the vote in the upcoming governmental reforms.

Margaret Cousins also helped organize the AIWC. The

WIA journal, *Stri Dharma*, had published an article which urged women to present the government with demands for female education. Cousins then wrote to all WIA branches suggesting that they hold local conferences and prepare resolutions on women's education, preliminary to an all-India conference on women in education. The All-India Women's Conference, which became the AIWC, was held in January of 1927. The list of delegates included the names of several women who were already part of the nationalist struggle or who would later become prominent nationalists.[27]

Many of these women insisted that their commitment to India's freedom was compatible with their concern for women's rights. It was strategically important to do this. To remain feminist while nationalist, it was necessary to resist step-child status: they did not want their organizations to become simply women's auxiliaries of a political party. At the same time, these women were well aware that criticism of Indian men or the male-dominated social system could be used by the British as justification for maintaining political control. An autonomous, apolitical stance would allow the women's organizations to maintain feminist priorities while permitting individual members to support the nationalist movement. Nevertheless, over the years situations and events caused leaders of these organizations to vacillate, redefine their aims, amend by-laws, argue with each other, and finally end up with organizations which were somewhere between separate and autonomous women's associations and women's auxiliaries of the Indian National Congress.

From the beginning, the WIA had an interest in Home Rule and women's suffrage and rhetoric that was clearly patriotic.[28] Women should have a full opportunity for civic service; they should accept their responsibilities as "daughters of India," and see the importance of their role in "training, guiding and forming the character of the future rulers of India."[29] Yet, even in the troubled times of 1928-29 the WIA insisted that their policy was to work for reforms through the Legislative Councils.[30] They were not ready to accept civil disobedience, for this would have jeopardized the relationship they had so carefully worked out with government to secure women positions as magistrates and on various councils and committees, and to urge the legislation they thought necessary for the improvement of women's status.

When the civil disobedience movement began in 1930, therefore, the WIA was faced with a dilemma. The officers tried to articulate a position "in support of political freedom for India." At the same time, they wanted to preserve harmony among a membership which included staunch Congress members, government servants, the dependents of government servants, and women opposed to Congress policies.[31] As could be expected, leaders of the WIA were never completely successful in juggling their contradictory aims nor the needs of this complex membership. In 1930, the WIA first requested that three of their members be appointed delegates to the proposed Round Table Conference. Then they reversed this stand, followed the Congress, and refused to participate. When the Gandhi-Irwin pact was concluded, they again reversed their stand and asked to be included in the Round Table Conference, but this time it was too late.[32]

The problems of balancing patriotism and deep commitment to women's issues can best be illustrated through the case of Dr. Muthulakshmi Reddi. Reddi, a medical doctor, a founder-member of the WIA, the first woman member of the Madras Legislative Council, and a serious social reformer, had definite ideas about the role of a women's organization. She believed that political activism was "flashy" and when the smoke had cleared, women would still suffer from oppression. Separate women's organizations were necessary, she asserted, because in women's organizations, women could speak freely, vent their grievances, discuss solutions, and develop powers of expression before they attempted to seek amelioration in the outside world.[33] In the 1920s, Reddi thought that women should keep away from party politics until their status had improved, although she approved of the nomination of women to decision-making bodies. Since women were mainly concerned with social issues, Reddi felt that British government help would be necessary for some time to come.[34] Yet Reddi, as Vice-President of the WIA, signed a protest in 1928 against the all-British composition of the Simon Commission. Not only did it lack Indians, it lacked an Indian woman, essential if the views of Indian women were to be considered.[35] Subsequently Reddi was nominated to the Hartog Committee, the Auxiliary Education Committee to the Simon Commission, and she accepted. Her acceptance was denounced by WIA officers.[36] Reddi, in turn, threatened to resign from the Association. She explained that she was not acting in a self-serving and capricious manner, but that she had always taken the stand that the WIA's main concerns were social issues and the education of women. She firmly believed that at this stage of their development, women should not assume an anti-government attitude, if such an attitude was detrimental to their cause.[37]

Before long, nevertheless, Reddi became disillusioned with government actions. When Sarojini Naidu was arrested in 1930, Reddi said, "We women, however moderate and law-abiding cannot afford to be quiet at this juncture." This illustrates the degree to which those who were predisposed to a loyalist position were alienated by the harshness of British reaction to civil disobedience. Reddi decided then that social reform would not be possible without political power, and to gain that she would throw in her lot with the nationalists. Though not in favor of civil disobedience, she resigned from the Legislative Council in 1930 because Gandhi had been arrested. She was fully supportive of *swadeshi, khaddar*, the anti-drink campaign and the anti-untouchability movement.[38] But she never believed that the Congress was fully committed to women's rights.

Reddi's distrust of the Congress influenced the WIA. The organization noted in 1937 that the Congress was not anxious to nominate women for general seats in the election. Furthermore, many Congress members, once elected, showed no concern for women's rights. In Madras, members of the Congress minority in the legislature initiated a measure to exempt Devadasis from the Immoral Traffic Bill. In the eyes of women who trusted the Congress, this was tantamount to legalizing prostitution.[39] While no one accused the Congress of misusing women, many made it clear that this instance had made them mistrustful of "politics."

The AIWC, an association that claimed to speak for all Indian women, and which was formed to recommend to government policies concerning women's education, was less avowedly "patriotic" than the WIA. And yet, it too went through as many changes vis-à-vis the Congress as did the WIA. During its first session in 1927, the AIWC decided to focus on social problems as well as female education, since it was impossible to isolate the two. When its constitution was accepted in 1929, the AIWC included a clause stating that it would not engage in party politics.⁴⁰ This neutral stand was defended in terms of female unity. Only an apolitical association could bring together maharanis and officials of princely states, Muslim women, employees of the educational and medical services, the wives of government servants, British women interested in women's rights, Congress women, and those who were indifferent to political questions. To have their resolutions and deputations taken seriously, AIWC leaders believed that they should be able to speak for all Indian women.

The president of the AIWC's eighth annual session, Lady Abdul Qadir, emphasized this feminist and apolitical stance. Educational and social reforms, she believed, needed the support of all women, and getting involved in controversial matters, like politics, could only weaken women's position. But professor Radhakrishnan, who spoke to the AIWC in the same year, bridged the conceptual gap, claiming that this sense of unity was the essence of nationalism. He was delighted to see in the AIWC all castes and communities: "the distinctions of high and low, Hindu and Muslim, European and non-European, official and non-official, are not observed." This was a great contribution to political emancipation because the removal of social and communal differences was one of the biggest tasks before India.⁴¹

Opposing this, a political stance were those women who wanted the AIWC to support the nationalist movement. They did not want the Conference to become part of the Congress, but many of them were personally devoted to the Congress and convinced that it was the true champion of women. They felt, as Nehru did, that "fence-sitting" served no purpose. If they continued to vacillate between support for the nationalists and collaboration with the British, someone else would always make their decisions for them.⁴² The political issue was debated with fervor and even anger at AIWC meetings throughout the 1930s. During the civil disobedience movement of 1930-31, many Congress women had to resign as members of the AIWC, but there was considerable opinion in favor of permitting members of the Congress to remain in the AIWC. In the matter of franchise, the AIWC was solidly in favor of women's suffrage, and most members did not wish to avoid this question as a "political" matter. The debates in the AIWC usually centered around an amendment to the constitution that would have allowed the AIWC as an association and its members to make political statements. The amendment failed to achieve the necessary four-fifths majority, however, until 1939.[43]

Clearly, the line between feminism and nationalism was a fine one, where it could be drawn at all. These two concepts, far from being mutually exclusive, were defined in terms of priorities. AIWC members expressed their opinions about political affairs with great frequency. They claimed that women could only be released from their shackles with "true political emancipation,"[44] and praised the Congress for its support of the women's movement.[45] The AIWC criticized the government for the Communal Award and its internment of prominent women, and praised Gandhi for inspiring the womanhood of India. The conference also approved of politically active women, such as Kamaladevi Chattopadhyaya, who held its highest offices.

The results of all this political activity for an organization that claimed to be apolitical included a government request that Indian women members of the educational service resign from the AIWC, which was branded as political.[46] Branches of the AIWC in some of the princely states withdrew from the organization, and a number of Muslim women resigned.[47] The Organizing Secretary noted in a 1940 report that some women members of the Muslim League were antagonistic to the perceived domination of the AIWC by Congress-minded Hindu women, who could by a majority vote rule on such topics directly affecting Muslim women's rights as the shariat legislation.[48] Other women also resented the organization's moving away from its original intention. Hilla Rustomji, a Parsi from Hyderabad, wrote that many political resolutions had nothing to do with educational and social matters. In her own branch, some thirty-five members had resigned after asking the branch to disaffiliate itself from the parent body. The AIWC is supposed to represent all women, she continued, and is "not supposed to take part in 'party politics,' yet if you look at the Resolutions passed during the last years, you will find that they are all absolutely Congress."[49] Resignations from Madras summed up dissatisfaction with the AIWC stand. In 1943, these included a prominent Muslim educationalist, Rahmatunnissa Begum; Mary Clubwalla a well-known social worker who was involved with a number of organizations which included British women; and a woman from a princely family, Yuvarani Saheba of Pithapuran.[50] Unfortunately, the opposition which objected to the "tilt" of the organization was often disparagingly referred to as the "Muslim women" or the "Bengal group," implying that it represented small groups and parochial interests. In taking such a stand the AIWC sacrificed its earlier claim to speak for all women, but refused to come to terms with the consequences both for feminist and national unity.

As serious as the question of unity was the question of priorities. Gradually, the advocates of "women's rights first" in the AIWC lost ground to those who looked upon freedom for women and freedom for the country as synonymous. The women's awareness of the divisive potential of feminist issues within the context of nationalism has already been noted. Sarojini Naidu, at the fourth session of the AIWC in 1931, asserted in no uncertain terms that she was not a feminist.[51] From then on, as the nationalist movement gathered increasing momentum, the official rhetoric of the AIWC repeated that its members were not feminists, not suffragettes, and did not intend to start a sex war with men. Western movements for women's rights, they felt, had pitted women against men and they were not anxious to adopt that model if it would damage the nationalist cause.

Dissenting voices nevertheless continued to advocate feminist priorities. "If India has suffered from foreign domination, if we have lost our manliness, our courage, our initiative individually, if we have become stunted for want of self-government and self-rule, no less disastrous results have been produced by one-sided laws and customs,"[52] said one member. Commenting on a debate in the Central Legislative Assembly on women's legal disabilities, Begum Hamid Ali, President of the AIWC in 1940 asked, "When will men of India realize that it is of no use asking a third party to play fair when they themselves are willing to close their eyes to all the wrongs the women suffer and have mental reservations when freedom is proposed for womanhood?....Sons of slave mothers will always remain slaves mentally, whatever their legal position in life." As far as she could see, Indians would not gain *swaraj* until they had set their own house in order and granted women legal equality.[53]

More common than these statements, however, were assertions that linked feminist and nationalist priorities: First, women's status could not be changed as long as India remained under foreign domination, and second, the nationalist movement was aiding the development of the women's movement. This point of view is illustrated by the following statement: "It is said that the French Revolution made the poor man proud. Our fight with the British has made us women human beings."[54]

The rapprochement between feminism and nationalism was threatened again in the 1940's by differences over strategy. The period of Congress governments after 1937 and renewed civil disobedience during the war led the AIWC to doubt the value of the Congress connection. The world of women had not been transformed in the Congress provinces, and civil disobedience would retard the passage of legislation advantageous to women and children. At the fifteenth session of the AIWC in 1941, the members deplored the failure of the British to grant India freedom, but voted to continue working with the government by drafting reform bills and urging sympathetic members of the Legislative Assembly, such as V.V. Joshi, Har Bilas Sarda, and C.V. Deshmukh, to introduce those bills.[55] For all their pronouncements about freedom first, the AIWC was willing to cooperate with the government to secure legal reform at a time when Congress members had resigned from the legislatures.

While the women's organizations found it easy to take a firm and consistent stand as patriots, they found it difficult always to accept the priorities and tactics dictated by male-dominated political parties. They accepted a subordinate but complementary role in political matters, preferring to work for women's issues. As long as the activities, timing, and rhetoric of the Congress were supportive of women's issues, they could be enthusiastic nationalists. But when cooperation with the Congress threatened women's issues and alienated their membership, the women's organizations looked to their own priorities. Feminism and nationalism were never mutually exclusive for these Indian women's organizations, however. There may have been conflict with the nationalists over priorities and tactics but not over ultimate goals. The congruence of these goals can be further clarified by examining in detail three women's issues:

child marriage, purdah, and legal reform.

IV. An Examination of Specific Issues

1. Child Marriage

The Child Marriage Restraint Act of 1929 can be regarded as the focus of the child marriage debate. Since the nineteenth century, there had been opposition to child marriage and to the consummation of marriage with girls below the age of puberty. Moral issues, problems of health, birth control, mistreatment of females, all became associated with the issue of child marriage.[56] Between 1922 and 1927 the Indian Legislative Assembly debated a number of bills concerned with raising the age of consent, or the age at which legal intercourse could occur. In 1927, Rai Saheb Har Bilas Sarda introduced the Hindu Child Marriage Bill which he claimed struck at the real problem of child marriage. This bill and one on the age of consent by Hari Singh Gour were relegated to a committee which, in its report to the Assembly in 1929, recommended that fifteen be the minimum age for marriage and twenty-one the age of consent outside marriage. The final bill was amended to read age fourteen for females and eighteen for males and approved. The Sarda Act came into effect in 1930.

This was an issue of major concern to those committed to women's rights. From their inception, both the WIA and the AIWC had recognized child marriage as a detriment to female education and health.[57] Thus as soon as the Sarda Bill was introduced, the women's organizations decided to mobilize to support its passage. They held meetings, presented petitions, sent delegations to meet members of the Assembly, presented evidence before the legislative committee, wrote articles in favor of the law, and sent visitors to attend debates in the Assembly. When the Sarda Act was passed, the AIWC referred to it as a "personal triumph."[58]

Influential nationalists also gave overwhelming support to the Sarda Bill. Motilal Nehru favored the reform; Lala Lajpat Rai insisted the reform be passed and enforced, and Muhammad Ali Jinnah condemned child marriage as contrary to the laws of Islam. Even the leader of the Hindu opposition to the bill, Pandit Madan Mohan Malaviya, was willing to accept a minimum age of twelve years.[59] Gandhi expressed his dislike of child marriage as early as 1926 and suggested that all child marriages be annulled.[60] A year earlier, he had confessed to the world: "It is my painful duty to have to record here my marriage at the age of thirteen... I can see no moral argument in support of such a preposterously early marriage."[61] Marriage, in his view, was only important for procreation and only adults were capable of making this kind of decision.[62] He suggested sixteen as the minimum age for marriage and claimed that an older age of marriage would protect females from premature old age, prevent Hinduism from sanctioning the birth of weak, rickety children, and help curb man's lust and develop his capacity for self-sacrifice.[63]

The primary opposition to the bill came from Muslims. According to the Muslim opposition, child marriage was not a problem among members of their community. Their law, derived from the Quran, specified that the two partners enter into a marriage contract knowingly, a clause that implies maturity. More important to their opposition was the notion that law is religiously-based and cannot be made or changed by the state. In this sense, the Sarda Act was a dangerous precedent. Home Department files are full of resolutions from Muslims protesting their inclusion in the provisions of the act, an outright violation of their moral obligation to follow shariat law. Following its passage, resolutions and deputations continued asking that it be amended to exempt Muslims.[64] While the British took these deputations seriously, there is little indication that Muslim women saw this issue as forcing them to make a choice between women's rights and national identity. Muslim "modernists," both men and women, argued that the Sarda Act would make no difference to Muslims who actually followed the shariat. Despite statistics to the contrary, Muslims insisted that child marriage was strictly a Hindu custom.[65]

The abolition of child marriage was a women's issue, but perhaps more important it was a measure which tested the desire of Indians to modernize. Support for the Sarda Act was significantly boosted by the publication of Katherine Mayo's book *Mother India* in 1927. Well-known as a muckraking journalist, Mayo argued that India's capacity for self-rule was severely hampered by the religion and customs of the people. She particularly focused on child marriage:

> Take a girl child twelve years old, a pitiful physical specimen... illiterate, ignorant, without any sort of training in habits of health. Force motherhood upon her at the earliest possible moment. Rear her weakling son in intensive vicious practices that drain his vitality day by day. Give him habits that make him, by the time he is thirty years of age, a decrepit and querulous old wreck—and will you ask what has sapped the energy of his manhood?[66]

Because of its exaggerated position, the book posed a problem for reformers. Women acknowledged that it contained some truth, but had to deny the total picture and protest its publication.[67] According to Manoranjan Jha, "Indians felt it was a scandalous libel on their civilization and character."[68] "Barbaric customs," as they had been styled by Mayo, could be used as justification for not granting Indians responsible government. Mayo summed up the potential of Indians to solve their own social problems thus:

> Today, however, few signs appear, among Indian public men, of concern for the status of the masses, while they curse the one power which, however little to their liking, is doing practically all of whatever is done for the comfort of sad old Mother India.[69]

Although women's organizations had supported reform long before the publication of Mayo's book, the protest against it helped bring women and nationalists together. Nationalist leaders, instead of remaining neutral or opposing the measure, had to agree with it. Eleanor Rathbone, a British Member of Parliament, feminist, and champion of Indian women, warned the British government that Indians would try to blame the evils of early marriage on British resistance to social reform in India.[70] In the Assembly debate, Sarda, Motilal Nehru, and E. L. Price stressed that world opinion would be influenced by the fate of the Sarda Bill.[71] By the late 1920s it seemed that moderates and even some defenders of tradition were willing to join social reformers in support of a bill that would set a legal age for marriage.

Women claimed the Sarda Act as their victory and felt that their easy victory was firm evidence of nationalist leaders' support for womens' rights. Nationalist leaders ignored the act after it was passed, however. There were few convictions under the Sarda Act, and it was always in denger of being amended to exempt certain groups. The women's organizations were concerned about the lack of enforcement, petitioned government to amend the act so that it would be easier to prosecute offenders, and formed vigilance committees, but despite their efforts, there were few prosecutions. The Sarda Act's greatest impact was perhaps to indicate to the women who supported it how powerless they actually were when it came to effecting social change by legislation.

2. Purdah

Purdah, the veiling or seclusion of women, proved quite a different kind of issue. This was not a custom that all "modernists" condemned nor one that all "traditionalists" supported. The women's organizations used this term to describe a whole continuum of custom, observed by about one-third of India's women, Hindu and Muslim: from veiling and seclusion to sex-segregated behavior. They further maintained that purdah lacked scriptural authority in Islam and in Hinduism and was a man-made custom.[72]

Purdah was derived from the Persian word for curtain, and the *zenana* or women's quarters entered India with Muslim rule. Many reformers consequently blamed the custom on foreign invaders, but there is considerable evidence that Hindu notions of modesty and female *dharma* encouraged females to remain inside the house, lower their head and eyes, and to cover the head and much of the face long before the Muslim conquest. With Muslim dominance, purdah was reinforced, partly due to the need to protect women in unsettled times, but also in imitation of the ruler's custom. Purdah was more widespread in the north and, like child marriage, was an eloquent symbol of the low status of Indian women in the view of India's colonial rulers.

Both the AIWC and the WIA attacked purdah and complained that the custom made it difficult to educate girls and to contact adult women. Identifying it as a serious social problem on a par with child marriage, the AIWC urged women to emulate Turkish women and break purdah.[73] They passed resolutions condemning purdah and stating that its abolition was essential for women's health and progress,[74] but they made no attempts to initiate legislation that would abolish the veil as Ataturk had done in Turkey. The reason for this was that purdah was a very special issue to these women. Many of them observed purdah at some time in their lives, and many continued to do so as members of women's organizations. Those who had never observed purdah often had close relatives, sometimes living in the same house, who did. Since AIWC members wanted to include purdah women in their organization, legal abolition was ruled out.

Another reason for this moderate stand was the realization that the institutions demanded by a sex-segregated society could serve the interests of women. From the beginning, the AIWC urged the government to provide schools for girls in purdah.[75] The organization provided facilities for purdah women to attend Conference meetings, planned purdah parks and initiated purdah fairs. These were important measures if the women's organizations wanted to represent all women, since many Indian women shared the view of Lady Abdul Qadir, that purdah was wrong not so much in principle but in the degree to which it was observed. Since change would necessarily be slow, she urged non-purdah women to be patient and encourage purdah women to join organizations and participate in activities to improve women's status.[76]

When the AIWC discussed ways in which social problems could be attacked, they mentioned four strategies: propaganda, protest meetings, legislation, and vigilance committees. Different strategies were appropriate for different issues. Purdah, they decided, needed to be "treated" with propaganda.[77] In Bihar and Bengal, where purdah was observed by the majority of Hindu women, there were attempts to break the custom with massive doses of propaganda. In Patna, women planned "anti-purdah" days. At one of these, the speeches delivered gave various reasons why women should abandon purdah: Women needed to gain physical and mental strength so they could defend themselves; Gandhi was opposed to the custom; it had not been observed in ancient times; and it led to illiteracy and bad health. The message was loud and clear: Women would have to seize the initiative and come out of purdah.[78]

In Calcutta, Marwari women had begun to celebrate an annual anti-purdah day in the 1930s. By 1940, their Anti-Purdah Conference attracted 5,000 women. Before the 1940 Conference, the President, Radhadevi Goenka of Akola, was driven through the streets by a Marwari lady driver. The car was followed by a procession of Marwari women led by girls riding horseback. At the conference itself, the Chairwoman of the Reception Committee, Rukmini Devi Birla, told the women that there could be no reform or progress until purdah was abolished. She urged social workers to help, and a resolution was passed to boycott weddings where purdah was practiced by women of the household.[79] All who attended were impressed with the success of the anti-purdah day.

Purdah was widespread but also widely condemned. Gandhi and Nehru were against it; many Muslim jurists demonstrated that it had not existed in classical Islam; Jinnah denounced it; and women's organizations sought its abolition. They criticized it as a custom without scriptural authority, as preventing female education, and as detrimental to the healthy development of women's minds and bodies, but few of them tried to analyze the custom and attack its roots. This sort of analysis can be found, however, in the writings of Mahatma Gandhi and Muthulakshmi Reddi.

In trips through U. P., Bihar, and Bengal, Gandhi attended a number of women's meetings and then commented in *Young India*:

> It pained and humiliated me deeply, I thought of the wrong being done by men to the women of India by clinging to a barbarous custom which, whatever use it might have had when it was first introduced, had now become totally useless and was doing incalculable harm to the country.[80]

He was appalled by the behavior of purdah women: they were disorganized, noisy throughout his speech, and at the end rushed to touch his feet.[81] He despaired of ever seeing uneducated women, confined to their homes, acting properly in the outside world. While Gandhi's tirade against purdah included comments common to most anti-purdah writings, he also ventured into the realm of sexuality and condemned purdah as an outmoded technique to protect female chastity. Time and again, he told his readers: "Chastity is not a hot-house growth. It cannot be superimposed."[82]

The most incisive comments on this custom were made by Dr. Muthulakshmi Reddi. She saw purdah as a custom left over from a more warlike period when women needed protection. With changed conditions, it had not disappeared but rather persisted and spread. The reason for this, Reddi thought, was that men were distrustful, suspicious, and jealous of women and had false notions of modesty and safety.[83] Women, because they were ignorant and helpless, followed the unnatural rules imposed on them by men. She elaborated:

> The existence of purdah is still kept up by a wrong feeling of sex superiority and tolerated on the assumption that women cannot take care of themselves, cannot resist temptation and women have no imagination to be fed and no mind to be trained, forgetful of the facts in our history that women have proved to be the best fighters in the raging battle when their honour was at stake and the best administrators when opportunities had been given to them.

Women kept from natural and easy association with men grew to see men, other than their fathers and brothers, as threats to their morals and chastity. Men saw women as mere reproductive machines, only there to cater to their physical needs. She concluded that there were no sound arguments for purdah; they all were founded on the baseless fear that women would abuse any freedom granted to them and become "unchaste and disloyal."[84]

Reddi's interpretation never caught on, however. The WIA, the AIWC, the Marwari women in Calcutta, and many others accepted the fact that women's separate world would continue to exist. In fact, they accepted the concept of "separate worlds" because it helped justify the existence of organizations for women only and the need for new women's institutions such as schools and hospitals. They did not think it wrong that men and women inhabited different worlds and had different functions, although the evils of child marriage and purdah needed to be abolished. Only a few individuals like Gandhi and Reddi related the separate worlds concept to deepseated notions about women's sexuality and irrationality. Acceptance of Reddi's interpretation might have led to that which was most dreaded by the women's movement leaders: antagonism between the sexes.

This did not happen because, instead of men or male-dominated culture being blamed for the evils of purdah, Islam became the scapegoat. The first versions of this interpretation of history were written in the nineteenth century.[85] It soon became commonplace to find articles claiming that women had moved about freely in ancient India and only began to practice purdah following the Muslim invasion.[86] This interpretation became so widespread that it continues in some of the most recent publications on Indian women. In 1972, Ila Mukherjee reiterated that:

> ... the institution of purdah or seclusion was completely unknown in the ancient Indian social life... The practice of purdah seems to have originated in the Hindu society after the advent of the Muslims in Hindustan.[87]

The issue of purdah might not contribute to war between the sexes, but it was bound to make a contribution to communalism. Lady Abdul Qadir had urged women to be patient and to make a place for purdah ladies in their organizations and conferences, and to a degree her advice was heeded. Certainly, a number of Muslim women joined the WIA and the AIWC and some of them, like Lady Abdul Qadir herself, came out of purdah. Hindu women found it easier to break purdah, especially once it had been labelled a Muslim custom, without roots in Hindu culture. At the same time, the protest movement led by Gandhi, which was responsible for bringing women out of seclusion to participate in demonstrations and picketing, attracted far more Hindu women than Muslim women. While propaganda urging women to seek education and take part in public life was very effective, and combined with the activism encouraged by Gandhi did much to mitigate the seclusion of Hindu women, it also helped to drive a wedge between Hindu and

Muslim. In a period when Muslim nationalism was intensifying, blaming Muslims for purdah did little to improve communal relations. Muslim women, in their own organizations, emphasized the importance of preserving Islamic traditions. They resented attacks on their religion, particularly when a number of modernist Muslim scholars claimed that strict purdah was not an Islamic custom but rather an ancient practice that persisted despite the Prophet's teachings.[88]

3. *Legal Reform*

Reform of women's legal status has been a chief issue for the Indian women's organizations from their inception. The child marriage controversy caused them to see women's legal position as an especially serious problem, and out of this grew demands that there be improvements in women's rights to divorce, and inherit and control property.[89] Throughout the 1930s the women's organizations formed committees on legal status, undertook studies of the laws, talked with lawyers, published pamphlets on women's position, and encouraged various pieces of legislation to enhance women's status. At first these demands were presented as part of the organizations' general efforts to uplift women, but by 1934, the AIWC passed a resolution demanding a Hindu Code that would remove women's disabilities in marriage and inheritance.[90]

This concern for reform was supported by a number of influential individuals: those members of the Assembly who had backed reformist legislation, Hari Singh Gour, Sir Morophant Joshi, Sir Har Bilas Sarda, and C. D. Deshmukh; members of the bar such as V. V. Joshi, a High Court pleader from Baroda, and a number of political moderates. These men were committed to the same ideals as the nineteenth-century reformers: socially they advocated the emancipation of women, and politically they favored the gradual extension of the institutions of self-rule. Many of them had legal backgrounds and believed that law was capable of bringing about social change.

In 1933, V. V. Joshi wrote a pamphlet for distribution by the AIWC. Hindu law, he stated, had developed when the requirements of society were quite different. Because the law was outdated, it was also unsuitable and needed to be overhauled.

Outlining women's position in personal and property law, he concluded that the only way to remove their disabilities was to alter the law. He advised women to concentrate on propaganda, locate and speak with members of the Assembly who would espouse their cause, and introduce reform bills. He concluded by advocating the appointment of a government committee to inquire into women's legal disabilities and to suggest reform.[91]

Women heeded his advice. In 1934, Lady Abdul Qadir, Rani Lakshmibai Rajwade, Charulata Mukherjee, and Renuka Ray issued an appeal for such a committee. They acknowledged their debt to those men who had introduced legislation on their behalf but felt that many of these bills had been reduced by the opposition to "half-measures." Palliatives and half-measures would no longer do. These women asked for a commission with a non-official majority and a strong representation of women to "enquire into the present disabilities of women in regard to marriage and inheritance." They asked for nation-wide support and also appealed to the government.[92]

In 1941 the government finally appointed a committee to consider certain points of Hindu law relating to inheritance and to clarify the previously-introduced Deshmukh Bill on separate residence and maintenance. This impressive committee was composed of chairman Benegal Narsing Rau, and members D. N. Mitter, J. R. Gharpure, and V. V. Joshi, who were to solicit the views of interested groups and prepare a report between January and June of 1941. The women's organizations were disappointed that no woman had been appointed to the committee but cooperated closely with it nonetheless. The Rau Committee Report of 1941 suggested the legislation that was subsequently incorporated into the Hindu Code.

The timing of the committee's appointment was perhaps the most significant factor in determining its impact on women in terms of the question of women's rights versus nationalism. In 1941, the Congress was boycotting the legislatures, leaving them to liberals, independents, Muslim Leaguers, and members of communal parties. When the committee was appointed in January, some Congress leaders were already in jail, and a few months later thousands of Congress members were engaged in civil disobedience. To cooperate with the British government while Congress members were being jailed presented the women with a dilemma. Congress had been committed to equality between the sexes since its Karachi resolution of 1931, but it had not supported comprehensive legislation, and particularly not now, when such reforms involved cooperating with the British government.

Gandhi regarded legislation to improve women's status as only a palliative; the real roots of the problem were man's greed for power and fame, and mutual lust. Gandhi hoped that women would come into public life as the embodiment of sacrifice and suffering and would purify public life. To Gandhi the liberation of Indian women was intimately tied up with the liberation of India, the removal of untouchability, and the amelioration of the poverty of the masses. He reminded women reformers that the masses had no child marriage, no prohibition against widow remarriage and some of the other "disabilities" suffered by high-caste women. He suggested that instead of focusing on their own lives, middle-class women descend and look at the lives of their poorer sisters. All in all, he did not support diverting time and energy from what he saw as India's more crucial problems to the question of women's legal status.[93] Jawaharlal Nehru gave higher priority to agrarian reform than to family law and opposed any cooperation with the British government.[94]

The women faced with the greatest dilemma were the members of the newly created Women's Department of the All-India Congress Committee. Set up in 1940 with the express purpose of "drawing into the Congress the unlimited number of enthusiastic national-minded women," the Women's Department planned to form an organization attached to each Provincial and District Congress Committee.[95] Soon after the government appointed the Rau Committee, Radhabai Subbarayan, one of the two women first appointed to attend the Round Table Conference and an indefatigable champion of women's rights, was invited to work on the committee. Congress, boycotting the Assembly, asked her not to accept the invitation. When she asked Gandhi, he dismissed the government effort as a device to divert public opinion. Amrit Kaur, a staunch follower of Gandhi, disagreed with her mentor however and said that the AIWC, particularly Sarojini Naidu and Vijayalakshmi Pandit, had worked very hard to get the government to appoint this committee, and thus women should cooperate.

It was clear that if women were only Congress members, they would boycott the committee, but if they were members of both Congress and the AIWC, the choice was more difficult. Mridula Sarabhai felt that Congress women, even if also members of the AIWC, would have to put their loyalties to the party first,[96] but this opinion was not shared by many members of the AIWC. At the sixteenth annual conference (1941-42), Vilasini Devi Shenai denied that Indian women should put the fight against the British before all other considerations: "Today our men are clamouring for political rights at the hands of an alien government. Have they conceded their wives, their own sisters, their daughters, 'flesh of their flesh, blood of their blood' social equality and economic justice?"[97] Thus, when the Rau Committee was reconstituted in January of 1944 to prepare a Hindu Code, the AIWC continued its helpful posture. The organization carried out a country-wide campaign in favor of codification, and approved a draft memo by Kitty Shiva Rau (sister-in-law of the chairman of the committee) which was submitted to the Hindu Law Committee. Rameshwari Nehru, Renuka Ray, and Chandrakala Sahmai testifed before the committee on the response of the AIWC's thirty seven branches to the proposed legal changes.[98]

Two women active both in the struggle to free India and the AIWC made comments about the Hindu Code which reflected a shift in women's priorities. Kamaladevi Chattopadhyaya stated in 1944 that the women's movement was changing. The important issues on which women were focusing: franchise, inheritance, entry into the professions, were part of the larger effort to overcome undemocratic practices. This was not a sex war, she stressed, but rather an integral part of the struggle of backward castes and long-oppressed classes.[99] Hansa Mehta, as President of the eighteenth session of the AIWC, told women not to forget that their goal was to emancipate women and through women, to emancipate the country.[100] This was a reversal of some of the statements made ten years earlier.

From examining this case, it would seem that many women supported women's rights vis-á-vis nationalism when forced to make a choice. Of course, many women boycotted the Assembly with Congress, but there were many patriotic women determined to cooperate with the government in developing a reformed Hindu Code. It was in reference to this issue that some of the most radical statements about women's position emerged. Comprehensive legal reform, however, unlike child marriage and purdah, generated a strong reaction on the part of the men. Women's rights to inherit and to divorce posed serious threats to patriarchal authority. AIWC members soon learned that they had few allies among the nationalists when it came to recodification of the law, and that their main supporters were the British government and those liberals and constitutionalists who were often called collaborators.

Although this issue caused more antagonism between women and nationalists than the others mentioned, the disagreement, again, was basically one over priorities. With independence, Nehru committed himself to passage of the Hindu Code which embodied the proposals of the Rau Committee. A Hindu Code became the symbol of modernization, and although Nehru was unable to overcome the opposition in the Constituent Assembly (the bill was allowed to lapse in 1951), he finally pushed it through Parliament piecemeal in 1955 and 1956.[101] The parliamentary debates made some women aware of the great hurdles that lay ahead, but for others, the passage of the Hindu Code was reassurance enough that the Congress was committed to women's rights.

V. Conclusion

In reviewing these three examples, one sees that women's issues, when they did not threaten patriarchal society or were couched in terms which did not seem threatening, could comfortably coexist with the nationalist movement. In addition, the relationship of women's rights to the nationalist struggle had a historical dimension which should not be discounted. The Indian nationalist leaders were sympathetic to women's issues, because they had inherited from the nineteenth-century social reformers an ideology that posited the advancement of women as an indicator of social and political progress. Women, in turn, lent the national movement tremendous support. In many cases, their numbers were not that large but their presence in processions and on pickets served to rally others to the movement. In addition to those women who actually joined demonstrations, there were many who wore *khaddar*, spun, worked tirelessly with untouchables, or simply shouldered more responsibility so that others could work for freedom. It seems clear that they gained the respect of Indian men for their activities and that a new sense of women's worth developed.

Women's issues were encouraged by the Congress but not at the expense of the nationalist struggle. Generally, the women's organizations also accepted *swaraj* as their first priority, although on the issue of the Hindu Code, *swaraj* slipped to second priority. While this issue emphasized potential disagreement over priorities, it was insufficient to damage permanently the alliance between women and nationalists.

In the last few years, the position of Indian women has been reassessed, and the goals and advances made by women during the independence movement re-examined. While women's efforts in those years were heroic, there has been much criticism of their middle-class preoccupation with legislation which has had little effect on the masses of Indian women. Some would fault the women reformers for not confronting basic socio-economic issues head-on. But it is difficult to see exactly how a head-on approach would have benefitted the women's movement, if this had meant analyzing the roots of women's oppression and concluding that the attitudes and institutions of a patriarchal society were to blame. Such a confrontation would have served little purpose in the midst of a nationalist struggle. The women involved in the movement rightly feared the development of sex antagonism at that time, but the lack of confrontation of such issues in the period since independence is another matter. In a perceptive article on women's organizations in Madras, Patricia Caplan has analyzed their inability to face current problems. Generally the members of these organizations lack any sense of female solidarity. The organizations are "a means of maintaining or gaining status" and "problems such as the high mortality rate of women, illiteracy, and lack of job opportunities are perceived by the middle and upper-class members of women's organizations as being confined to lower class women, and accordingly, members direct their efforts towards 'uplifting' these women."[102]

This ambiguous legacy does not make the efforts of Indian women during the inter-war years any less significant. The definition the women's organizations had of women's emancipation: first, removing obstacles to women's growth and second, allowing for the development of women's special nature, meant that their strategies suited their goals. The gains they made have been of benefit to India's middle-class women. The value of these gains for the masses of Indian women is much less apparent. but documents such as the Report of the Committee on the Status of Women (1974) illustrate deep concern about the present situation. The national women's organizations are no longer the leaders of the women's movement, and if one is looking for activity that suggests female solidarity, the search should begin with local women's organizations and in women's labor unions.

NOTES

[1] Aparna Basu, "The Role of Women in the Indian Struggle for Freedom," in B.R. Nanda, ed., *Indian Women : From Purdah to Modernity* (New Delhi : Vikas, 1976), p. 40.

[2] The "Indian Women's Movement" remains a vague and poorly defined concept. To date, most authors use it as a blanket term to include those associations and events between 1905 and 1947 which included a number of women. The activities that women engaged in ranged from picketing foreign cloth and liquor shops, to petitioning for social reform, to carrying out raids planned by terrorist groups. See, e.g., Geraldine Forbes, "The Ideals of Indian Womanhood : Six Bengali Women During the Independence Movement," in J.R. McLane, ed , *Bengal in the Nineteenth and Twentieth Centuries*, South Asia Series, Occasional Papers, no. 25 (East Lansing : Michigan State University, 1975), pp. 59-74.

[3] As in the case of the terrorists. Geraldine Forbes, "Goddesses or Rebels ? The Women Revolutionaries of Bengal," *The Oracle* II, 2 (April, 1980).

[4] "Report of the Desh Sevika Sangh, the Volunteer Branch of the Rashtriya Stree Sabha, 1931-34," All-India Congress Committee (AICC) Papers, File no. 33/1934, Nehru Memorial Museum and Library (NMML), New Delhi. A few records exist, but they are incomplete. As this particular report, written for the Congress Working Committee, states, this organization and the Rashtriya Stree Sabha were both declared illegal and this prevented them from publishing anything. In addition, most of the records and leaflets were destroyed during the Bombay riots of May, 1932.

[5] For example, my information on the Women's Swadeshi League of Madras is derived mostly from interviews with Mrs. S. Ambujammal, the first President of the League. Interviews. January 19, 22, and 26, 1976, Madras.

[6] Sandra C. Danforth, "Muslim Women in Violent Conflict : Participation Without Transformation," unpub. paper presented at Third World Conference, University of Nebraska at Omaha, October, 1977, p. 9.

[7] Joy Paulson, "Evolution of the Feminine Ideal," in Joyce Lebra, Joy Paulson, and Elizabeth Powers, eds., *Women in Changing Japan* (Boulder, Colorado : Westview Press, 1976), pp. 17-19.

[8] Suzette Leith, "Chinese Women in the Early Communist Movement," in Marilyn B. Young, ed., *Women in China* (Ann Arbor : University of Michigan Press, 1973), p. 66.

[9] Vina Mazumdar, "The Social Reform Movement in India—From Ranade to Nehru", in Nanda, ed., *Indian Women*, p. 54.

[10] Sheila Rowbotham, *Women, Resistance and Revolution* : *A History of Women in the Modern World* (New York : Vintage, 1974), p. 51.

[11] Rev. E. Storrow, *Our Indian Sisters* (London : The Religious Tract Society, nd.), pp. 154-167.

[12] Sir Herbert Risley, *The People of India*, ed. by W. Crooke (2nd ed, Calcutta : Thacker, Spink and Co., 1915), p. 171.

[13] Romila Thapar, "Looking Back in History," in Devaki Jain, ed., *Indian Women* (New Delhi : Government of India Publication Division, 1975), p. 14.

[14] Gail Omvedt, "Caste, Class and Women's Liberation in India," *Bulletin of Concerned Asian Scholars* (BCAS) VII, 1 (January-March, 1975), p. 47.

[15] Maria Mies, "Indian Women and Leadership," BCAS VII, 1 (January-March, 1975), pp. 58-59.

[16] Laksmi K. Menon, "Women and the National Movement," in D. Jain, ed., *Indian Women*, p. 23.

[17] Vina Mazumdar, "Social Reform Movements from Ranade to Nehru," p. 66.

[18] Aparna Basu, "Role of Women in the Indian Struggle for Freedom," p. 37.

[19] Gail Omvedt, "Caste Class and Women's Liberation," p. 43.

[20] V. Mazumdar, "Social Reform Movements," p. 66.

[21] Devaki Jain, ' Introduction," in D. Jain, ed., *Indian Women*, p. xv.

[22] Aparna Basu, "Role of Women. . .," p. 40.

[23] *Ibid.*, Pratima Asthana, *Women's Movement in India* (New Delhi : Vikas, 1974), p. 129.

[24] For a fuller treatment of these organizations, see G. Forbes, "From Purdah to Politics : The Social Feminism of the All-India Women's Organizations," forthcoming in Hanna Papanek, ed., *Purdah in South Asia : The Segregation of Women.*

25See e.g. Saraladevi, "A Women's Movement," *Modern Review* (October, 1911), pp. 344-350.
26*NCWI Report*, 1930-32, p. 22, NMML ; *AIWC Report*, 1929, p. 26, AIWC Library (AIWCL), New Delhi.
27*AIWC Report*, 2nd Session, 1928, p. 2, AIWCL.
28*WIA Report* 1917-22, p. 7, Private collection of Mrs. Manda Krishnamurthy (MK), Madras.
29*WIA Report*, 1928-29, frontispiece, MK.
30*Ibid.*
31*WIA Report*, 1930-31, p. 3, MK.
32*Ibid.*, p. 8
33Muthulakshmi Reddi, "The Need for Women's Organizations," nd, Reddi Papers, file no. 11, NMML.
34"Note by Dr. Reddi," Reddi Papers, file no. 8, NMML.
35"Women's Protest Against the Statutory Commission," Reddi Papers, file no. 8, NMML.
36"Statement issued by Smt. Malata Patwardhan, Honorary Secretary, WIA;" Anna Thomas (Madurai WIA) to Dr. Reddi, June 1, 1928, Reddi Papers, file no. 8, NMML.
37Dr. Reddi to Honorary Secretary, WIA, June 5, 1928; Dr. Reddi to Mrs. Patwardhan, June 8, 1928, Reddi Papers, file no. 8, NMML.
38Dr. Reddi to Mrs. Faridoonji, May 23, 1930, Reddi Papers, file no. 11, NMML.
39*WIA Report*, 1936-38, p. 23, MK.
40*AIWC Report*, 3rd Session, 1929, p. 76, AIWCL.
41*AIWC Report*, 8th Session, 1933-44, p. 34, AIWCL.
42*AIWC Report*, 14th Session, 1940, p. 29, AIWCL.
43*AIWC Report*, 12th Session, 1938, p. 87; 13th Session, 1938-39, p. 64, AIWCL.
44*AIWC Report*, 7th Session, 1932-33, p. 30, AIWCL.
45*AIWC Report*, 12th Session, 1938, p. 25, AIWCL.
46Letter from Mrs. Rustomji Faridoonji, October 26, 1933; Letter to Mrs. Rustomji, October 21, 1933; Letter from Mrs. Rustomji, October 17, 1933, AIWC Files, AIWCL.
47Miss B. Ayesha Bibi to Mrs. M.E. Cousins, nd, AIWC Files, AIWCL.
48Report of the AIWC Organizing Secretary, 1940, Half-Yearly Report, AIWC Files, no. 225, AIWCL.
49Mrs. Hilla Rustomji Faridoonji to, December 23, 1947, AIWC Files, no. 410, AIWCL.
50AIWC Madras Memo, 1947, AIWC Files, no. 410, AIWCL.
51*AIWC Report*, 4th Session, 1930-31, p. 21 AIWCL.
52*AIWC Report*, 14th Session, 1940, p. 20, AIWCL.
53*Ibid.*
54*AIWC Report*, 20th Session, 1947-48, p. 13; 12th Session, 1938, p. 25, AIWCL.
55*AIWC Report*, 15th Session, 1941, pp. 10, 48, 60 AIWCL.

[56]While there is considerable controversy regarding which particular text should take precedence, there are statements in many of the authoritative law books which enjoin the father to arrange his daughter's marriage before she reaches puberty. Youthful marriages were preferred for a number of reasons: They made it easier to find a bridegroom who fit the various prescriptions demanded in a caste system. Since a female was always to be under the protection of a man (father, husband or son), this transferred the responsibility to the husband before there was any possibility of the girl becoming pregnant; it upheld the society's obsession with female chastity; and promoted family harmony by having young daughters-in-law brought up in their husband's households. In most cases, there were two marriages : the formal betrothal and the later ceremony of consumation.

Reformers opposed child marriage from the mid-nineteenth century. They argued that it had not existed in ancient India and was not demanded by the sacred texts. Pressuring the British authorities, they first attained a provision in the Indian Penal Code (1860) that defined statutory rape as sexual relations with a woman, married or unmarried, below the age of ten. In what became known as the "Age of Consent controversy," this statute was amended in 1891, raising the age to twelve years. See K.M. Kapadia, *Marriage and Family in India*, (Calcutta: Oxford University Press, 1966), pp. 138-66; and Geraldine H. Forbes, "Women and Modernity: The Issue of Child Marriage in India," *Women's Studies International Quarterly* II, 4 (1979), pp. 407-419,

[57]*AIWC Report*, 2nd Session, 1928, pp. 37, 40; 3rd Session, 1928-29, p. 6, AIWCL.

[58]*AIWC Report*, 3rd Session, 1928-29, p. 65, AIWCL; *WIA Report*, 1930-31, App. D, MK; Kamalabai L. Rau, "Memoirs of a Brihan Maharashtrian," tr. by Indira M. Rau, (unpub. ms.), pp. 16-17.

[59]During the 1920's when "age of consent" and child marriage were being considered as possible targets for legislation, much was written regarding these customs and about menarche in Indian females. Many of the "studies" reported that Indian females began to menstruate after age twelve. This allowed some orthodox Hindus to accept age twelve as a minimum age for marriage. *AIWC Report*, 1929, pp. 75-78, AIWCL,

[60]"Sorrow of Girl Wives," *Young India*, October 7, 1926.

[61]M.K. Gandhi, *The Story of My Experiments with Truth* (Boston: Beacon, 1957; first serialized in 1925), p. 8.

[62]S. Shridevi, *Gandhi and the Emancipation of Indian Women* (Hyderabad: Gandhi Sahitya Prachuraralayam, 1969), p. 67.

[63]M.K. Gandhi, *Women and Social Injustices* (Ahmedabad: Navajivan Publishing House, 1957), pp. 31-32; D.G. Tendulkar, *Mahatma* II (New Delhi : Government of India Publications Division, 1961), pp. 366-67.

[64]Government of India, Home Department (Judicial) File Nos. 65/ 1930; 740/1930; 272/1931; F44/1931, National Archives of India (NAI),

[65]*AIWC Report*, 2nd Session, 1928, p. 37; 4th Session, 1930 p. 15, 5th session, 1931, p. 43, AIWCL; *MIA Report*, 1930-31, App. D, MK.

[66]Katherine Mayo, *Mother India* (New York; Harcourt Brace, 1927), p. 16.

[67]"A Protest Against 'Mother India", *Stri Dharma* X, 2 (September, 1927), p. 162.

[68]Manoranjan Jha, *Katherine Mayo and India* (New Delhi : People's Publishing House, 1971), p. 26.

[69]Mayo, *Mother India*, p. 20.

[70]Eleanor Rathbone to Wedgewood Benn, April 15, 1930, Rathbone Papers, folder no 2, Fawcett Collection at the City of London Polytechnic (FCCLP).

[71]*Legislative Assembly Debates* 1929, I, January 29, 1929, p. 197; IV-V, September 11, 1929, pp. 679-80; September 19, 1929, p. 1110.

[72]"Purdah," *Roshni*, Special Number, (1946), pp. 92-95.

[73]*AIWC Report*, 1st Session, 1927, p. 18, AIWCL.

[74]*AIWC Report* 4th Session, 1928, p. 17, AIWCL.

[75]*AIWC Report*, 2nd Session, 1928, p. 44, AIWCL.

[76]Lady Abdul Qadir, "Muslim Views on Purdah and Marriage," *Stri Dharma* XIV (February, 1931), p. 184.

[77]*AIWC Report*, 4th Session, 1930, pp. 49-50.

[78]"Bihar Women's Crusade Against Purdah," *The Indian Social Reformer* XLV (July 20, 1935), pp. 746-47.

[79]"Anti-Purdah Conference," *Roshni* II, 3 (October, 1940), pp. 9-11.

[80]M.K. Gandhi, "Tear Down the Purdah," *Young India* (February 3, 1927), p. 37.

[81]M.K. Gandhi, "Ladies Meeting," *Young India* (September 19, 1929), p. 306.

[82]Gandhi, "Tear Down the Purdah."

[83]Many of these themes have been explored in the modern context in the writings of Sylvia Vatuk, Hanna Papanek, Doranne Jacobson, Carroll Pastner, Mary Jane Beech, and others in a forthcoming book edited by Hanna Papanek, *Purdah in South Asia : The Segregation of Women*.

[84]Muthulakshmi Reddi, "Purdah," nd, Reddi Papers, file no. 11, NMML.

[85]See Peary Chand Mittra, "A Few Desultory Remarks on the 'Cursory Review of the Institutions of Hinduism Affecting the Interest of the Female Sex' Contained in the Rev. K.M. Banerji's Prize Eassy on Native Female Education," in Goutam Chattopadhyay, ed., *Awakening in Bengal in Early Nineteenth Century* (Selected Documents), I (Calcutta : Progressive Publishers, 1965), pp. 273-297.

[86]"Seclusion of Women," *The Indian Social Reformer* (March 18, 1900), 221; Klash Sobha, "Indian Women Yesterday and Today," *Roshni* II, 10 (December, 1947), p. 4.

[87]Ila Mukherjee, *Social Status of North Indian Women, 1521-1707, A.D.* (Agra : Shivlal Agarwala, 1972), p. 57.

[88]"Muslim Women Today," *The Hindu* (April 17, 1938), p. 3; "The Purdah System in Islam, I-III," *The Indian Social Reformer* (May 5, 1933), p. 582; (May 12, 1933) p. 598; (May 26, 1935), p. 633.

[89]*WIA Report*, 1928-29, p. 3, MK; *AIWC Report*, 1st session, 1927, p. 22; 2nd session, 1928, p. 73, AIWCL.

[90]Jana Everett, "The Indian Women's Movement in Comparative Perspective," (Ph.D. dissertation, Ann Arbor : University of Michigan, 1976), ch. VII; published as *Women and Social Change in India* (New Delhi : Heritage Publications, 1979).

[91]V.V. Joshi, *Legal Disabilities of Hindu Women* (pamphlet, 1933), AIWC Files, no. 36, AIWCL.

[92]"Legal Position of Women," *The Indian Social Reformer* XLIV (April 28, 1934), p. 551.

[93]M K. Gandhi, "Liberate the Women," *The Indian Social Reformer*, (May 25, 1939); Gandhi, "The Position of Women," *Young India* (October 17, 1929), p. 340.

[94]Harold Levy, "Indian Modernization by Legislation : The Hindu Code Bill," (Ph D. Dissertation, University of Chicago, 1973).

[95]"Note on AICC Women's Department," nd, AICC Papers, no. WD-9, NMML.

[96]Mridula Sarabhai to Kripilani, March 14, 1941, AICC Papers, no. WD-9, NMML.

[97]Report of the AIWC, 1944-45, AIWC Files, AIWCL.

[98]"AIWC Evidence Before the Hindu Law Committee," AIWC Files, no. 314, AIWCL.

[99]*AIWC Report*, 17th Session, 1944, p. 20, AIWCL.

[100]*AIWC Report*, 18th Session, 1945-46, p. 11, AIWCL.

[101]Lotika Sarkar, "Jawaharlal and the Hindu Code Bill," in Nanda, ed , *Indian Women*, pp. 87-98; cf. *Towards Equality : Report of the Committee on the Status of Women in India* (New Delhi : Government of India, 1974), ch. IV.

[102]Patricia Caplan, "Women's Organizations in Madras City, India," in Patricia Caplan and Janet M. Bujra, eds., *Women United, Women Divided : Cross-Cultural Perspectives on Female Solidarity* (Bloomington : Indiana University Press, 1979), p. 100.

4
Sisterhood or Separatism? The All-India Muslim Ladies' Conference and the Nationalist Movement

GAIL MINAULT

In examining the relationship of the women's movement in India to the movement for national independence from British rule, the question arises, were the two contradictory or complementary? It seems unquestionable that, though priorities and personalities clashed from time to time, the movements for women's rights and for national emancipation in India were complementary. Indian nationalist men were the successors to the nineteenth-century social reformers whose efforts on behalf of women were, in part, designed to revalidate their own culture and society in the eyes of their British rulers. The status of women in India thus became symbolic of India's preparedness to rule itself. Women were the passive beneficiaries of this trend, but being passive symbols was clearly not enough. Only when women became actively involved in the movement for Indian political freedom did society begin to accept for them an increased range of roles and rights.[1]

The women's movement in India, in fact, provides yet another example of the confluence of educational and social reform movements and politics in modern India.[2] In the men's world, educational institutions and social reform organizations provided the recruiting ground and organizational base for many of the leading lights of the Indian nationalist movement. Fund-raising skills were developed in trying to get support for schools, styles and techniques of public action were evolved in promoting social reform causes, and the ground work laid for political mobilization when successive governmental reforms made overt political action possible.³

The same points can be made about the women's movement. Organizations to promote women's education, or to bring about legal and social reforms, provided a training ground, a way for women to meet with other women, to develop organizational skills, to become socially active in ways which were limited but acceptable to their society. Political action was not far behind. The emphasis of various women's organizations remained upon social and educational developments, for these were areas related to women's traditional social roles; they could not be as overtly political as their males without exciting opposition. But social reform movements and nationalist politics were inextricably entwined. The priorities of certain individuals or organizations might vary, but one form of public action usually entailed the other. This is an argument which I have pursued at greater length elsewhere, in attempting to show the relationship between certain Muslim educational movements in India and the evolution of Muslim political groupings.⁴ It is also a phenomenon found among Hindu social and educational movements. Geraldine Forbes has discussed the close relationship between social reform and political action in the all-India women's organizations. The Women's Indian Association (WIA) and the All-India Women's Conference (AIWC) found that political considerations were inescapable: constituencies had to be rallied, their position as spokeswomen for an interest group established, compromises among the members reached, deals made with the government, or with the nationalists, or both.⁵ In short, these women's organizations were political. Polite petitioning may have been one of their chief means of expression, but such approaches to the British administration did not prevent some of their membership from taking part in boycotts of British goods or marching in processions of non-cooperators. It would be interesting to know more about the factions and divisions within such organizations, in addition to what the organizations stood for as collectivities. A study of such divisions within women's organizations would doubtless show how they related to political divisions within the nationalist movement as a whole.

This article proposes to do this for one small component of the Indian women's movement, on the theory that movements as heterogeneous as "Indian nationalism" or "the Indian women's movement" must be broken down in order to be fully understood. This kind of scholarship has become a growth stock in South Asian history lately with the appearance of numerous studies of provincial politics, of factions in the various national parties, and of the interplay between personal or local considerations and nationwide politics.[6] In showing the conflicts and controversies which lie beneath the surface of such broad categories as "Indian nationalism" or "imperial administration," these studies reveal the complexities of the movement for Indian freedom and try to answer questions unanswered, or unasked, by earlier works dealing with greater aggregates.

Until recently, scholarship on the Indian Muslims has been particularly prone to a monolithic approach.[7] Muslims are the most significant religious minority in India, and British administrators and historians of all stripes had a tendency to treat them as an undifferentiated mass. This approach saw Indian Muslims becoming politically mobilized in the twentieth century, and the gradual but inexorable development of a separate nationalism under the aegis of the Muslim League, which culminated in the partition of India in 1947 and the establishment of the state of Pakistan. But just as the Muslim community in India is ethnically, linguistically, and doctrinally diverse, so too was it politically fragmented. To look upon it as solidly separatist and behind the Pakistan movement is to read history in reverse. Not all Muslims were followers of the Muslim League nor separatist in their politics, no matter how strong their religious faith or their consciousness of themselves as Muslims. The study of political divisions within the Indian Muslim community yields greater insights into the emergence of separatism—as well as the eventual breakup of Pakistan—than does an oversimplified, monolithic approach.

The Muslim League claimed to speak for all Indian Muslims, a claim disputed by the National Congress, which claimed to represent Indians of all castes, classes, and religious affiliations.

Neither claim was wholly accurate, but they were indicative of separate efforts to create political constituencies with national proportions, and hence they were to some extent self-fulfilling prophecies. To place the Indian women's movement within this political context, one may say that the All-India Women's Conference followed the pattern of the Indian National Congress in claiming to represent all Indian women, regardless of caste or community. This too was a claim more indicative of aspiration than actuality. The activities of the AIWC did result, however, in a broadened social and political consciousness among a particular class of women, and thus its aspirations helped to shape reality.

Looking at the case of the All-India Muslim Ladies Conference (Anjuman-e-Khawatin-e-Islam),[8] one may say that it was, in some respects, to the AIWC what the Muslim League was to the Congress. The Anjuman claimed to speak for all Muslim women in India. That it did not is perhaps self-evident given the pattern sketched above. The Anjuman was composed of women of the urban, educated, professional class, just as were the other all-India women's organizations. But this is less important than other questions about the Anjuman's role, such as: Did the Anjuman's claim to represent all Muslim women reflect an effort to create a social consciousness where none had existed? If so, then did the consciousness which the Anjuman fostered emphasize a separate Muslim identity, or rather an identity of sisterhood with Indian women of all religious communities? In other words, in the case of Muslim women, the problem of the conflict between women's rights and national freedom takes on an added dimension, and that is the question of the rights of a religious minority. Did Muslim women concentrate on Muslim rights to the detriment of their rights as women, or were the two seen as inalienable? And where does Indian freedom fit into this scheme of things?

There are several ways to find answers to such questions from the sources available.[9] One is to look at the professed goals of the Anjuman and check those against what was actually accomplished, if that can be determined. Another way is to analyze the divisions and disagreements within the Anjuman and try to discern whether they reflect divisions within the Muslim community concerning social reform and the political future of the community, or whether they reflect divisions within the Indian women's movement concerning women's rights and how to achieve them. The danger of such a line of analysis is that factions may not be based on ideological considerations at all, but rather on personality clashes, family feuds, or whether the secretary of the organization is a relative. But this fact should not lead one to discount the importance of factional divisions as indicators of what was happening, for factions based on personal or kinship conflicts can easily take on ideological or tactical dimensions.[10]

The All-India Muslim Ladies' Conference was founded on March 1, 1914 as part of a colorful ceremony inaugurating a new residence hall for Aligarh Girls' School. Aligarh had been a center of the movement for modern education among Indian Muslims since Sir Sayyid Ahmad Khan founded Aligarh College there in 1875. The college became the premier institution for Muslim boys' education in India, and Aligarh headquarters for such offshoots of Sir Sayyid's movement as the Muhammadan Educational Conference founded in 1886, the Muslim University movement launched in 1898, and the Muslim League begun in 1906. The Muhammadan Educational Conference had begun a section to promote women's education in the late 1890s in response to the growing desire of western-educated Muslims to find educated wives. The Secretary of this section was Shaikh Abdullah, a Kashmiri Brahmin who had converted to Islam, attended Aligarh College for the BA and law degrees, and married into an enlightened Mughal family of Delhi. Among his other activities, Shaikh Abdullah helped organize exhibitions of women's crafts at the annual Muhammadan Educational Conference meetings—to raise money for women's education and to point out that Muslim women were capable of doing useful and beautiful work. In 1905, he started an Urdu journal for women, *Khatun*, and in 1906, he founded a primary school for Muslim girls in Aligarh. He was assisted by his wife who, though she observed strict purdah, had been educated at home by her father, and who believed along with her husband that women's education was the key to the reform and advancement of the Muslim community in India.[11]

The Shaikh and Begum Abdullah encountered many obstacles in their efforts to establish a girls' school: attacks on their morality in the Urdu press, physical and verbal assaults on the Shaikh, indifference and lack of monetary support from fellow Muslims. Eventually, however, the Shaikh secured the patronage of the Begum of Bhopal, a Muslim woman who, through the inability of her princely house to produce male heirs, was the ruler of a small Central Indian state. The Begum was highly educated herself and had started a school for girls in her own state of Bhopal. She granted Aligarh Girls' School a monthly stipend and also gave generously toward the construction of a residence hall. The British Indian government matched the grant, and in 1914 the new edifice was ready. This was a milestone in the development of women's education among Muslims, for many Muslim parents had objected to sending their daughters out of the house every day to school. Now, however, the parents could be assured that their girls had proper purdah arrangements behind the high double walls of the new hall, and proper supervision under the watchful, maternal eyes of Begum Abdullah (who had five daughters of her own), and her two sisters.[12]

This then was the background to the founding of the Anjuman-e-Khawatin-e-Islam. Shaikh Abdullah had invited prominent Muslim women from all over India to grace the occasion of the opening of the new building, and the Begum of Bhopal to preside. Purdah arrangements were stringent, and the list of women present reads like a who's who of the wives of the educated, professional elite of Muslim India. Many had arrived by train in special purdah compartments and were ferried from the Aligarh station in closed, curtained carriages to the homes of local purdah-observing families. The arrangements for holding the meeting, and for the accommodation and transport of purdah-observing women, had to be detailed and precise, and were consequently very time-consuming, testifying to the dedication of the local organizers. In addition to Begum Abdullah, the wives of other Aligarh luminaries present included Begum Aftab Ahmad Khan and Nafis Dulhan Sherwani, whose husbands were both local trustees of Aligarh College, and Begum Sayyid Mahmud, widow of the son of Sir Sayyid Ahmad Khan. From Lahore came Begum Mian Muhammad Shafi, whose husband was a leading member of the Muslim League and a future Education and Law Minister in the Government of India, and her sister Begum Shah Din, wife of a Justice in the Punjab High Court. From Bombay came the Fyzee sisters, Zohra and Atiya, who had been educated in England, thrown off the veil, and become active in women's social and educational causes. Fatima Arzu Begum, private secretary to the Begum of Bhopal and sister of the well-known Urdu journalist, Abul Kalam Azad, was also there, as were a number of women active in Urdu journalism in their own right. These included Waheeda Begum Yaqub, editor of *Tahzib-e-Niswan* of Lahore,[13] and Fatima Begum, editor of *Sharif Bibi*, another Lahore journal for women.[14]

Foremost in the concerns of these women was the promotion of women's education in the Muslim community throughout India. The Begum of Bhopal in her ribbon-cutting speech quipped that the doors of the new hall (which had stuck when she tried to open them) symbolized the obstacles in the way of Muslim girls' education. Muslims in India had not yet realized the importance of women's education for the progress of the community as a whole. The government was willing to help, but could do little without initiative from the people concerned. Even the Muhammadan Educational Conference, she said, would continue to pass resolutions but do very little else until Muslim women become active in their own behalf. They, as educated women, had an obligation to spread the word, to organize meetings, to make speeches, to write articles, to raise funds for schools. But the propaganda aspect was only one part of work. They should also start schools and pay special attention to the training of teachers, to religious and moral instruction, and to insuring adequate purdah arrangements. The Begum's emphasis was upon education, but also on the art of the possible: Without adequate religious instruction and proper purdah restrictions, Muslim parents would not send their daughters to school. Their job was to promote and to supervise their daughters' education.[15]

Following the inaugural ceremony, the women reassembled to found the Anjuman, which was dedicated to the advancement of education and rights for Muslim women. The Begum of Bhopal again presided and reiterated the primacy of her concern for education, for without it, Muslim women would not know the rights granted to them under Islamic law. The advancement of the entire community was at stake; they could do little without the aid and cooperation of their men, but neither would the men do much until they themselves began the work of propagating education. She urged them to start schools in their families, extended kin groups, and neighborhoods, and to pay special attention to education in health care.[16]

The meeting then elected officers and decided upon a program of action. In addition to the President, the Begum of Bhopal, and the Vice-President, Waheeda Begum Yaqub, there was an Honorary Secretary, Nafis Dulhan Sherwani, a Joint Secretary, Begum Abdullah, and a Working Committee of Aligarh residents.[17]

Since headquarters of the Anjuman were in Aligarh, and Muslim women in purdah would have difficulty traveling to out-of-town meetings, the centralization of the Anjuman in Aligarh was understandable, but it was also indicative of the main concerns and control of the organization. Shaikh Abdullah had been active behind the scenes and was anxious to see the Anjuman contribute to the prestige and patronage of his girls' school. He had also hoped that his wife might be named Secretary of the Anjuman, but then did not push it, on the advice of the Begum of Bhopal. She felt that Begum Abdullah had enough to do at the girls' school and with her own family, without taking on this added burden, but also that opponents of the Shaikh's work would then oppose this new endeavor as well.[18] But the fact remains that the directorate of Aligarh College, Aligarh Girls' School, and that of the Anjuman remained closely associated. Nafis Dulhan, the Honorary Secretary, was the wife of Habibur Rahman Khan Sherwani, a local landowner and trustee of Aligarh College, an Islamic scholar, and close collaborator and well-wisher of Shaikh Abdullah. As Joint Secretary, Begum Abdullah was in close contact with whatever the Anjuman did. And other women on the local Working Committee included Begum Sayyid Mahmud, Begum Aftab Ahmad Khan, Begum Muhammad Ishaq Khan, Bilquis Begum (a sister of Aftab Ahmad Khan), and Begum Haji Musa Khan. All were married or related to members of the powerful group of local trustees who controlled Aligarh College and the Muhammadan Educational Conference.[19] In addition to these Aligarh women, there were several women from other towns elected to the committee including Nazar Sajjad Hyder, wife of a well-known Urdu writer and an author herself, Zohra Fyzee of Bombay, and Begum Shah Din of Lahore. These women helped broaden the scope of the organization, but control was definitely centered in Aligarh.[20]

The program too was tilted in the direction of Aligarh. The general aims of the Anjuman were broad enough: to work for unity and agreement among all Indian women; to support those working for women's education, and to insure that both religious education and practical training were included in the curriculum; to promote the improvement of homemaking generally. The Anjuman also resolved that, in its opinion, no Muslim girl should be married before the age of sixteen, for earlier marriages were detrimental to girls' education. In this way, Muslim women identified with the movement to raise the age of marriage, even though the struggle to raise the age of consent in the 1890s had been carried out by Hindu reformers and Muslim reformers usually maintained that child marriage was a Hindu problem. Still, the problem of a premature end to education due to early marriage was one that affected all Indian women, Hindu and Muslim. In this issue, therefore, the Anjuman identified their cause with that of Indian women in general.[21]

The specific objectives which the women formulated to give effect to the Anjuman's general aims, however, reveal more Aligarh bias: To have a conference every year in a different city, or failing that, to meet at Aligarh Girls' School; to found branches of the Anjuman in major cities and towns in India; to urge the community to found more girls' schools and to contribute to the progress of Aligarh Girls' School; to see that girls from different regions are admitted to Aligarh Girls' School, so that the entire community might benefit from its work; and in support of this purpose, to endow scholarships for Aligarh Girls' School; to increase the publication and circulation of journals aimed at the spread of education and reform among women; and to promote the writing and publication of books for women which contained up-to-date ideas on child-rearing, health care, and homemaking.[22]

The composition of the committee and a good many of the program resolutions emphasized Aligarh. They would build up the girls' school, its scholarship fund, and student body, and broaden its base of support to include all regions of India. This paralleled the effort on the part of the Aligarh trustees to make their college into a university which would be the cultural and educational center for a reformed and self-conscious Muslim community in India. Aligarh was symbolic of all-India Muslim regeneration. Further, the other program resolutions would also benefit Aligarh Girls' School. For example, the publication of books for women would not only aid the work of women's education generally, but would also provide appropriate textbooks for the girls' school, one of Shaikh Abdullah's major concerns. The increased circulation of journals for women was of direct interest to a number of members of the Anjuman, but also to Shaikh Abdullah, whose Aligarh-based journal, *Khatun*, was floundering.[23]

The Anjuman was founded at a momentous time for India,[24] as well as for the British Empire. World War I broke out in the summer of 1914, submerging for a moment other political considerations. But Indian nationalists expected further concessions to come after the war, prepared their own joint Congress-Muslim League program of reforms at Lucknow in 1916, and in 1917, began a Home Rule movement which gave the British administration something to worry about. The Secretary of State, Edwin Montagu, then promised eventual political reforms. Politically active Muslims kept a low profile early in the war, but they were disturbed by the conflict between their British rulers and the titular head of the Islamic world, the Ottoman Caliph. Concern for the fate of the caliphate after the war prompted more outspoken Muslims, at Aligarh and elsewhere, to favor greater cooperation with the nationalist movement. For women in Britain, the war meant a culmination of the suffrage movement with the attainment of a still limited franchise in 1918.[25] Indian women, Hindu and Muslim, took note of all these developments. In 1917, the WIA was founded and sent a delegation to meet Montagu during his political fact-finding visit to India. The delegation asked for the franchise in addition to other demands affecting women's status, such as greater opportunities for education and public service.

The Anjuman met annually during the war years and passed well-intentioned resolutions in favor of more educational institutions for Muslim girls, and voicing approval for a type of purdah as prescribed in the Islamic holy law, the shariat. Purdah as observed in India, they said, was based on custom and was entirely too strict. There was some disagreement over the degree of purdah prescribed in the shariat, but no disagreement at all about their desire to see a lessening of purdah restrictions. Education was impossible if women were never allowed to go beyond their walls. A new style *burqa*, patterned on Turkish ones, was coming into fashion among the women who belonged to the Anjuman. A coat with a detachable cape-like headpiece and veil, it permitted women to go out in urban areas and even on public transportation and be modestly covered. Members of the Anjuman were still mainly concerned with improving Muslim women's education and with facilitating their access to it. The momentous political events of the war years had as yet made little impression on them, nor was there much evidence of discontent with their traditional roles. When the WIA sent its deputation to Montagu in 1917 to ask for the franchise, the Muslim women who participated in it were the wives of Congress Muslims, rather than representatives of Muslim women or of the Anjuman *per se*.[26]

Other work by the Anjuman during these years included the formation of local branches in Lahore, Delhi, Meerut, Jullundhur, Dehra Dun, and a few other towns, and the setting up of small girls' schools by members of those branches. The Working Committee continued its work of supporting the girls' school in Aligarh, which expanded. The attendance at the annual meetings, in Aligarh in 1915, in Meerut in 1916, and in Delhi in 1917, dropped off. Finally, in 1918, the Anjuman received a new lease on life when a group of prominent Punjabi Muslim women invited the conference to convene in Lahore. The sisters Begum Shafi and Begum Shah Din, and their daughters, Begum Shah Nawaz and Begum Muhammad Rafi composed a local arrangements committee of remarkable skill and energy. They had been active in educational and social causes in the Punjab, and with this effort, sought to broaden the Indo-Muslim women's movement beyond the confines of the walls of Aligarh Girls' School.[27]

The conference was held in Faridkot House, Lahore, March 3-5, 1918, and over 500 women attended, more than twice that at any previous conference. The women who attended from out of town all stayed at Faridkot House, which not only simplified purdah arrangements, but also heightened the sense of community. Women from the Punjab had a chance to meet women from Delhi, Calcutta, Bombay, and Hyderabad, and to stay up all night talking if they wished. Further, the local committee had asked that all women wear only plain clothes—no gold, no heavy silks—in the interest of symbolizing their sense of equality and desire for community service, as opposed to showing off their wealth and privilege. Accounts of the meeting noted the sense of solidarity and enthusiasm among the participants.[28]

The conference itself provided several interesting developments. The all-India aspirations of the Anjuman were reemphasized when girls' schools in Calcutta, Jullundhur, Lahore, and Meerut were all mentioned as recipients of financial aid from the membership. The question of social reform in the Muslim community was faced in an outspoken resolution against the evils of polygamy proposed by Jahanara Shah Nawaz and passed by acclamation, to the effect that:

> ... the kind of polygamy which is practiced by certain sections of the Muslims is against the true spirit of the Quran and of Islam and that it is inimicable to our progress as a community. And that it is the duty of educated women to exercize their influence among their relations to put an end to this practice.[29]

The resolution condemning polygamy caused a terrific flap in the Muslim press. *Tahzib-e-Niswan*, the leading Urdu journal for women in the Punjab, came out in favor of the resolve, but others were scandalized. Most notably, Rashidul Khairi, editor of *Ismat*, an Urdu literary journal for women published from Delhi, attacked the resolution as anti-Islamic, and declared that the women of the Anjuman were only seeking to impress their Western and Christian educational mentors, and that he would disown any daughter of his who supported it. This objection was the sort of criticism that had been levelled at Hindu social reforms in the nineteenth century, that they emanated from sources outside the culture and were consequently illegitimate. Reformers were extremely sensitive to this criticism and tried to show that, on the contrary, the reforms proposed were in consonance with the great textual traditions. The women of the Shafi family, in this case, rejoined that no Western woman or teacher had been present when the resolution was drafted or passed, and that they were following their consciences as Muslims. To be sure, the Quran allows polygamy, but the spirit of the Quran, if not the letter, supports monogamy. What man could possibly treat multiple wives equally, as enjoined by the Quran? This argument was one that had been advanced by Muslim reformers since the nineteenth century, among them Sir Sayyid Ahmad Khan and Ameer Ali. Traditionally-trained Muslims were inclined to sneer at such revisionism. Rashidul Khairi, a reformer insofar as he favored education for women to improve their minds and their domestic skills, was not about to follow Sir Sayyid theologically.[30]

The polygamy resolution was as outspoken and unanimous as the Anjuman ever became. The resolution remained on the books, but did not become subject of a campaign for legal reform until much later. In other areas of social change and reform, the women of the Shafi family left purdah in 1920, but the Anjuman itself never went beyond saying that the kind of purdah practiced in India was excessive. Most members did not challenge purdah, but rather clung to it as symbolic of Muslim culture, or of their own status.

There were other rumblings at the Lahore meeting. One resolution, aimed at challenging the dominance of Aligarh in the Anjuman, proposed that the headquarters be moved every five years to a different city, but it was voted down.[31] There was another unpleasant moment over the election of an officer. Waheeda Begum, the Vice-President of the Anjuman, had died suddenly during the year, and the conference replaced her by her sister-in-law, Asaf Jahan, who had also replaced her as the editor of *Tahzib-e-Niswan*. This move was attacked by Fatima Begum, editor of another women's journal, *Sharif Bibi*. There had never been much love lost between the two journalistic families of Lahore, and at this juncture Fatima Begum may have felt doubly put out, for she had been active in the Anjuman since its inception, and undoubtedly thought she deserved the post more than Asaf Jahan. But Fatima Begum had also been among those who had opposed putting Begum Abdullah in as Secretary of the Anjuman four years previously, so it is difficult to imagine how the Aligarh group could have worked with her. She also had opposed the anti-polygamy resolution, so ideological factors joined with the power of the Aligarh group to exclude from office this able Punjabi woman.[32]

Sayyid Mumtaz Ali, the founder of *Tahzib-e-Niswan*, commented on the entire proceedings in the pages of his journal. The Anjuman was in a position to do significant work, he said, but had so far done little. This year the women had shown that they were alive to their national and community duties, and had symbolized their devotion to social service by wearing plain clothes, by patronizing numerous girls' schools, and by taking a firm stance on polygamy. The Anjuman was one of the few opportunities for purdah-observing women to get to know their sisters from different regions or of different points of view, and it was beginning to foster an increased social consciousness among Muslim women, and hence he wished it well. But, he cautioned, symbolism and resolutions are not enough. The women should also work actively in their neighborhoods, raising money, hiring teachers, and seeing to the education of all classes of girls. The Anjuman itself needed to start more branches and get away from the dominance of Aligarh. He felt that the women's Anjuman had become too much like the Muhammadan Educational Conference, which was tightly directed by the local trustees of Aligarh College. He claimed that this group dictated the resolutions and speeches to be given at the Educational Conferences every year, and allowed few, if any, dissenting voices.[33] Mumtaz Ali did not say so, but this group: Shaikh Abdullah, Aftab Ahmad Khan, the Sherwanis, and including too Mian Muhammad Shafi of the Punjab, were generally loyal to the British connection, moderate in their politics, and desirous of cooperating with the British administration in political and social reforms which would benefit the Muslim community. They were out of sympathy, or out of touch, with the newer currents of Muslim politics which, in the post-World War I era, would see Muslim collaboration with the Congress under Gandhi in an anti-British political movement.

The weaknesses in the organization noted by Mumtaz Ali became more noticeable the following year when the Anjuman met in Calcutta, February 10-12, 1919. Nafis Dulhan, the Secretary, had moved to Hyderabad, where her husband had taken up the post of chief judicial officer in the Nizam's government. With the invitation to hold the meeting in Calcutta from Mrs. Sakhawat Husain, Principal of the Sakhawat Husain Memorial Girls' School, one might presume that the influence of the Aligarh group would be diminished, and—as in the Punjab the previous year—here in Bengal too, the new sense of an all-India Muslim community, and social service to it, would be enhanced. Such, however, was not the case. The woman chosen to preside, Begum Khediv Jang, was the wife of another prominent Hyderabad official, but had strong family links to the Aligarh movement.[34] She remained neutral in the controversy which followed, but as a close friend of Nafis Dulhan and with her ties to Aligarh, she would do nothing to diminish the control of the Aligarh group.

Nafis Dulhan arrived in Calcutta a few days before the conference was to begin and found that the local arrangements committee had arranged for it to be held in a large house and compound on Ripon Street, where tents could be erected and adequate screening assured for all the purdah-observing women to attend the meeting in security. Nafis Dulhan's hostess, Naziri Begum Arif, however, objected to the place, saying that the house on Ripon Street was not private enough, and it would thus be a problem for women in purdah to go there. Begum Arif's husband, Sulaiman Arif, and his brother, Ghulam Husain Arif, were like brothers to Nafis Dulhan's husband, and the Sherwanis had stayed with the Arifs on a previous visit to Calcutta.[35] The two women thus looked upon each other as sisters, and Nafis Dulhan felt bound to respect her friend's wishes. She asked that the meeting place be changed.

Mrs. Sakhawat Husain balked at this last-minute change in plans, for it would mean that many women who had already received invitations would not know where the meeting was, and attendance would be reduced. She further argued that it cast aspersions on the judgement of the local committee. What kind of a national organization is this, she said, if the local committee's decisions are not respected by the central committee, and if our carefully-laid plans are thrown into confusion once the Honorary Secretary arrives on the scene? Mrs. Sakhawat Husain was a woman of considerable pride and independence, and Nafis Dulhan's decision had angered her, but there was more than anger and hurt pride involved in her criticism of the Honorary Secretary. If Nafis Dulhan insisted on making last-minute arrangements herself, as she did in this instance, it would be extremely difficult for the Anjuman to build up a nationwide network of active local branches, which would feel free to make arrangements for the annual conference to meet in their cities. The organization would be so dependent on the central committee's decisions, or whims, that it could not grow and broaden its influence in other localities.

Mrs. Husain's criticism was in part, therefore, based on friction between the center and the branch over the issue of autonomy, and in part also on the regional rivalry between Bengali Muslim educators and the Aligarh-dominated Muslim educational movement. But there was another, more parochial reason for this delicate state of affairs. The Arif family did not get along with the prosperous Muslim family who lived in the house on Ripon Street. Nafis Dulhan, out of affection for her friend, and also because as a purdah-observing woman she could not adequately check out the location for herself, took Naziri Begum's word that the place was unsuitable. The venue of the conference was changed by a self-appointed committee composed of the Arif family and friends; Mrs. Sakhawat Husain and her thriving girls' school were permanently alienated from the Anjuman; and as Mrs. Husain had predicted, the attendance at the Calcutta conference was seriously curtailed.[36] At the meeting, the officers who had served for five years were re-elected for another five-year term, and Aligarh's control over the Anjuman was reaffirmed.[37]

The Calcutta incident could be passed over as simply an example of petty, local bickering, or more broadly, as a disagreement over control of the Anjuman. But there is another issue in evidence here as well, and that is the acceptance of purdah itself. These upper-class, educated women, quite accustomed to traveling about India on trains, albeit in special compartments or accompanied by male relatives, were more concerned about proper screening than they were about the success of the meeting or, it would seem, about the future of the Anjuman itself. And yet, they had a point. If purdah-observing women did not feel secure at a meeting of the Anjuman, they would never return to it. If Muslim society felt that the Anjuman was lax in this respect, all their work, including the growing acceptance of women's education, might be undone. Purdah was not just a social institution the boundaries of which they had to observe if they were to be effective, but it was also symbolic of their identity as Muslims, of which they were proud, and of their class status as well. Symbols of religious identity and social status were not dispensed with lightly, especially when one's program required public acceptance.

The Anjuman was never quite the same after the Calcutta meeting. In 1920, a projected conference in Madras did not materialize, so the Aligarh women pulled together a conference in Agra on April 2-3, 1920, under the presidency of Begum Shafi.[38] Thereafter, meetings petered out. In 1921, Nafis Dulhan journeyed to Bombay to drum up a conference there, but plans were dropped when "it was decided that under present conditions, a meeting would not be successful." Then there were efforts to hold a meeting in Poona, and even in Hyderabad, Nafis Dulhan's residence, without success. The Anjuman continued to collect a modest amount of annual dues and other contributions for women's education and supported girls' schools in various cities, as well as regularly granting 50 rupees per month to Aligarh Girl's School.[39]

A Punjabi woman, writing in *Tahzib-e-Niswan* in late 1923, criticized the state of the Anjuman. Why, she asked, has it become so impossible for the All-India Muslim Ladies' Conference to hold a meeting? Certainly, in these three years, even if invitations had not come from elsewhere, it should have been possible to hold a conference in Aligarh, and a number of members had requested just such an arrangement, but to no avail. The Anjuman, she said, is not an All-India Ladies' Conference at all, but rather a "Nafis Dulhan Conference." The real reason for the inaction is that the Secretary, and Shaikh Abdullah, Secretary of the Women's Education Section of the Muhammadan Educational Conference, are out of sympathy with the political currents of the time.[40] The Anjuman may not have become simply a "Nafis Dulhan Conference," but it certainly had always been Aligarh-dominated. This fact explains the reluctance of officers to summon a meeting of Muslim women during the heat of the non-cooperation and Khilafat movement, a time when Hindus and Muslims alike were very much involved in anti-government political agitation. With Muslim women of different political stripes brought together, anti-government opinions might be expressed and resolutions passed which might jeopardize the hard-won government patronage of Aligarh Girls' School. The Khilafat movement had brought about the defeat of loyalism in Muslim politics, but Muslims who believed in collaboration with the government clung to their positions of influence in the Educational Conference and the Women's Anjuman, both still headquartered in Aligarh.

Summarizing the career of Anjuman, one may say that it had certainly fostered an increased sense of community and social consciousness among Muslim women. It had provided a respectable meeting place for purdah-observing women from many provinces, branching out from North India and the Punjab to include representatives from Calcutta, Central India, Bombay, and Madras. But the Aligarh faction had remained tightly in control, and as Aligarh waned in importance as a political center for the Muslims of India during the Khilafat movement, with Muslims turning to anti-British political activity, the Anjuman too lost whatever representativeness it had had, and became moribund. The members stopped sending in their dues and drifted away, and without the attraction of an annual meeting, where women could meet new-found friends from other cities and provinces, there was little to hold the Anjuman together. Educational work continued. The Anjuman, or what was left of it, continued to donate to Aligarh Girls' School. Local branches of the Anjuman supported girls' schools in their localities, whether they still acknowledged their connection to the All-India Anjuman or not. Members whose political views differed from those of the Aligarh clique went their own way politically. A number of Muslim women were active in the Khilafat-Noncooperation movement, even from behind the veils of purdah;[41] and in 1927, when the All-India Women's Conference was founded, a few Muslim women became active in it.

The Begum of Bhopal presided over the second annual AIWC meeting in Delhi in 1928 and in her speech called on all the women there to avoid the religious divisions and bickering which affected Indian political life. They should work with solidarity to improve the quality of women's education, and to gain greater rights for women. In other words, involvement in politics was dangerous to their sisterhood; they should concentrate on social matters. She particularly called for support of the Sarda Bill, then in the legislature, designed to raise the legal age of marriage. In the matter of purdah, she said that the way it was practiced in India was much too strict. This was quite an admission for a woman who had been an observer and defender of purdah all her life.[42] She said that the needs of the times dictated a moderation of the custom, and that she now believed that purdah as it was practiced in India had been harmful to the cause of women's education.[43]

The Begum and some other Muslim women had become aware of an all-India sisterhood in which Muslim women could support Hindu women in their campaign to raise the age of marriage, while calling upon Hindu women to support their efforts to lessen the restrictions of purdah.[44] This did not mean the abandonment of purdah altogether, however, but rather—they continued to maintain—a return to the kind of purdah sanctioned in the shariat. The desire for the enforcement of the shariat as Muslim personal law, rather than any thought of a uniform civil code, was an issue which separated Muslim women from their Hindu sisters. If the shariat were in force instead of customary law, Muslim women felt, then their rights to property, inheritance, and choice in marriage would be assured. Hence in this matter of legal reform, Muslim women's sense of separate community identity was reinforced. The recognition of the shariat as the operative Muslim personal law was a matter which concerned both Muslim men and women. In this instance Muslim women's rights were identified with those of the Muslim minority. Though Muslim women joined the AIWC, they were few in number, and they were considered a group apart within the AIWC membership.[45]

The Anjuman-e-Khawatin-e-Islam, meanwhile, faded into oblivion. In 1929, the first All-India Muslim Ladies' Conference since 1920 was held in Hyderabad, but it was all-India in name only, since only a half-dozen women from elsewhere attended. Nafis Dulhan, who had been re-elected Secretary for a third five year term in 1923, offered to resign in favor of anyone else who would take the job, but was again re-elected. Resolutions were passed, and the women went home.[46] The Begum of Bhopal, long a patron of the Anjuman, ceased her stipend to it just before she died in early 1930. That meant that the Anjuman went broke and had to cease its monthly grant to Aligarh Girls' College. In 1931, Nafis Dulhan reported that there were still three branches of the Anjuman, in Poona, Berar, and Calcutta, in addition to headquarters in Aligarh. People compared the Anjuman unfavorably to the rapidly expanding AIWC and said that the Anjuman had failed because it had become wholly the concern of one person.[47]

This was borne out in 1932 when Rahmatunnissa Begum, Secretary of the Madras Muslim Ladies' Association, invited the Anjuman to hold an all-India conference in her city. She organized a local arrangements committee, raised money, and seemed to have injected new life into the corpse of the Anjuman. But Nafis Dulhan objected to the fact that Muslim men were to be permitted to attend certain sessions, but to sit behind a screen in a kind of purdah in reverse. Even though the men in question were well-wishers of the Anjuman and had donated money to hold the conference, this was unacceptable, she said, not because the men might see the women, but because they could hear them. This would be a violation of purdah, strictly speaking, and was also objectionable since it might inhibit discussion.[48]

The Madras incident illustrates the fact that purdah was a rapidly changing institution. When the Anjuman was founded in 1914, most of its membership observed stringent purdah, and even those women who did not observe purdah themselves accepted it as necessary for the conference because it needed social approval. The new style *burqa*, however, was beginning to make it easier for purdah-observing women to get out, and helped increase their confidence beyond their walls. In Calcutta in 1919, the members still accepted strict purdah as part of the requirements of meeting, but there was obviously disagreement over the degree of strictness. With the spread of women's education, the very success of the Anjuman's mission, and with growing political activism among women in the 1920s and 30s, more and more Muslim women began to regard purdah as a nuisance, if not intolerable. The case of the Begum of Bhopal is illustrative of this growing consciousness that purdah was a burden. Further, there were regional variations in its observance. Madras was an area where purdah was not observed as strictly as in UP or Hyderabad. The idea that men should not even hear women, a standard that Nafis Dulhan insisted upon, must have been regarded as ludicrous by many on the local arrangements committee.

The Madras meeting folded. So did the Anjuman. There is no further reference to the all-India conference, but the Madras Anjuman-e-Khawatin-e-Islam flourished under the leadership of Rahmatunnissa Begum.[49] The Punjab branch too, which had always maintained an autonomous existence under the energetic direction of Begum Shah Nawaz, remained active. In 1936, the Punjab Anjuman-e-Khawatin transformed itself into the women's branch of the Punjab Muslim League.[50] Their causes included support for the Shariat Bill in 1937 and thereafter the Pakistan movement.

What conclusions can be drawn about the significance of the Anjuman for Muslim women's rights, or for the Indian nationalist movement, during the years of its existence? During its early years, the Anjuman contributed to a sense of solidarity and community among Muslim women from different regions of India. There were also references in their resolutions to Indian womanhood as a whole, but by and large, the specific measures they espoused had to do with Muslim education and social reform. The Anjuman, therefore, doubtless contributed to a growing sense of Muslim identity, but whether that implied political separatism in the period before 1920 is very questionable. The politics of the Muslim community, however, were reflected closely in the factional divisions within the Anjuman. The period of the Khilafat movement, 1919-1924, was crucial for Indo-Muslim politics. This period saw a trend away from the loyalists and moderates centered at Aligarh and in the old guard of the Muslim League and the Educational Conference, toward a group of Muslims who were more actively nationalist, who collaborated with Gandhi in non-cooperation and civil disobedience. During this period, Shaikh Abdullah, Aftab Ahmad Khan, Habibur Rahman Khan Sherwani, and Mian Muhammad Shafi all withdrew from political activity to spend full time in educational pursuits or government office.[51]

The Anjuman-e-Khawatin was hampered by its association with one faction of Muslim political life, and it was especially hindered by its directors who, during the Khilafat movement and thereafter, would not permit control of the organization to expand so that it would become representative of Muslim women of various points of view and regional affiliations. That the Anjuman avoided association with any one political party seems irrelevant. The AIWC too avoided direct political affiliation as long as possible, but found it impossible to be completely divorced from the pressures of Indian nationalist politics. The Anjuman, then, began the work of awakening a social consciousness among a certain class of Muslim women. It ultimately failed, not because it was elitist, but because it did not become representative of a large enough spectrum of opinion within that elite. In the long run, the Anjuman probably contributed little either to the movement for women's rights or the nationalist movement in India.

The career of the Anjuman, however, does demonstrate the parallelism between the divisions within, and the concerns of, women's associations, and the factions, controversies, and political alliances among the men. It serves as an excellent example of the close interaction between social reform organizations and political parties in India. It shows the class nature of Indian social and political movements at the time, the importance of status, and of personal alliances and kinship in the making of factions, all of which are important in understanding the course of Indian nationalism. It is thus an excellent example of the way in which the study of women's history can illumine the history of society as a whole. One can be disappointed that the Anjuman-e-Khawatin did not accomplish more, and dismiss it as ineffectual, or one can learn something about Muslim political and social life from its vicissitudes. The latter seems a more worthwhile pursuit.

NOTES

The author is grateful to the American Institute of Indian Studies for a Senior Research Fellowship for the year 1977 which made possible the research on which this paper is based. An earlier version of this paper was presented at the Fourth Berkshire Conference on the History of Women, Mt. Holyoke College, August 23-25, 1978.

[1] On the question of women's political mobilization and the social acceptance thereof, see Gail Minault, "Purdah Politics: The Role of Muslim Women In Indian Nationalism, 1911-1924," forthcoming in Hanna Papanek, ed., *Purdah in South Asia: The Segregation of Women.*

[2] For an examination of an aspect of this theme, see Gail Minault and David Lelyveld, "The Campaign for a Muslim University, 1898-1920," *Modern Asian Studies* VIII, 2 (April, 1974), pp. 145-189.

[3] Classic studies of the relationship between social reform, English education, and the rise of Indian nationalism are: Charles Heimsath, *Indian Nationalism and Hindu Social Reform* (Princeton: Princeton University Press, 1964); and Bruce T. McCully, *English Education and the Origins of Indian Nationalism* (Reprint. Gloucester, Mass.: Peter Smith, 1966).

[4] See Gail Minault, *The Khilafat Movement: Religious Symbolism and Political Mobilization in India* (New York: Columbia University Press, forthcoming), intro., ch. I.

[5] See Geraldine Forbes, "The Indian Women's Movement: A Struggle for Women's Rights or National Liberation," above; and her "From Purdah to Politics: The Social Feminism of the All-India Women's Organizations," forthcoming in Hanna Papanek, ed., *Purdah in South Asia.*

[6] The bibliography of recent scholarship on Indian nationalism is very extensive. To list a few examples: J. H. Broomfield, *Elite Conflict in a Plural Society: Twentieth Century Bengal* (Berkeley: University of California Press: 1968); Anil Seal, *The Emergence of Indian Nationalism* (Cambridge: Cambridge University Press, 1968); Anil Seal, Gordon Johnson, and John Gallagher, eds., *Locality, Province and Nation* (Cambridge: Cambridge University Press, 1973); C.A. Bayly, *The Local Roots of Indian Politics, Allahabad, 1880-1920* (Oxford: Oxford University Press, 1975); John R. McLane, *Indian Nationalism and the Early Congress* (Princeton: Princeton University Press, 1977).

[7] New works which serve as a corrective to this are: Peter Hardy, *The Muslims of British India* (Cambridge: Cambridge University Press, 1972); Paul Brass, *Language, Religion, and Politics in North India* (Cambridge: Cambridge University Press, 1974) part III; Francis Robinson, *Separatism Among Indian Muslims, The Politics of United Provinces' Muslims, 1860-1923* (Cambridge: Cambridge University Press, 1974); David Lelyveld, *Aligarh's First Generation: Muslim Solidarity in British India* (Princeton: Princeton University Press, 1978).

[8] The name of the conference was thus translated into English by its members. It will be referred to hereafter as "the Anjuman."

[9] Proceedings of the Anjuman's meetings in the Urdu press or in published pamphlets, coverage of and comment upon the meetings in the Urdu press and journals for women, published speeches, and personal memoirs.

[10]See Minault and Lelyveld, "The Campaign for a Muslim University;" and David Lelyveld, "Three Aligarh Students: Aftab Ahmad Khan, Ziauddin Ahmad, and Muhammad Ali," *Modern Asian Studies* IX, 2 (April, 1975), pp. 227-240.

[11]Shaikh Abdullah, *Sawanih-e-Umri-e-Abdullah Begum* (Aligarh: Privately Printed, 1954), pp. 14-19.

[12]Shaikh Muhammad Abdullah, *Mushahidat wa Ta'asurat* (Aligarh; Female Education Society, 1969), pp. 186-88, 198-240; *Khatun* (Aligarh) VIII, 1 (January, 1912), pp. 33-42.

[13]Begum Yaqub was the daughter of the first marriage of Sayyid Mumtaz Ali, who founded *Tahzib-e-Niswan* in 1898. Mumtaz Ali's second wife, Muhammadi Begum, had been the editor of *Tahzib* until her untimely death in 1908.

[14]Fatima Begum was the daughter of Maulvi Mahbub Alam, the editor of *Paisa Akhbar*, one of the most popular Urdu newspapers in the Punjab.

[15]*Khatun* (Aligarh) X, 2-3 (February-March, 1914) pp. 44-54.

[16]*Risala-e-Anjuman-e-Himayat-e-Islam* (Lahore) XXX, 3-4 (March-April, 1914), pp. 18-24

[17]*Khatun* X, 2-3 (February-March, 1914), p. 28.

[18]Shaikh Abdullah, *Sawanih-e-Umri-e-Abdullah Begum*, p. 59.

[19]Begum Muhammed Ishaq Khan was the wife of the Honorary Secretary of Aligarh College. The mother and sister of Nafis Dulhan were added to the committee at its first six-monthly meeting in August, 1914. *Khatun* X, 8 (August, 1914), pp. 18-20.

[20]*Khatun* X, 2-3 (February-March, 1914), pp. 61-63.

[21]*Ibid.*, pp. 57-63,

[22]*Ibid*.

[23]*Khatun* ceased publication at the end of 1914. Shaikh Abdullah cited as reasons the press of work in his law practice, and at Aligarh College and Girl's School.

[24]The Anjuman was the first organization of Indian women with all-India aspirations, although Tagore's niece, Sarla Devi Chaudhrani, had begun the Bharat Stri Mahamandal in 1910, with membership from a limited area.

[25]Women who were thirty years of age and householders, or the wives of householders, were given the vote in 1918: They did not attain equal suffrage in Britain until 1928, William L. O'Neil, *The Women Movement* (Chicago: Quadrangle Books, 1971) P. 85.

[26]The composition of the women's deputation to Montagu in 1917 is open to question. One list of members mentions Mrs. Mazharul Haq, wife of a prominent lawyer and leading Congress Muslim of Bihar, as the Muslim delegate. Another list mentions Begum Hasrat Mohani as the sole Muslim. Hasrat Mohani was an Urdu paet and journalist, pro-nationalist and pro-*swadeshi*, who was intened during World War I for his political writings. In either case, the women were more closely indentified with the nationalist movement then with women's social and educational reform efforts. Eor a comparision of the two versions of the

deputation's membership, see Geraldine Forbes,"Votes for Women: The Demand for Women's Franchise in India, 1917-1937," in Vina Mazumdar, ed., *Symbols of Power: Studies in the Political Status of Wamen in India* (Bombay: Allied Publishers, 1979), pp.5, 21, note 8.

[27] Begum Shah Nawaz's autobiography, *Father and Daughter* (Lahore: Nigarishat, 1971), details her family's social and political history during this period.

[28] *Tahzib-e-Niswan* (Lahore) XXI, March 30, 1918, pp. 199-201, hereafter cited as *TN*.

[29] *TN* XXI, April 20, 1918, pp.245-49.

[30] *TN* XXI, May 11, 1918, pp. 298-302.

[31] *TN* XXI, March 9, 1918, p. 164.

[32] *TN* XXI, March 9, 1918, p 163; May 11, 1918, pp. 303-06. *Tahzib-e-Niswan*, however, is hardly a neutral source in this instance. It gives no details on why Fatima Begum opposed Begum Abdullah as Secretary of the Anjuman. As for the polygamy issue, Fatima Begum had good personal reasons for the ideological position. She was childless, and so permitted her husband to take a second wife.

[33] *TN* XXI, February 16, 1918, pp. 117-19; April 6, 1918, pp. 221-24.

[34] Her father, Imad ul-Mulk, Sayyid Husain Bilgrami, had been the Director of Education in the Nizam's government. The Bilgrami Sayyids had been patrons and trustees of Aligarh College over the years.

[35] *TN* XXI, February 9, 1918, pp. 94-96.

[36] *TN* XXII, April 5, 1919, pp. 218-23; April 12, 1919, pp. 241-50.

[37] *TN* XXII, March 15, 1919, p. 165.

[38] *TN* XXIII, March 13, 1920, p. 164; April 17, 1920, pp. 243-48.

[39] *TN* XXVI, February 3, 1923, np.

[40] *TN* XXVI, December 8, 1923, pp. 775-77.

[41] See Minault,"Purdah Politics," cited above, note 1.

[42] Sultan Jahan Begum, *Al-Hijab, or Why Purdah is Necessary* (Calcutta: Thacker and Spink, 1922). The Begum observed purdah while conducting the business of her state, and even went veiled to London in 1911 to attend the coronation of King George V. At the end of her life, in the late 1920s, however, she gradually came out of purdah, saying that one had to change with the times, and she wanted to urge the women of Bhopal to come out of purdah and educate their children. Doranne Jacobson, "The Veil of Virtue: Purdah and the Muslim Family in the Bhopal Region of Central India," in Imtiaz Ahmad, ed., *Family, Kinship, and Marriage Among Muslims in India* (New Delhi: Manohar, 1976), pp. 202-03.

[43] *TN* XXXI, February 18, 1928, pp. 158-66.

[44] *TN* XXXII, May 18, 1929, pp. 465-68.

[45] For Muslim membership in the AIWC, see Geraldine Forbes' article, above; for a detailed treatment of the place of shariat legislation in Muslim politics in the 1930s, see David Gilmartin's article, below.

[46]*TN* XXXII, March 2, 1929, pp. 225-26; March 16, 1929, pp. 249-53.

[47]*TN* XXXIV, April 5, 1931, pp. 345-47; April 25, 1931, pp. 385-88; May 9, 1931, pp. 441-50.

[48]*TN* XXXV, August 6, 1932, pp. 770-71; November 12, 1932, pp. 2002-03; December 10, 1932, pp- 2098-2100.

[49]Rahmatunnissa Begum, Ms. of Autobiography, pp. 7-11. I am grateful to Geraldine Forbes for this reference.

[50]*TN* XXXIX, May 2, 1936, p. 430; Jahanara Shah Nawaz, *Father and Daughter*.

[51]Aftab served on the Secretary of State's India Council in London (1917-1924) and later returned to Aligarh as Vice-Chancellor of the Muslim University (1924-1927). Habibur Rahman Khan Sherwani joined the Nizam's government in 1919. Mian Muhammad Shafi joined the Government of India as Education Member in 1920 and later served as Law Member (1922-24), and was knighted. Shaikh Abdullah served as Treasurer of Aligarh College and the Muslim University, and continued to direct the Girls' School and College.

5

Catalysts or Helpers? British Feminists, Indian Women's Rights, and Indian Independence

BARBARA N. RAMUSACK

During the closing decades of the nineteenth century some foreign, mainly British, women come to India to work for improved social conditions for Indian women. In contemporary terms they were feminists since they wanted to broaden the range of opportunities available for Indian women. They usually had pursued professional careers, especially teaching, in Great Britain and frequently had been active in the suffragette campaign which was the most prominent aspect of an expanding women's movement that sought equality under the law for women. These individuals were not associated with either missionary or official networks in India and either became attached to Indian-based groups and leaders or worked as independent agents.

Social reform in India had been intertwined with imperial politics and colonial culture since the early nineteenth century when Ram Mohun Roy, the Bengali religious and social reformer, had propagandized for the abolition of sati. By the 1890s the controversy over a bill to raise the age of consent to consummation within marriage illustrated the complex relationship between social reform and nationalist politics in a colonial setting. Shortly thereafter, the agitation over the partition of Bengal from 1905 to 1911 demonstrated the growing strength of Indian leaders as adversaries of British rule in India. Foreign women who wished to pursue the apparently straightforward goal of changing women's status and rights quickly discovered that they had to confront the personal and institutional implications of the nationalist movement for their efforts.

This essay will focus on three British women—Eleanor Rathbone, Margaret Gillespie Cousins and Agatha Harrison—who worked both for women's issues and for progress toward Indian self-rule. Throughout a delineation of their backgrounds, activities, and interaction with Indian women and men, there will be an effort to analyze how these women sought to reconcile their feminist concerns with the achievement of political independence. Was more to be gained by cooperation with the imperial power or by opposition? Were their goals capable of being pursued and achieved simultaneously or consecutively? If the latter option were preferred, which objective would have the higher priority and with what results? What would be the response of Indian women personally and through their organizations? Would foreign women, particularly those from the imperial power, be able to contribute to a women's movement in a colonized country? On one level, the answers to these questions will illuminate what areas of cooperation might be possible among women of various nations, cultures, and societies. On another plane, they will extend the understanding of the intricacies of imperial relationships.

I

Eleanor Rathbone came from a Lancashire liberal family that had long been associated with business, humanitarian activities, and legislative politics in Liverpool.[1] The William Rathbone family had extensive financial resources, a firm commitment to nonconformist sects, and a tradition of the men marrying strong-willed, independent-minded women. The family fortune was based on a shipowning business which gradually extended into various forms of merchandising. By the late 1700s William Rathbone IV had shifted from Quakerism to Unitarianism and had enhanced the family reputation for liberalism by attacking the slave trade which was a significant source of income in the triangular trade between Liverpool, West Africa, and the West Indies. William Rathbone V assaulted electoral corruption in municipal politics and became the first Rathbone to sit on the Liverpool City Council after the passage of a reform act in 1835. The Rathbone name and interests extended beyond Liverpool. When Ram Mohun Roy came to England in 1831, he went first to Greenbank, the estate of the Rathbones known for their gracious hospitality and sympathy for Unitarianism.[2] William Rathbone VI became a Liberal member of Parliament representing Liverpool, and thus Eleanor Rathbone was born in London on May 12, 1872. Her youth was divided between London and Greenbank. Because of this peripatetic lifestyle, her early education was private and sporadic. The ancient English universities had been opened to nonconformists and in a more limited way to women, so in 1893 Eleanor went to Oxford and became one of forty-seven students at Somerville College. By this point she was no longer a committed Unitarian and was already smoking cigarettes, her one acknowledged vice. She chose the Oxford Greats, concentrating on philosophy and was awarded a second. She had a reputation as a quick and imaginative thinker, but a scholar with limited strength in textual analysis.

Her classmates at Somerville were a select group of dedicated, precedent-breaking young women. Eleanor formed close friendships with such feminists as Margery Fry, eventually the principal of Somerville, and Barbara Bradley Hammond, the coauthor of several influential studies of the industrial revolution. Eleanor was also a founding member of a small discussion group known as the APs whose title, supposedly only the members knew, stood for Associated Prigs. At their third meeting, Eleanor compared public and private schemes of poor relief and social service.[3] Their wide-ranging discussions were a stimulating forum for the maturing Rathbone woman, who seemed inclined to maintain the family tradition of social service.

In 1896 Eleanor returned to Liverpool where she became involved in public roles, first as an assistant to her father now retired from Parliament, and then in her own spheres. From this period until her death fifty years later, she pursued concurrently her interests in social welfare programs, feminism, and legislative politics. In 1897 she became secretary to the Liverpool Women's Suffrage Society. She soon was the dominant force in this group which was affiliated with the moderate National Union of Women's Suffrage Societies (NUWSS), headed by Millicent Fawcett. In the ongoing struggle for the extension of the franchise to women, the strategy of the NUWSS was dramatically challenged after 1905 by Emmeline Pankhurst and her daughters Christabel and Sylvia. Their militant Women's Social and Political Union (WSPU) advocated confrontation and direct action, including windowbreaking on government property. Eleanor, however, remained committed to constitutional processes and compromises designed to achieve the possible.

After the death of her father in 1902, Eleanor pursued research on topics which came to her attention while serving as an officer in various social welfare organizations. She was dissatisfied with temporary solutions, and her formal education directed her to look for underlying causes and to seek remedies for them, as well as to provide palliative measures. Her reports focused on concerns ranging from the problems of casual laborers—as experienced by the dockworkers of Liverpool, to the degrading conditions of widows under the poor laws. During World War I Eleanor worked with wives and dependents of military personnel in Liverpool. Her research on widows and her wartime experiences led her to advocate family allowances paid in cash directly to mothers as one means to recognize the social contributions of mothers and to provide some basis for their economic independence. Her most famous book, *The Disinherited Family* (1924), contained both supporting statistical data and critical arguments for this scheme which was eventually enacted by Parliament in 1945.

Eleanor's entry into legislative politics came in 1909 when she was elected to the Liverpool City Council as an Independent, becoming its first woman member. During World War I she began to move beyond Liverpool when she joined the Executive of the NUWSS in London. With the grant of partial suffrage to women in 1918 the NUWSS became the National Union of Societies for Equal Citizenship (NUSEC), and in 1919 Rathbone succeeded Millicent Fawcett as president. Much of her ten-year tenure was devoted to two broad objectives: First, she wanted to widen organizational goals from winning the franchise to achieving true equality between men and women. The program was labelled the "new feminism". Since it could encompass a myriad of reforms, the NUSEC Council identified six priority areas.

1. Equal pay for equal work.
2. Equal standards in sexual morality.
3. Allowances for civilian widows with dependent children.
4. Equalization of the franchise and the election to Parliament of women pledged to equality.
5. Legal recognition of mothers as equal guardians with fathers of children.
6. Opening of the legal profession and magistracy to women.[4]

Besides working toward these goals, Rathbone sought and secured the collective support of NUSEC for her scheme of family allowances, even though Millicent Fawcett opposed this proposal from her protégé.

A second objective was to expand the territorial horizons of NUSEC from Great Britain to Europe and eventually to Latin America, Asia, and Africa. Once the franchise had been won for women in Great Britain and the United States, there was growing pressure to support the fight for this political right elsewhere. As president of of NUSEC, Rathbone attended the triennial meetings the Women's International Suffrage Alliance in Various European capitals, Geneva, Rome, Paris and Berlin. In July, 1928 Rathbone stated to NUSEC members that :

> ...So long as imperialism is an unescapable fact, its responsibilities are also an unescapable fact, and these, for the women of this country, include the welfare of all those women in India and the East whose wrongs, as compared to the worst wrongs of our past, are as scorpions to whips.[5]

There is some evidence that Eleanor Rathbone might have attended meetings in London during 1919 when Herabai Tata, a Parsi women's leader from Bombay, and her daughter sought British support for the extension of the franchise to Indian women in the Indian Councils Act then under Parliamentary consideration.[6] These meetings, however, do not seem to have made a lasting impact on her. It was only in 1927 that Rathbone began to concentrate her attention on the situation of Indian women. The instrument was a widely-read book, *Mother India*, by Katherine Mayo, an American journalist who had also written investigative studies of the Philippines and the Pennsylvania State Police. Her book aroused considerable debate because of its negative analysis of the political capacity of Indians for self-government. Mayo argued that all Indian problems including "poverty, sickness, ignorance, political minority, melancholy, ineffectiveness [and] a subconscious sense of inferiority" could be attributed to "his manner of getting into the world and his sex-life thenceforward."[7] She then depicted in graphic detail the physical devastation which early marriage and motherhood had imposed on Indian women.[8] British officials and reviewers generally praised Mayo's book. Most Indians and a few British critics either deemed her a conscious or unconscious tool of British imperialists or an unsympathetic observer who maligned Hindu society by distorting the impact of particular social and religious customs.[9] Rathbone's immediate response to Mayo's exposé was, characteristically, to try to ascertain the accuracy of her data. Her subsequent actions were conditioned by her longstanding habits of social research and her existing organizational networks.

Rathbone called a small conference of British Women's groups to discuss the problems illustrated in *Mother India*. NUSEC then launched a survey of social conditions affecting Indian women which included questionnaires sent to Indian groups. These activities quickly elicited unfavourable comments from Indian women who were not consulted, as well as reticence from some who were. Rathbone attempted to make amends by inviting six prominent Indian women in London to tea. These included Lady Mehrbai Dorab Tata and Hannah Sen, a Bengali educator who was serving as the representative of Indian women's groups in London. Eleanor felt that they "had a vigorous hammer and tongs discussion, but parted good friends." It is difficult to evaluate whether or not her impression was shared, since even British feminist co-workers remember her as being one who lectured rather than discussed.[10] Writing from India, Sri Maya Devi emphasized the importance of acknowledging Indian national identity as a basis for friendly cooperation, and advised Rathbone to visit India to meet Indian women in their own setting.[11] Even from English colleagues, Rathbone received cautionary advice. Ellen Wilkinson, a Labour MP, declined to sign a letter to *The Times* on the issue of child marriage arguing that "however well-intentioned the people of the governing country and however necessary the reform may be," in a colonial situation, "the governed elevate the abuse into a principle to be maintained against the oppressor."[12]

Eleanor, however, proceeded with plans for a conference sponsored by NUSEC which she would chair. This meeting was for all British women's organizations interested in Indian social reform and was held at Caxton Hall in Westminister on October 7 and 8, 1929. Dhanvanthi Rama Rau, then living in London while her husband was assisting the Simon Commission write its report on proposed Indian constitutional reforms, and herself later the leading figure in the family planning movement in independent India, has vividly described her reaction to these proceedings.

> I was comparatively young, excitable when slighted, somewhat rash and certainly courageous enough to face so important a person as Eleanor Rathbone in the chair, and women in the audience like Sylvia Pankhurst and Mrs. Pethick-Lawrence.... I asked for permission to speak, and was graciously allowed five minutes. I did not speak on any of the subjects on the agenda, but merely disputed the right of British women to arrange a conference on Indian social evils in London, when all the speakers were British and many of them had never even visited India. Not one of them had even asked if there were any Indian women's organizations that were dealing with the problems on the spot, the same problems that British women were exploring

from the great and deceptive distance of fifteen thousand miles.... We were already assuming the responsibility ourselves, and we were sure we could be more successful than any outsiders, especially those who were ignorant of the cultural patterns of our social groups and therefore could not be as effective as our own social reformers.[13]

After this unfortunate confrontation with a representative of the rising generation of Indian feminists, Eleanor Rathbone showed greater concern for Indian leaders and their efforts as she pursued her goal of raising the minimum age of marriage for Indian women. During the earlier debate on this issue in 1891 some Indian nationalists such as B. G. Tilak protested against any government interference in such a private, religious matter, while other Indians eagerly sought British support for such legislation.[14] The 1891 Age of Consent Act did not resolve the situation, and so the issue had been debated in the Central Indian Legislative Assembly since 1921. By the time of the Caxton Hall Conference, it was the subject of two bills and one investigative committee chaired by M. V. Joshi. In 1929 the Legislative Assembly approved the Child Marriage Restraint Act, known by the last name of its sponsor, Rai Sahib Harbilas Sarda, the member from Ajmer-Merwara, the British enclave in Rajputana. The Sarda Act set fourteen as the minimum age at marriage for females but it was not to come into effect for six months after passage. Its initial impact was to stimulate an increase in child marriages as parents sought to escape its provisions.[15] While the existence of the Act may have prevented some marriages, it was generally deemed ineffective. Most basically it was difficult to enforce since registration of births and deaths was largely confined to urban areas, and because it was difficult to find an individual willing to register a complaint that an illegal marriage had taken place. As in 1891, enforcement of this legislation acquired political implications.

In 1930 the Indian National Congress under the leadership of Mahatma Gandhi had launched a civil disobedience movement against the British Government of India demanding self-government immediately. When Eleanor Rathbone advised Wedgwood Benn, the Secretary of State for India, that she proposed to ask three questions in Parliament on the Sarda

Act, he asked her to withdraw them since "bringing any sort of pressure to bear, will add incalculably to the embarrassment of the GOI and all the local Governments, and do much to hinder the return of a calmer atmosphere we all wish to see."[16] Rathbone forcefully expressed her indignation to Mabel Hartog, a feminist colleague and wife of Philip Hartog, the educator who served as a most dynamic Vice-Chancellor of the University of Dacca and headed the Education Subcommittee of the Simon Commission, when she confided that she felt "distracted at the thought of all the wretched little brides who are likely to be sacrificed on the altar of India's political aspirations."[17] Rathbone did not want reforms improving the condition of women to be delayed by British or Indian concerns for self-rule. She continued to badger Samuel Hoare, Benn's successor at the India Office, for firmer government implementation of this measure.[18] Hoare did advise Lord Willingdon, the Viceroy, that he had "considerable sympathy with Miss Rathbone's objective," and piously hoped that Delhi could promote the objective of the Sarda Act without making political trouble.[19] Delhi remained indifferent.

As one with a reputation for political realism and a comprehensive approach to social problems, Rathbone explored other devices for achieving her aims. In March, 1930 she suggested the establishment of a Minister for Maternity and Child Welfare on Indian Provincial Executive Councils.[20] She broadened her contacts with women in India first through correspondence and then during a tour of India in the first months of 1932. After repeated responses from both the India Office and the Government of India that Indians alone could provide leadership on this issue, Rathbone published *Child Marriage: The Indian Minotaur*. It was a harsh, polemical work intended to stimulate people to action, but its author argued differently from Mayo in that she apportioned blame for the evils associated with child marriage not just to Hindu custom, as Mayo had done, but to Hindus, Muslims, and especially to the British Government.

Rathbone apparently wrote this book without asking any Indian woman leader to read it in draft form. Once it was published she sent copies to many such leaders including three women who had been in London to testify before the Joint

Select Parliamentary Committee on Indian Constitutional Reform during the summer of 1933: Muthulakshmi Reddi, a physician, active worker for the *devadasis* of Madras, and president of the All-India Women's Conference in 1934; Shareefah Hamid Ali, a member of the Tyabji family and active in Bombay women's groups; and Rajkumari Amrit Kaur, an Indian Christian from a Punjab princely family who had become a follower of Gandhi. She acknowledged that it was a "terribly outspoken little book" but hoped it would not annoy them since most of her criticism was directed against the British authorities, "as an Englishwoman's responsibility is limited to them." Rathbone wanted their reactions to proposals she had made, especially the one to set up a propaganda and lobbying organization devoted solely to the issue of child marriage. She realized that it might not be appropriate for an Englishwoman to make such suggestions but she pleaded "where sufferings and injustices affecting women are concerned, I as an old suffragist simply cannot remember or bother about national distinctions."[21]

Many Indian women expressed their personal appreciation for Rathbone's concern.[22] The All-India Women's Conference (AIWC), founded in 1927 and by 1934 the most prominent women's organization in India, discussed Rathbone's proposal for a new organization and her offer of financial assistance to pay an employee to establish such a venture. The Standing Committee of the AIWC decided that it was not appropriate to accept such foreign funds and that they lacked the personnel to set up a separate organization.[23] This decision was not unanimous as Lakshmi Menon, a young lawyer just beginning to practice in Lucknow, argued, "If we could appeal to foreign countries for help for the loss sustained by the earthquake (in Bihar), I did not see any reason why we should reject the offer of voluntary help from one sister abroad." She added, "I hope you'll understand the attitude of women who feel some kind of inferiority in these things and forgive them."[24] The AIWC Standing Committee had appointed an All-India Sarda Subcommittee with Shareefah Hamid Ali as its convener, but she soon resigned because of her commitment to village uplift work and was succeeded by Lakshmi Menon.[25]

In early 1935, N.M. Joshi, the labor leader and member of the Servants of India Society who had come to know Rathbone on the voyage to India in January, 1932, asked Rathbone if she was arranging for the drafting of legislation to amend the Sarda Act and volunteered his assistance.[26] In London, Eleanor secured the help of Henry Polak, a lawyer and follower of Gandhi from his South African years, and William Wallach, an advocate at Allahabad, in drafting a suitable amending bill. Rathbone specifically requested that her name not be associated with this project since it might be prejudicial to the bill if it appeared to be engineered by English politicians.[27] Joshi was able to obtain the cooperation of Bhubanananda Das, a Congress legislator from Orissa, as sponsor of the bill. Even before she received requests from Rajkumari Amrit Kaur and Muthulakshmi Reddi to do so, Rathbone urged the India Office to pressure the Government of India to support the Das Amendment Bill.[28] It was enacted in 1938 and revealed that foreigners could play a positive role in securing legislation but not necessarily in rendering it effective.

When requesting Rathbone's assistance with the Das Bill, Muthulakshmi Reddi had lamented that:" Unfortunately, there is not even a single woman in the Assembly, to represent the woman's point of view."[29] Rathbone herself had long argued that women in the legislature would mean the passage of more laws improving the social and legal conditions of women. She first ran unsuccessfully for Parliament in 1922 and then won a seat seven years later as an Independent from the Combined English Universities constituency. In 1941 she recalled that she had decided to seek office largely because of her "desire to help Indian women to secure social reforms and a political status equivalent to those which British women had achieved."[30] Her motives were probably more mixed, since her opening campaign speech focussed on domestic concerns with emphasis on social and economic goals, such as improving the quality of municipal administration and dealing with unemployment.[31]

Once in Parliament, where she remained until her death in 1946, Eleanor juggled internal and external issues. Her early years there paralleled the extended debate over constitutional reforms for India which began with the appointment in 1927 of the Indian Statutory or Simon Commission, an investigative body, evolved into three Round Table Conferences in London, produced a White Paper in 1933, dragged on through eighteen months of hearings before a Joint Select Committee of Parliament and culminated in the Government of India Act of 1935. Rathbone was a firm advocate of measured constitutional advances toward Indian self-government,[32] though she was not a supporter of the 1930 civil disobedience movement.[33] Her independence in domestic politics carried over into Indian politics. She admitted to Carl Heath, the respected Quaker leader of the India Conciliation Group which sought to maintain effective dialogue between British officials and Indian leaders, that when speaking to Hoare, she was "always provoked into talking purely pro-Indian." When in contact with the other side such as Heath, however, she was anxious that they work to help Indians understand the strength of the Conservative opposition in Parliament to Indian aspirations for self-rule. Rathbone wanted British friends of India "to act as interpreters and links between the best elements among the Indians and the British Government alike."[34] Following her own advice, she worked with others to secure the continued cooperation of Indian liberal leaders such as Tej Bahadur Sapru, M.R. Jayakar and N. M. Joshi in the constitutional consultations of the 1930s.[35] Agatha Harrison, the secretary of the India Conciliation Group, sought Rathbone's support for conciliatory measures in the Parliamentary debates on India.[36] Even though she did not countenance the civil disobedience movement, Rathbone expressed repeated concern to the India Office about the embittering effect of the arbitrary ordinances which the British used to maintain law and order in troubled provinces, and the allegations of harsh treatment of political prisoners. Her liberalism also led her to oppose any special protection offered to autocratic Indian princes as an inducement to join the proposed federation of British India and princely states.[37] Her position on these last three items was similar to that of the Indian National Congress.

In the sphere of Indian affairs during the early 1930s, however, Rathbone directed most of her attention toward the expansion of the franchise among Indian women. From 1921, Indian provincial legislatures had begun to grant the franchise to women on a very restricted basis. In 1931, the British appointed a Franchise Committee to study and make recommendations to be incorporated in the forthcoming constitutional revisions. Some sources speculate that Rathbone expected to be on this committee but the one woman member was Mary Pickford, a Conservative MP. Rathbone undertook her only visit to India in January 1932, ostensibly "to see something of the work of various women's organizations and to learn how the Act to prevent child marriage in India is working."[38] She traveled on the same ship as did members of the Franchise Committee, chaired by Lord Lothian, and her tour in India generally preceded or paralleled that of the Franchise Committee.[39] Rathbone met with women's groups in Bombay, Madras, Calcutta, Nagpur, Patna, Lucknow, Delhi, Lahore, and except for Bombay, generally had a friendly reception. She found it "amusing how our own ideas and arguments are brought up to us after a few days or even hours, having taken root and sprouted."[40] Elizabeth Vallance, author of *Women in the House*, has characterized Eleanor Rathbone as a pragmatist. On the issue of franchise reform Rathbone argued that "we are so used here to working to get what we can as we can and making it the basis for more, that we can only go on that method and hope for the best."[41] The AIWC, the Women's Indian Association, Congress women members led by Sarojini Naidu, the Bengali poet who had been the second woman to serve as president of the Indian National Congress in 1925, and a meeting of prominent women in Bombay on April 17, 1931, generally asked for equality and no special privileges for women. They specifically called for full adult suffrage in any new constitution.[42] Rathbone accepted the proposed reservation of legislative seats for women and argued that since adult suffrage was unlikely to be obtained, women's groups in England and India should lobby for as broad an extension of the franchise as possible within the existing political atmosphere. Rathbone was greatly dismayed by the gradual reduction in the proposed ratio of men to women voters from 1:2 in the Simon Commission Report, to 1:4½ in the Franchise Commission Report, to 1:7 in the White Paper of 1933.

The White Paper reflected objections from the provincial bureaucrats in India about the administrative difficulties involved in a broader extension of the vote among women. Both British and Indian women's groups were outraged by the White Paper's recommendations, which in some provinces meant an actual ratio of 1:20. In April, 1933 the Indian women's groups met once again in Bombay and modified their demands to adult franchise in the towns, and similar literacy and property qualifications for both sexes.[43] In London, Rathbone coordinated the dispatch of a letter of protest to *The Times*[44] and the establishment of the British Committee for Indian Women's Franchise (BCIWF). After Margaret Wintringham, an early woman MP, declined to serve as chairperson, Rathbone presided over this coalition of female and sympathetic male MPs, leaders of British women's organizations, and others with Indian contacts such as the Hartogs. The BCIWF sought such technical concessions related to women's enfranchisement as a simple literacy test, as opposed to a secondary degree or matriculated status; the inclusion of wives, widows, and mothers of military personnel and wives of property owners who had the vote; and the elimination of the need for eligible women to apply for their vote. They also obtained six reserved seats for women in the Council of State, the upper house of the proposed federal legislature, as well as the nine reserved seats for women in the Federal Assembly and the forty-one reserved seats in the provincial Legislative Assemblies already granted by the British Government.[45]

Rathbone agreed with Indian women leaders that adult franchise in urban areas would be more realistic than their earlier demand for complete adult suffrage, but was not sanguine about their chances of obtaining it.[46] The issue of granting the vote to wives of certain categories of males continued to divide Rathbone and the BCIWF from Indian women's groups and their British supporters. Rathbone pleaded that this measure was a helpful intermediate step, since in England it had led in five years to complete adult franchise, while also improving the status of married women by recognizing them as their husbands' partners in citizenship.[47] Muthulakshmi Reddi countered that one could not compare Indian with English wives since their legal, social, and educational conditions were so different.[48] Their conflicting opinions were reflected in their testimony before the Joint Select Committee in 1933. When the report of that Committee was issued in 1935, it was a disappointment to Rathbone as well as Indian women. She continued to lobby until the ratio of men to women voters was set at 1:5 and other adjustments were made in the method by which women would be chosen for the reserved seats. Shareefah Hamid Ali in London and Rajkumari Amrit Kaur in India dismissed these concessions as minor details in a Government of India Bill generally deemed unacceptable.[49] Amrit Kaur repeatedly expressed her appreciation of Rathbone's efforts on behalf of Indian women but advised her about compromises: "in a free country like yours—yes—but in a subject country—no—because a start on the wrong basis means disaster *ab initio* and can never lead to the ultimate true goals."[50] Rathbone found it personally impossible to accept an overriding commitment to the goal of Indian independence at the expense of intermediate social and political gains. Some moderate Indian women leaders such as Radhabai Subbarayan in Madras, Sarala Ray in Bengal, and Lakshmi Menon in Lucknow agreed with her strategy, but they were not in leadership positions within the major women's organizations.[51] Rathbone's effectiveness as a political lobbyist was thus limited by her reluctance to sacrifice short-term gains for long-term ones.

During the late 1930s Eleanor Rathbone kept in touch with Indian affairs through Grace Lankester, a missionary wife who had lived in Peshawar and later served as the liaison officer for the AIWC in Great Britain. Rathbone gradually became "absorbed in other perplexing questions in the international sphere."[52] She emerged as a sharp critic of both appeasement and its idealistic opponents, and as a forthright advocate for Jewish refugees. Her last significant contact with Indian affairs was during 1941 when she wrote an open letter asking Indian friends to forget past wrongs and to join Britain in its fight against a common foe. This appeal written in the aftermath of the highly destructive Battle of Britain produced a sharp condemnation from Rabindranath Tagore and a lively exchange with the jailed Jawaharlal Nehru.[53] But Rathbone also had critics in her own country. Carl Heath lamented that English people including Rathbone "believe that if *they* do things *for* India which *they* think are good for India, they deserve to be met with thankfulness. They dislike the idea that this well-wishing towards India should be regarded as imperialism and resented as it certainly is . . ." He added that "British people seem unable to realise how baffling and infuriating insistent paternalism is to grown-up India..."[54] Rathbone remained unable to understand the desire of Indians to do things for themselves and to refuse to compromise on the goal of national independence.

II

Margaret Gillespie Cousins presents sharp contrast to Eleanor Rathbone, though they both were active in the suffragette movement in Great Britain, appalled by child marriage and its consequences in India, and active in working to extend the franchise to Indian women. Their differences ranged from those of personality, to nationality, to religious and cultural orientation. Eleanor Rathbone wore her white hair in a bun at age forty and wore matronly black dresses from her thirties, while Margaret Cousins liked to have her auburn hair done at a hairdresser whenever possible and sometimes wore *khaddar*, the rough handspun and handwoven Indian cotton. Margaret was born on November 7, 1878, in Boyle, Roscommon County, Ireland of Protestant, Unionist parents. As a child she deeply imbibed the romance of Irish culture and the drama of Irish nationalism, read biographies, and grew up wanting to be a cheerful saint.[55] In 1898 she went to the Royal Irish Academy of Music in Dublin, and four years later received her degree in music.

During her years in Dublin she had met James Cousins, an active participant in the Irish dramatic and literary revival which was adding artistic expression to the Irish freedom struggle. They married in 1903 and at her wedding reception she announced that she had accepted her husband's ideas and was becoming a vegetarian. Shortly afterwards, Margaret and then James began to read *The Secret Doctrine* by Helena Blavatsky, the Russian aristocrat who had founded the Theosophical Society in 1875. While they were living in Manchester during 1906, Margaret attended the National Conference of Women and soon became a sympathizer with the militant suffragettes, headed by the Pankhursts. When they returned to Ireland, she became treasurer of the Irish Women's Franchise League in 1908. She was a frequent speaker at public meetings, an active participant in windowbreakings in London, and an inmate in English and Irish prisons.[56] Her feminism extended to the religious sphere. In Liverpool in 1914, Margaret helped to found the Church of the New Ideal, a religious organization where women were the ministers and policy board but both men and women could be members of the congregation.[57] On the central question of what priorities should be given to Irish freedom and votes for Irish women, Cousins declared that:

> The introduction of a Home Rule Bill supported by the Liberal Party looked very hopeful for the gaining of the freedom of Ireland at long last. But the Bill made no mention of Irish women being made citizens of their own country. We stumped the country pointing out the injustice of the omission and demanding an amendment in the proposed Home Rule Bill .... We were as keen as men on the freedom of Ireland, but we saw the men clamouring for amendments which suited their own interests and made no recognition of the existence of woman as fellow citizens. We women were convinced that anything which improved the status of women would improve, not hinder, the coming of real national self-government.[58]

Margaret Cousins had gradually shown great interest in psychic phenomena and in communicating with spirits beyond the material world. She and James continued to read Theosophical works and attended a Theosophical convention in London on July 6, 1907 where they first met Annie Besant. After the death of Helena Blavatsky in 1891, Annie Besant, an extraordinary Irish-English woman who had a multiplicity of interests ranging from socialism to birth control, eventually became head of the Theosophical Society and shifted its world headquarters to Adyar near Madras.[59] During her years in India, Besant became increasingly involved in Indian nationalist politics and in September, 1915 founded a Home Rule League which sought the then radical goal of self-government for India within the British Commonwealth. Meanwhile, the Cousins became members of the Theosophical Society in 1908 and founded a Lodge of it in Ireland. They moved from Dublin to Liverpool in 1913, since James had taken a position with a vegetarian food factory in anticipation of proceeding to India to establish a branch factory there. The impact of the war ended that plan, but in 1915 Margaret received a psychic impulse which urged them to write to Annie Besant and to volunteer their services as journalists. Besant replied by asking them to come to India for three years.[60]

Henceforth India became the permanent home for the Cousins, though they would return to England and Ireland for visits, take a couple of world tours, and spend a year in New York City. In India, Margaret Cousins remained an active musician, teaching and giving concerts for Theosophists and Indian princes. She became an author, writing books on women and on music,[61] but gradually came to devote much of her time and energy to the Indian women's movement. Her principal spheres of activity were the organization of women on a local, regional, and national levels; the editorship of *Stri Dharma*, the journal of the Women's Indian Association; lobbying for the franchise for women, then seats for women in the legislature, and places on committees and commissions; and public relations work in India and abroad.

James Cousins began his life in India as literary editor of *New India*, a newspaper published by Annie Besant to whom James referred as "the Chief," and he soon developed an enthusiasm for modern Indian art. Besant, however, became increasingly involved in nationalist politics and was elected the first woman president of the Indian National Congress in 1917. She then decided that George Arundale, a collaborator in the establishment of the Central Hindu College at Benares, should replace the apolitical Cousins on the staff of *New India*. The Chief offered to pay their return passages but Cousins asked for that sum as severance pay since they wanted to stay in India. He soon took a position teaching English at a Theosophical college in Madanapalle, a small town near the Madras-Mysore border also famous as the birthplace of J. Krishnamurti, Besant's controversial protégé. Margaret obtained a similar position at the affiliated high school.

Once in Madanapalle, Margaret was entertained by local women at tea parties. They were on a different scale than the one held by Eleanor Rathbone for six Indian women in the shadow of Westminister Abbey. Margaret's

> first reaction was to follow up our tea-parties, which had shown me that Indian women were just as human as my-

self and as interesed in one another, by bringing together the wives of the teachers and some of their friends in the town, and seeing what would happen. What happened, after some preliminary meetings that created enthusiasm in those who attended them, and criticism in those who stayed away, was a society which called itself the Abala Abhivardini Samaj—the Weaker Sex Improvement Society, an inferiority title that took me some time to get used to.[62]

This misnamed group soon became the prototype of the Women's Indian Association (WIA) which Dorothy Jinarajadasa, an English Theosophist married to a Sinhalese Buddhist scholar who was also a Theosophist, organized with Annie Besant as its first president in 1917. Jinarajadasa was the general secretary.

Soon afterwards, in August, 1917 Edwin Montagu, the Secretary of State for India, announced that he would go to India to survey political conditions with Lord Chelmsford, the Viceroy, in preparation for formulating recommendations for constitutional changes in India. After consulting with Indian women and male social reformars such as D. K. Karve of Poona, Margaret Cousins applied for an interview with this august pair to press for the extension of female education. When she was refused because the tour was only concerned with political issues, James suggested that she apply to discuss votes for women. The answer was now affirmative and Margaret organized a deputation headed by Sarojini Naidu, who was emerging as the most prominent Indian woman in the Indian National Congress, and wrote its petition.[63]

Their interview on December 18, 1917 with Montagu and Chelmsford was only the opening skirmish in a long campaign which Eleanor Rathbone entered at a much later stage. Cousins reflected that

> Curiously enough, though I had the backing of some of the best women of India, I was the one voice publicly explaining and proclaiming the suffrage cause; not because I had any special fitness, but simply because the womanhood of India had not yet found its authoritative voice.[64]

Margaret was understating her past suffragette experience which now proved most valuable. She faced challenges from close associates as well as support from Indian collaborators. Putting political freedom first, Annie Besant refused "to make votes for Indian women a plank in the platform of her Home Rule League."[65] Herabai and Mithan Tata went to London in 1919 to lobby for support from British women's organizations and MPs for a women's franchise provision in the Indian Councils Bill.[66] When it was enacted, this legislation left it up to individual provincial legislatures in India to grant the franchise to women. Margaret then organized campaigns in key provinces, beginning in Madras and proceeding to Bombay and Bengal, arranged public meetings, produced sample resolutions, lobbied Indian legislators, and solicited funds from Indians and foreign suffrage groups.[67] In 1921 the Madras Legislative Council led the way, and by 1929 all provinces and a few princely states had granted some form of limited franchise to women.

The next step was to enable women to sit in the legislatures. Here again, Madras led the way, and Margaret Cousins, now a General Secretary of the WIA along with Jinarajadasa, and the WIA hurriedly sought candidates for the 1926 elections. Cousins quickly approached Kamaladevi Chattopadhyaya, a musician and actress married to a brother of Sarojini Naidu, whom she had first met while teaching in Mangalore, and Hannah Angelo, the secretary of the Nurses' Association in Madras and an Anglo-Indian.[68] Kamaladevi lost 4461 to 4976 and Cousins asked the Governor of Madras to nominate four women including Kamaladevi to the Madras Legislative Council.[69] He passed over Komaladevi who was already acquiring a reputation as a possibly dangerous revolutionary, and nominated Dr. Muthulakshmi Reddi, who had recently returned from a year of medical study and work in London. Cousins also had a close personal relationship with Reddi. In June 1927 Margaret asked her for a monetary gift instead of a promised sari so that she could undertake a pilgrimage from Srinagar to Amarnath, the sacred site where the god Siva is worshipped in a phallic symbol of ice. She wanted to take advantage of this special experience of Indian life and hoped Muthulakshmi and other Indian women would think of her "as a sannyasi kind of sister."[70]

When the Simon Commission was first announced in 1927,

it provoked a loud outcry in India because it contained no Indian members even though it was to study Indian conditions. Margaret Cousins was one of the three WIA officers who signed a protest against the lack of any Indian women members. They also objected to "the exclusion of a British woman, particularly at this time when Miss Mayo's false generalisations about the womanhood of India are being made political material antagonistic to India's claim for Home Rule."[71] The NUSEC in London also pressed for the appointment of women assessors or technical advisers to the Simon Commission and eventually some invitations were issued though no changes were made in the actual membership of the Commission.[72]

1927 also witnessed the emergence of the All-India Women's Conference (AIWC). Originally organized by Margaret Cousins to discuss the educational needs of women and to develop more suitable curricula and institutions, the AIWC became a permanent association when those present at its initial session realized that improvement in education required a broadening of objectives. The AIWC came to be a more nationally representative group than the WIA, which tended to be concentrated in South India and closely linked to the Theosophical movement. After a world tour during 1928 and 1929, Margaret further extended her organization network and convened an All-Asia Women's Conference in Lahore in January, 1931.

During the early months of the 1930 civil disobedience movement, Margaret briefly skirmished with the British authorities in Madras because of her support for the nationalists. She then had a respite from Indian politics while James taught at the City University of New York during the 1931-32 academic year. Margaret established contacts with American feminist groups and spoke to a wide variety of audiences about the women's movement in India. Upon her return to India she encountered the special ordinances which sharply restricted free speech and had alarmed Eleanor Rathbone. On her way from Bombay to Madras, Cousins had an interview with the jailed Gandhi and told him of her plan to challenge this ban on free speech. On December 7, 1932 at a public meeting on the seashore in Madras, Margaret urged her listeners to exercise their right to free speech. She was promptly arrested and was sentenced to a year of simple imprisonment. Her trial occasioned outcries by Indian leaders and newspapers, as well as by American feminists such as Alice Stone Blackwell.[73] Cousins was willing to endure prison to protest against not only the general curtailment of civil rights, but also specific discrimination against women.

After her release in 1933, Margaret continued to divide her energies among music, the Theosophical Society, and work for women's organizations. She presided over the WIA in 1933 and was elected president of the AIWC in 1936. The latter office was in recognition of her previous work for the organization but also because she was a neutral candidate at a time when personalities and different attitudes toward political involvement were fostering tensions among Indian women within the AIWC.[74] By 1943, Cousins was beginning to withdraw from prominent participation in political and feminist activities. As she related:

> The Indian situation went steadily worse. Gandhiji had again been made to take on another fast. I went on a sympathetic fast. Ammu Swaminathan and other friends in Madras were arrested. I longed to be in the struggle against such foreign imbecility; but I had the feeling that direct participation by me was no longer required, or even desired, by the leaders of Indian womanhood who were now coming to the front, and, as we saw it, were being marshalled by what Tagore in "Jana gana mana" called the "dispenser of India's destiny" for some national service that was not far below the horizon.[75]

She also became discouraged by what she viewed as a dominance of AIWC meetings by a Bombay clique who, she felt, did not present a balanced view of the opinions of Indian women.[76] Then in August, 1943 she suffered a brain hemorrhage from which she only partially recovered. She died in 1954.

III

Born in 1885, Agatha Harrison was the daughter of Charles Harrison, a Methodist minister and Greek scholar.[77] She was educated briefly at Jersey Ladies' College and then at Redland High School in Bristol. When her father died suddenly in Jersey leaving his wife with a large family, Agatha's opportunity for a college education evaporated. She began to earn her living from the age of sixteen, working during the day and studying in the evenings for a Froebel certificate. She then taught kindergarten for several years before shifting to welfare work among women employed in factories. In October, 1917 she joined the London School of Economics (LSE), despite her lack of a college degree, as a welfare tutor. Her international career began in 1921. The YWCA in China wanted someone to undertake an investigation of working conditions for women and children in Shanghai. When Agatha was first asked to go, she was reluctant to leave her work at the LSE and her widowed mother. During her interview, some of the World YWCA Committee staff were apprehensive about her lack of commitment to organized Christianity, but their fears were allayed when she admitted sometimes attending the Guildhouse founded by Dr. Maude Royden, the suffragist preacher, in 1921.[78]

On February 24, 1921 Agatha left for China via the United States, since the American YWCA was funding her project and she would be working with the American YWCA in Shanghai. She later recounted the importance of this experience since she "had... to face for the first time what other people thought of my country and people.... Gradually some of my insularness [sic] dropped from me...."[79] During her two years in China, Harrison undertook a survey of child labor in Shanghai and developed techniques of informally arousing public opinion in order to alleviate social evils — in this case child labor. She interviewed millowners, both British and Chinese, organized women's groups and secured the establishment of a Child Labor Commission by the Shanghai Municipal Council. Harrison left China before this Commission was stymied by the taxpaying voters of the Shanghai International Settlement, and before the effort by Chiang Kai-shek and the Kuomintang to unite China militarily.[80]

Upon her return to England, Agatha was approached by the National Christian Council of India to undertake similar industrial welfare work in India. She refused mainly because her experiences in China altered her views on Christianity and she did not want to go to India where she would have "to lead out the Christian forces."[81] Her ambivalent relationship to organized Christianity would only be formally resolved in 1940, when she was accepted into the Society of Friends. Meanwhile, she went to the YWCA headquarters in New York and from 1925 to 1928 organized its department for social sciences and economics. Once back in London in late 1928, she embarked upon a six-month speaking tour for the Women's International League to help organize a pre-election campaign which would stimulate public debate on issues related to international peace.

Agatha Harrison's first significant contact with India came in 1929 when she accompanied the Royal Commission on Labour in India as the personal assistant to one member, Beryl Power, a former organizer for NUWSS and an official in the British Ministry of Labour. Since the Commission was leaving for India in September, 1929, when the British refusal to consider the Congress demand for self-government was straining political relations, Power thought that Harrison would be helpful in informally contacting political and trade union leaders who would not meet formally with the Commission. Agatha was successful first in meeting herself with Indian trade union leaders, and then in persuading them to talk unofficially with Power and J. H. Whitley, the Chairman of the Commission.[82]

Besides the innumerable and often incongruous dinners and parties with British officials and industrialists and Indian industrialists, Harrison took time to meet or at least see some Indian political leaders. She and Beryl went to see Mahatma Gandhi at a public meeting, and Agatha noted that, "I'll always remember that sight—a surge of people, and then suddenly a roar as the slight, emaciated figure came in."[83] It is noteworthy that she unconsciously shared Gandhi's concern for proper sanitation: Sir Victor Sasson, an industrial member of the Labour Commission, dubbed Agatha "the Latrine Queen" because of her insistence on inspecting them at factory compounds. Harrison also met Jawaharlal Nehru at breakfast and wrote to her sister, "Remember this name, for you are likely to hear a good deal about him in the future."[84] Thus her six months in India gave her bird's-eye views of its major cities and industrial centers, as well as contacts with British officials, Indian labor leaders, and with two of the three men who would be so dominant in her later work for India.

Agatha's decisive association with India began in London during the summer of 1931. Her mother had recently died and their household of four sisters was breaking up. Agatha was temporarily employed by Mrs. Alexander Whyte, the widow of a prominent Presbyterian minister and the mother of Alexander Frederick Whyte who had been the first president of the Indian Legislative Assembly from 1920 to 1925. Mrs. Whyte directed her to assist Charles F. Andrews, an Anglican priest who had begun his career in India as an educator, evolved into a passionate champion of overseas Indians, and developed into a follower of both Rabindranath Tagore and Mahatma Gandhi.[85] Andrews had recently arrived in London as a modern St. John the Baptist to prepare the way for Gandhi who was coming to attend the Second Round Table Conference. Thus, through Andrews, Harrison came to know the leader who had made such a striking impression on her in 1929. She quickly became a devoted friend of both of them.

Harrison's quite efficiency brought order into Andrew's intense and peripatetic life. She handled his voluminous correspondence, typed his book manuscripts, secured a clean cassock and surplice when needed for a wedding ceremony, and generally tried to arrange that he would meet appointments. Gandhi once wrote to her, "I have always told Andrews that he is in need of a care-taker. I do not therefore wonder at all about the funny experiences you are having with him. But that is precisely why he is never tired of describing you as an ideal care-taker."[86] Some friends of Charlie had hinted that he should marry Agatha who cared so well for him. She, however, sensitively realized his "need for being alone" and how he hated "to be 'managed' or 'possessed' in any way."[87] As Hugh Tinker, the most recent biographer of Andrews, relates, "She had accepted some of the burdens of a wife without any of the benefits."[88]

Meanwhile Gandhi had decided that Agatha would be helpful as a permanent resource in London and secured some funding for her position from G. D. Birla, the Marwari industrialist who was a major financial supporter of other Gandhian projects. She soon assumed the duties of the secretary of the India Conciliation Group (ICG). During the Second Round Table Conference, some members of the Society of Friends and others sympathetic to Indian nationalism had decided to form the ICG to maintain channels of communication between Indian political leaders and British officials in both London and India.[89]

Agatha's chief task was to interpret Indian and British leaders to each other. She maintained close relations with the India Office, concerned British political figures such as Lord Irwin and Lord Lothian,[90] and MPs including Eleanor Rathbone whom she viewed as one ally in the effort to achieve a political solution in India acceptable to all parties.[91] As a result of her carefully cultivated contacts, Harrison was able to obtain interviews at key junctures to discuss controversial developments, and to introduce visiting Indian leaders to a wider array of influential people than they would ordinarily meet. For example, she arranged for both Birla and Jamnadas Mehta, the president of the National Trade Union Federation, to meet Rathbone.[92] British officials as well as Indian politicians respected her knowledge and integrity, although Lord Allen, a close friend of Prime Minister Ramsey MacDonald, once ventured "very courteously to beg you in the name of India's welfare to be a little cautious before you, as an English woman, become almost over anxious about the sensibility of Indians."[93] Many sought her counsel. When Sir Stafford Cripps was preparing to leave for India in early 1942 on a mission to secure the support of the Indian National Congress for the war effort, he discussed the proposals which he was taking with members of the ICG. Agatha bluntly advised him that he was six months too late. That outburst was prophetic.[94] It was, however, uncharacteristic, since most of her associates remember her as saying very little in the meetings which she coordinated and attended.[95]

Possibly Agatha's most difficult challenge was to interpret Gandhi's ideas and actions to British officials and the British public and vice versa. During the waning months of the second civil disobedience movement, when Indian terrorists had assassinated some British officials, Harrison tried to explain to the Mahatma how his views on the causes of terrorism appeared to many British as encouragement to terrorists. She seems to have influenced Gandhi to make a moderate statement when there was a subsequent attack on Sir John Anderson, the Governor of Bengal.[96] At the same time she argued that the British government had to deal with Gandhi and the Congress or else had to face a revolution.[97] She was put to a critical test, as was Eleanor Rathbone, by Gandhi's refusal to support the British during World War II. She eventually sent Gandhi, through his jailers—

the Secretary of State for India, Lord Amery, and the Viceroy, Lord Linlithgow—sympathetic letters asking him for a fuller explanation of his actions so that she might understand them, and for a gesture of reconciliation.[98]

Harrison also performed many of the functions which might be done by a public relations consultant or firm. She cultivated receptive newspaper journalists and editors such as James Bone, the London editor of the *Manchester Guardian*, and supplied them with articles and memoranda explaining the viewpoints of Indian leaders on specific events and proposals. One example was a cable from Tej Bahadur Sapru questioning the possible end to mutual consultation between Indians and British on constitutional issues, for which she obtained extensive coverage.[99] She put together pamphlets and joint letters to the editors by British public figures who were supportive of Indian independence. Working alone or sometimes with Krishna Menon and the India League, she coordinated the London visits of such varied Indian leaders as the AIWC witnesses before the Joint Select Parliamentary Committee in 1933, Subhas Chandra Bose, and Jawaharlal Nehru.

After their brief, wordless introduction in 1929, Agatha did not again meet Jawaharlal Nehru until the autumn of 1935. On September 2, 1935, Harrison received word that Kamala Nehru was in alarming condition at a sanatorium in Badenweiler in the Black Forest. Her daughter Indira, then a young woman of eighteen, was in a nearby *pension*, but her husband was in prison because of his activities during the civil disobedience movement. Intervening with Irwin—now Lord Halifax—and with the India Office, Agatha helped to secure the immediate release of Jawaharlal, and then hurried herself to Badenweiler to assist him and Indira.[100] Thus began a close relationship with the Nehru family. During the remainder of the 1930s Agatha was a surrogate mother, travelling companion, and hostess to Indira who moved between Switzerland, Germany, and England in order to improve her health and to prepare for the entrance examinations for Oxford.[101] She also helped to arrange introductions for Jawaharlal in London in late 1935 and during his more extended visit in 1938. At times she assisted him with the details involved in publishing his books, and at one point tried to mediate between Nehru and Krishna Menon and Nehru's publishers.[102]

Harrison did not confine her sphere of activity solely to London, but travelled to India in 1934, 1936, 1938, 1945, January, 1949, and November, 1949. During these trips she went primarily "To listen and to learn."[103] She moved from tours with Gandhi of earthquake-devastated Bihar and Harijan areas in Orissa, to lunches with Presidency governors, to negotiations over political crises in princely states such as Rajkot. Although few British women did so, she took intermediate class trains purposely, "for it teaches me a lot and they [Indian women in Purdah] are so friendly and much amused by my clothes and typewriter."[104] Her travels were not only learning experiences, since gradually she came to serve as messenger and interpreter between Gandhi and British officials including the Viceroy, and between Gandhi and other Indian leaders such as Subhas Chandra Bose, during the 1938 crisis over Congress leadership.

Although India's political independence was clearly her primary commitment, Agatha also maintained wide contacts with Indian women and their organizations. Rajkumari Amrit Kaur, Muthulakshmi Reddi, and Shareefah Hamid Ali were greatly helped by her during their stay in London in 1933 when they presented evidence before the Joint Select Committee. Harrison agreed with their position that only adult suffrage was acceptable, while Eleanor Rathbone and the BCIWF allied themselves with Sushama Sen, a Bengali Brahmo and social worker in Bihar, who spoke on behalf of the Bengal Women's Franchise Groups and accepted the wife vote as an interim measure.[105] Agatha afterwards encouraged those three women to widen their contacts and influence by attending some international meetings. Muthulakshmi Reddi went to a women's conference in Chicago where she was reported to have made a great impression, and Shareefah Hamid Ali and Rajkumari Amrit Kaur returned to India by way of the League of Nations at Geneva, in an effort to secure more representative Indian women on League committees and commissions.[106] Harrison also helped in a wider campaign to secure more appointments of Indian women to international committees.[107] As Rathbone moved away from Indian affairs, Harrison served as a link between Indian women and British feminist leaders such as

Margery Corbett Ashby, who had succeeded Rathbone as president of NUSEC and was head of the International Woman's Suffrage Alliance.[108] During her visits to India, she attended meetings of the National Council of Women in India (March, 1934) and the AIWC (1936, 1938, 1945). She enjoyed close personal relations with prominent Indian women across the political spectrum. Two in particular were Rajkumari Amrit Kaur and Sarojini Naidu. Rathbone was also friendly with Amrit Kaur, even though they did not always agree. Harrison wrote to the Rajkumari after their first meeting that, "Every now and then in life one meets a friend whose presence in a tangled world seems to bring new life and hope. This is what I feel about you Amrit and I am deeply thankful that we have met."[109] Although Rathbone had described Naidu as "a poisonous woman,"[110] Agatha found her "like a tonic," and in 1949 expressed her sense of shame that the British had been responsible for the waste of her power and influence.[111] Still Harrison was not active in promoting a particular woman's issue or organization over an extended period, as were both Rathbone and Cousins. She functioned more as a facilitator and a confidante than as an initiator or organizer.

IV

Eleanor Rathbone, Margaret Cousins, and Agatha Harrison represent three different resolutions of the question whether women's rights or national independence should be the dominant priority for British women active in Indian feminist and political affairs. Varied factors influenced each to choose and to act as they did. Primary were their previous involvement in the suffragette movement and other feminist activities, and the place of India in their world view. Secondary were age, personality, social background and religious views.

Eleanor Rathbone was the oldest of this trio and came from a generation for whom the vote for women was crucial and had been secured only after a protracted struggle. That experience colored her evaluation of other campaigns for the franchise.[112] Eleanor also came from a social class which had the resources to educate its women and to permit them to devote their time and energy to unpaid humanitarian service. Her family background and college experience must have heightened her sense of having the right answers to the problems of others. Because of her own experience in social welfare service, Rathbone early argued that the vote must be utilized to secure legislation to improve the social and economic status of women. Her feminist vision was broad in both goals envisioned and classes included. Her preference was for moderation in goals and compromise in methods. This orientation was reflected in both her association with the NUWSS and the NUSEC and her status as an Independent in the Liverpool City Council and the House of Commons.

Although her father was only a government official, Margaret Cousins had a family situation which allowed her to attend college. She taught intermittently throughout her life, but the income of her husband also enabled her to volunteer much time to vegetarian, political, and suffrage organizations. Along with hundreds of Englishwomen, Cousins became involved in radical suffragette campaigns including militant public meetings and windowbreakings, and suffered police harassment and imprisonment. Her own Irish heritage and her activist husband led her to an equally passionate interest in Irish home rule. Margaret Cousins, therefore, learned at an early stage of her life to balance two key commitments. She supported her English sisters, worked to organize suffragette groups in Ireland, and struggled to convince sometimes unsympathetic Irish nationalists to accept female franchise and home rule as parallel objectives. For Cousins, suffragism was closely linked to a struggle for equality and political independence, and social welfare legislation affecting women was a more distant goal.

Agatha Harrison was thirteen years younger than Eleanor Rathbone and had to work from an early age to support herself and assist her mother. Her first career as a kindergarten teacher was a traditional choice for women of her social situation, and only gradually did she emerge as a pioneer when she shifted to industrial welfare work. By this point, in 1915, the extension of the franchise was immanent. Agatha recalled once that she had been a member of the WSPU but there is no evidence that she was as prominent in the suffragette movement as either Rathbone or Cousins were.[113] Her age and her need to work full-time possibly precluded such commitment. Her later work in China and in the United States with the YWCA and in England with the Women's International League exemplified the "new feminism," with its concern for economic equality and for international sisterhood. Thus for Harrison, women's issues were important but they were diffused in her personal and professional life.

Each woman had encountered India through different channels although all eventually travelled or lived there. Rathbone met Indian women most dramatically through a book written by an American woman and suffered in Indian eyes from her association with that journalist. For her, the political rights and social condition of Indian women became a continuing concern as they were for no other prominent British feminist and politician. Her chief commitment to India was to its women. As a member of Parliament which had ultimate responsibility for the governance of India, she was also concerned about political conditions and constitutional reform. She was a vocal opponent of the Conservative opposition to constitutional reforms in India, led by Winston Churchill in Commons and Salisbury in Lords. Rathbone, however, could not understand the impatience or sense of grievance of leaders such as Mahatma Gandhi and Jawaharlal Nehru or accept the extralegal tactics of the Congress. She was dedicated to legal processes and even-handed justice, as reflected in her concern for proper treatment of political prisoners, the end of arbitrary ordinances, and the continued cooperation of Indian moderates such as Sapru in constitutional discussions. Nonetheless, she was willing to accept the compromises of the 1935 Government of India Act in both the spheres of responsible government and women's franchise. There is little evidence that she read widely or deeply about Indian culture, and so India remained only one of many strands in her multifaceted career. It was then possible for her commitment to Indian women and Indian self-government to recede into the background as conditions in Europe became more foreboding.

Margaret Cousins came to know India through Theosophy and had studied the Bhagavad-Gita, the Hindu classic so beloved by Gandhi, in Ireland long before she thought of going to India. Although she had wide-ranging experiences in the feminist movement in England and Ireland, she did not go to India to work on feminist issues. She went because her husband wanted a change of employment and because of their mutual interest in Theosophy. Rathbone had wanted to alleviate certain conditions and set out to gather data through a questionnaire conceived in London and through debates conducted there on these issues. Cousins moved permanently to India, met Indian women in large and small urban centers, allowed Indian women to voice their concerns, and then proceeded to devote herself to the women's movement in India. Both women focused on franchise issues and both disliked the consequences of child marriage. Cousins, however, sympathized with the dilemma faced by the parents of young girls. Unlike Rathbone, she gave proper weight to the force of custom sanctioned by religious authority. Though like Rathbone, she committed herself "to do all I could to forward all circumstances calculated to bring women into public and particularly legislative life, so that this evil [of early motherhood] and others might be rectified."[114] While women's concerns gradually became a dominant theme in her work, Cousins was equally committed to political independence for India. It appears that she did not think that as a foreigner she could or should play as prominent a role in that sphere as in the feminist one.

Agatha Harrison arrived in India as an assistant to others. First it was to Beryl Power, and then more importantly to Charles Freer Andrews and Mahatma Gandhi. Their goals shaped her focus. With Power she was concerned about industrial welfare work, and with Andrews and Gandhi she shifted her attention to political independence. Her sacrificing, flexible personality seems to have ideally fitted her to the role of interpreter and mediator. She was firmly committed to Indian independence but did not seek to voice her own opinions on that or other subjects. Women's issues were one aspect of a complex situation and she allowed them to be sidelined by more pressing problems which were given higher priority by her superiors. Because of her total commitment to Indian independence, it was fitting that she was able to visit with Jawaharlal Nehru, Amrit Kaur, and Sarojini Naidu as government leaders in an independent India.

The responses of Indian women to these three British

women yield insights into factors which foster helpful cooperation between women of many cultures and countries. First, all must be sensitive to and tolerant of cultural as well as personality variations. Rathbone tried to apply British models and experiences to the Indian situation without giving adequate consideration to the impact of cultural and political differences. Cousins and Harrison were more willing to allow Indian women to formulate their own goals and then to suggest possible strategies and tactics to accomplish them. Second, it appears to be important for personal encounters to take place on the home soil of the women in the colonial or post-colonial countries. Cousins and Harrison spent far more time in India than did Rathbone and earned greater trust from Indian women. Even Rathbone's single tour of India had a positive effect in extending and improving her personal and working relationships with Indian women leaders. Third, foreign women are best suited to the roles of intermediaries and moral supporters. Cousins unconsciously found this position and Harrison consciously sought it. Rathbone first tried to initiate a campaign in London utilizing her personal network and institutional resources there. Once she began to seek advice from India and to respond to Indian initiatives, Indian women were more willing to accept her assistance.

From an institutional perspective, British women made limited contributions to the women's movement in India when Indian independence was the major focus for most active Indian feminists. These foreign women demonstrated the value of and contributed technical skills when the Indian women possessing such skills were few and overextended in their commitments. Rathbone illustrated the use of survey research, propaganda, and lobbying in support of a specific demand for social change. While her insensitivity to the feelings of others reduced her personal effectiveness, her suggestions for a woman-oriented ministry and a single-issue organization were ideas which were too far ahead of the times and were only implemented in the 1970s and 1980s. Cousins used her organizing and literary skills to focus and present the case for Indian women. In the area of goals these British women were more successful in gaining political reforms than social change. Cousins and Rathbone were more useful in the battle to win and to extend the franchise than they were in the effort to raise the minimum age at marriage. Outsiders can intervene more easily in the legal processes than in social customs.

British supporters were able to keep women's issues in the center of the political stage when most Indian women were occupied with the nationalist movement. It would not be unpatriotic or disloyal for them to do so. Eleanor Rathbone's concentration on women's rights had some impact on British officials when they were still making decisions which affected both Indian men and women. Rathbone could also ask hard questions about the lack of females among the Congress candidates in the 1935 and 1936 elections. Such gadfly inquiries did not bring her any personal popularity, but perhaps they pricked the consciences of some Indian males and stimulated some Indian women to be more forceful in their demands for political office and power. Rathbone, Cousins, and to a more limited extent Harrison served as surrogate publicists for Indian women and their concerns when distance, lack of financial resources, and time made it difficult for them to present their own case abroad.

These British women were also useful in urging and supporting Indian women to become active on women's issues in the international sphere. They saw the need for Indian women to contribute their unique insights on women's issues as well as to gain international support for their goals. It was impossible for Indian women leaders to participate on a continuing basis during the independence struggle but the way was paved for their distinguished service at the United Nations as representatives of a free India.

Most significantly, the effectiveness of British women was strongly determined by the stage at which they encountered the Indian women's movement. In 1917, Margaret Cousins met women anxious to voice their diffuse concerns. She understood the need for an organizational framework and for experiences which would enable Indian women to speak with authority. She acted to provide that framework and those experiences. In 1927, Eleanor Rathbone ignored a decade of intense Indian organizational activity and thereby damaged her ability to win support from Indian women for her efforts. Modifying some aspects of her style, she became an ally of moderate Indian women leaders and a useful auxiliary in the parliamentary area of the colonial power. By the time that Agatha Harrison met Indian feminists in the early 1930s, she shrewdly realized that the Indian women's movement did not need advisers or organizers but only sympathetic sisters in other lands.

NOTES

The author wishes to acknowledge with appreciation a Senior Research Fellowship from the American Institute of Indian Studies in 1976-77 and a Summer Stipend from the National Endowment for the Humanities in 1979 which made possible the research in India and in England on which this article is based. The Taft Faculty Fund at the University of Cincinnati also provided a timely grant-in-aid. An earlier version of this article was presented at the Fourth Berkshire Conference on the History of Women, Mount Holyoke College, August 23-25, 1978.

[1] The basic published source on Eleanor Rathbone is Mary D. Stocks, *Eleanor Rathbone : A Biography* (London: Victor Gollancz, 1949). Most of the papers relating to her work on Indian issues are at the Fawcett Library at the City of London Polytechnic but papers on her other activities are in the Sydney Jones Library at the University of Liverpool.

[2] Roy's visit is mentioned in J. Estlin Carpenter, *The Life and Work of Mary Carpenter* (London: Macmillan, 1879), p. 30. Rathbone once recalled that his portrait hung in her family home. Circular letter from Eleanor Rathbone, February 23, 1932, Jones Library, Liverpool, Rathbone Collection. I am grateful to Geraldine Forbes for sharing with me her copy of Rathbone's circular letters from her Indian tour in 1932.

[3] Stocks, *Eleanor Rathbone*, pp. 42-46.

[4] *Ibid.*, p. 106.

[5] In *Women's Leader*, July 13, 1928, quoted in *ibid.*, p. 127. The *Women's Leader* was the journal of the National Union of Societies for Equal Citizenship (NUSEC).

[6] Eva Hubback, the parliamentary secretary of NUSEC, arranged a meeting and press conference for Herabai Tata on October 21, 1919 and Rathbone as president of NUSEC must have been aware of this meeting even if she did not personally attend. Hubback to Herabai Tata, October 20, 1919, All-India Women's Conference (AIWC), Files, New Delhi. There is no mention of contact with the Tatas in 1919 in the collection of the Rathbone papers at the Fawcett Library.

[7] Katherine Mayo, *Mother India* (London: Jonathan Cape, 1927), p. 22.

[8] Margery Corbett Ashby, a successor of Rathbone as president of NUSEC, recently noted that one reason Mayo was considered so shocking was her frank description of sexual relations between husbands and wives when such things were not discussed openly. Geraldine Forbes generously shared her notes from an interview with Dame Corbett Ashby on August 10, 1978 at "Wickens" Sussex, England.

[9] There is some analysis of the controversy which surrounded Mayo and her books in Manoranjan Jha, *Katherine Mayo and India* (New Delhi: People's Publishing House, 1971).

[10] Dame Corbett Ashby interview, August 10, 1978.

[11] Stock, *Eleanor Rathbone*, p. 138.

[12] Ellen Wilkinson to Rathbone, undated but probably September 1929, Fawcett Library (FL), Rathbone Papers (Rathbone), Box 92, Folder 3.

[13] Dhanvanthi Rama Rau, *An Inheritance* : *The Memoirs of Dhanvanthi Rama Rau* (New York: Harper & Row, 1977), pp. 170-171, and an interview in Bombay on March 16, 1977.

[14] There is an excellent overview of the continuing debate over the issue in Geraldine H. Forbes, "Women and Modernity: The Issue of Child Marriage in India," *Women's Studies International Quarterly* II (1979), pp. 407-419.

[15] Eleanor Rivett, principal of the United Missionary Girls' High School in Calcutta, reported on this phenomenon to Rathbone on August 3, 1930, FL, Rathbone, B 92, F 3. J.H. Hutton, the Commissioner for the 1931 Census, later advised that "The figures on infant marriage at this census show a great increase as a result of the rush of marriages intended to anticipate the operation of the Sarda Act." Hutton to Rathbone, July 9, 1932, *Ibid.*, B 93, F 8, No. 14.

[16] Wedgwood Benn to Rathbone, May 15, 1930, *Ibid.*, B 92, F 2

[17] Rathbone to Mabel Hartog, May 26, 1930, *Ibid.*, B 93, F 4.

[18] Rathbone sent Benn similar letters on May 16, June 2, July 8, July 17, 1930, *Ibid.*, B 92, F 2, and continued to receive evasive replies. She wrote to Samuel Hoare, November 30, 1931, *Ibid.*, B 93, F 6, and asked thirteen questions in Parliament in four years, Rathbone to K. Radhabai Subbarayan, February 29, 1934, *Ibid.*, B 93, F 5, No. 7.

[19] Hoare to Lord Willingdon, August 3, 1933, India Office Library (IOL), Templewood Collection, MSS Eur. E 240/3.

[20] Rathbone to John Simon, March 29, 1930, IOL, Simon Collection, MSS Eur. F 77/86.

[21] Rathbone to Muthulakshmi Reddi, Shareefah Hamid Ali, RajKumari Amrit Kaur, February 29, 1934, *Ibid.*, B 93, F 9; Rathbone to Lakshmi Menon, February 29, 1934, *Ibid.*, B 93, F 14, No. 30.

[22] Reddi to Rathbone, March 20, 1934, *Ibid.*, B 92, F 1; Amrit Kaur to Rathbone, April 2, 1934, July 5, 1934, *Ibid.*, B 93, F 12, No. 24, Menon to Rathbone, May 24, 1934, *Ibid.*, B 93, F 14, No. 30, Hamid Ali to Rathbone, August 8, 1934, *Ibid.*, B 93, F 9, No. 18, Rameshwari Nehru to Rathbone, August 23, 1934, *Ibid.*, B 93, F 13, No. 29.

[23] Amrit Kaur to Rathbone, September 3, 1934, *Ibid.*, B 93, F 12, No. 24.

BRITISH FEMINISTS AND INDIAN WOMEN'S RIGHTS 145

[24] Menon to Rathbone, September 13, 1934, *Ibid.*, B 93, F 14, No. 30.
[25] Hamid Ali to Rathbone, February 1, 1935, *Ibid.*, B. 93, F 9 No. 18.
[26] N.M. Joshi to Rathbone, January 3, 1935, *Ibid.*, B 93, F 15, No. 34.
[27] Rathbone to Joshi, January 23, 1935, *Ibid.*
[28] Rathbone to Joshi, March, 22, 1935, *Ibid.*, Amrit Kaur to Rathbone, May 31, 1936, *Ibid.*, B 93, F 12, No. 24; Reddi to Rathbone, July 29, 1936, *Ibid.*, B 92, F 1.
[29] *Ibid.*,
[30] "An Open Letter to Some Indian Friends" by Eleanor Rathbone, May, 1941, reprinted in Stocks, *Eleanor Rathbone*, p. 337.
[31] *Manchester Guardian*, April 25, 1929.
[32] Collective letter from Eleanor Rathbone and eleven others to Tej Bahadur Sapru, M.R. Jayakar and N.M. Joshi, July 29, 1932, FL, Rathbone, B 93, F 8, No. 16.
[33] Rathbone to Hoare, June 11, 1932, *Ibid.*, B 93, F 6.
[34] Rathbone to Carl Heath, August 9, 1932, *Ibid.*, B 93, F 8, No. 16.
[35] See the joint letter of July 29, 1932, cited in note 32 and N.M. Joshi to Rathbone, August 13, 1932, *Ibid.*, Rathbone to Jayakar, August 25, 1932, *Ibid.*
[36] Agatha Harrison to Rathbone, December 20, 1932, Library of the Religious Society of Friends, London (LSF), Agatha Harrison-India Conciliation Group Papers (Harrison-ICG), Box 47, Rathbone File. (This collection is in Temporary MSS Boxes 41-51 and may be rearranged at some future date but there is a current handlist of the general contents. Private papers of Agatha Harrison and the papers of the India Conciliation Group are intermingled.)
[37] Rathbone to R.A. Butler, Undersecretary of State for India, March 1, 1935, FL, Rathbone, B 93, F 6, about the princes, and Rathbone to Hoare, April 8 and May 6, 1932, *Ibid.*, and to Lord Lothian, Undersecretary of State for India, April 9, 1932, *Ibid.*, B 93, F 7, No. 13, about the impact of the special ordinances and the treatment of political prisoners.
[38] *Manchester Guardian*, January 16, 1932.
[39] Circular letter from Rathbone, January 17-19, 1932, Jones Library, Liverpool, Rathbone Collection.
[40] Circular letter from Rathbone, February 15, 1932, *Ibid.*
[41] Elizabeth Vallance, *Women in the House: A Study of Women Members of Parliament* (London: The Athlone Press, 1979), p. 79. Rathbone to Amrit Kaur, January 9, 1932, FL, Rathbone, B 93, F 12, No. 24.
[42] Subbarayan to Rathbone, May 1, 1931, *Ibid.*, B 93, F 5, No. 7, and Reddi to Rathbone, May 6, 1931, *Ibid.*, B 92, F 1.
[43] Rathbone to Lord Lothian, April 28, 1933, *Ibid.*, B 93, F 7, No. 13.

[44] Rathbone advised Lord Lothian that she had "pulled every string I can think of," March 7, 1933, *Ibid.* "Letter to the *Times*," March 25, 1933. The organizing meeting of the British Committee for Indian Women's Franchise was on April 17, 1933, FL, Rathbone, B 93, F 11 No. 23 (1).

[45] The protracted negotiations over these issues are fully documented in the minutes and correspondence of the BCIWF, *Ibid.* The position of the BCIWF is in Great Britain, *Joint Committee on Indian Constitutional Reform* Volume II^C, *Evidence*, paragraphs 2258-2288 (London: His Majesty's Stationery office, 1934). There is a convenient summary of points gained and those denied, "Review of Action Taken Concerning Women During the Progress of the Government of India Bill," in the Pamphlet Collection on Franchise, FL, 396. 11 (54).

[46] Rathbone to Reddi, Begum Shah Nawaz, Sarala Ray, Amrit Kaur, April 7, 1933; Rathbone to unspecified correspondent but possibly Sarala Ray since correspondent was located in Calcutta, April 13, 1933, FL, Rathbone, B 93, F 13, No. 26; Rathbone to Butler, February 15, 1934, *Ibid.*, B 93, F 6. The main objection to complete adult franchise for women in the towns was that it would upset the balance between urban and rural voters.

[47] Rathbone to Reddi, February 9, 1933, *Ibid.*, B 92, F 1.

[48] Reddi to Rathbone, March 31, 1933, *Ibid.*

[49] Agatha Harrison to Horace Alexander, Friday sometime in May 1935, Nehru Memorial Museum and Library, New Delhi (NMML), Horace Alexander Papers. Unfortunately for the historian, Agatha Harrison did not precisely date her letters during the 1930s.

[50] Amrit Kaur to Rathbone, February 11, 1935, FL, Rathbone, B 93, F 12, No. 24.

[51] Sarala Ray to Rathbone, January 26, 1933, *Ibid.*, B 93, F 9, No. 21; Kailash Srivastava, President of YWCA in Lucknow, to Rathbone, January 30, 1933, *Ibid.*, B 93, F 9, No. 22; Subbarayan to Rathbone, February 26, 1933, and December 26, 1933, *Ibid.*, B 93, F 5, No. 7; Sushama (Mrs. P.K.) Sen, May 25, 1935, *Ibid.*, B 93, F 16, No. 38.

[52] Rathbone to Mrs. Copeland, June 24, 1938, *Ibid.*, B 93, F 16, No. 40.

[53] Jawaharlal Nehru to Rathbone, June 22, 1941, Rathbone to Nehru, August 28, 1941, and Nehru to Rathbone, November 9, 1941, reprinted in Stokes, *Eleanor Rathbone*, pp. 342-369.

[54] Carl Heath to Rathbone, September 17, 1941, LSF, Harrison-ICG Box 47.

[55] James H. Cousins and Margaret E. Cousins, *We Two Together* (Madras: Ganesh, 1950), is the basic source on Cousins's life especially as there is no central collection of her papers. Her childhood is recounted on pp. 22-26. A helpful bibliographic source is Alan Denson, *James H. Cousins (1873-1956) and Margaret Cousins (1878-1954)*: *A Bio-Bibliographical Survey* (Kendal, Westmoreland: By the author, 1967)

[56] Cousins and Cousins, *We Two Together*, pp. 128, 163-195. A more precise chronology is in Denson, *Cousins and Cousins*, pp. 23-26.

[57] Cousins and Cousins, *We Two Together*, pp. 228-231.
[58] *Ibid.*, p. 185.
[59] A basic source on Annie Besant is Arthur H. Nethercot, *The First Five Lives of Annie Besant* and *The Last Four Lives of Annie Besant* (Chicago: University of Chicago Press, 1960-1963).
[60] Cousins and Cousins, *We Two Together*, p. 242.
[61] Her books include *The Awakening of Asian Womanhood* (Madras: Ganesh, 1922); *The Music of Orient and Occident* (Madras: B.G. Paul, 1935); and *Indian Womanhood Today* (Allahabad: Kitabistan, 1941). Articles by Margaret and by James Cousins individually and collectively are listed in Denson, *Cousins and Cousins*, pp 127-223.
[62] Cousins and Cousins, *We Two Together*, p. 299.
[63] *Ibid.*, pp. 308-314, *Mrs. Margaret Cousins and her Work in India* compiled by One Who Knows [Muthulakshmi Reddi] (Madras: Women's Indian Association, 1956), pp. 1-12. Montagu's remarks which were more concerned with their physical appearance and their political affiliations than with their petitions are in Edwin S. Montagu, *An Indian Diary* (London: William Heinemann, 1930), pp. 115-116.
[64] Cousins and Cousins, *We Two Together*, p. 370.
[65] *Ibid.*, p. 331.
[66] There is a file of correspondence between the Tatas and various British suffrage activists at the AIWC Headquarters in New Delhi. I am grateful to Nargis Kumar for giving me access to this file when it was in storage while their new building was being constructed.
[67] Cousins and Cousins, *We Two Together* pp. 370, 408-409. *Mrs. Margaret Cousins and Her Work in India*, pp. 12-55; Margaret Cousins to "My Dear Sisters," May 28, 1919, AIWC Files, New Delhi. An example of the response from branches of the Women's Indian Association (WIA) is the resolution passed by the Thirumeyachur Branch, Peralam Post Office, WIA, and sent to Cousins on June 25, 1919, NMML, Muthulakshmi Reddi Papers, File No. 8.
[68] Cousins and Cousins, *We Two Together*, pp. 378-380, 446-447; Jamila Brijbhushan, *Kamaladevi Chattopadhyay: Portrait of a Rebel* (New Delhi: Abhinav, 1976), pp. 9-13, 30-31; *Mrs. Margaret Cousins and Her Work in India*, pp. 58-63.
[69] Cousins to Viscount Goschen, Governor of Madras, November 12, 1926, *Ibid.*, p. 61.
[70] Cousins to Reddi, June 6, 1927, NMML, Reddi, File No. 8.
[71] Women's Protest against the Statutory Commission, signed by Muthulakshmi Reddi, Dorothy Jinarajadasa and Margaret Cousins, *Ibid.*
[72] Stokes, *Eleanor Rathbone*, p. 135.
[73] Letter by Alice Stone Blackwell dated February 27, 1930 in *Springfield Republican* (Massachusetts), March 3, 1933, p. 10.
[74] Amrit Kaur to Hansa Mehta, October 17, 1936, NMML, Hansa Mehta Papers, Subject File No. 5.
[75] Cousins and Cousins, *We Two Together*, p. 740.
[76] Cousins to Srimati Nimbkar, February 11, 1943, AIWC Files, New Delhi.

[77] The basic published source is a brief biography, *Agatha Harrison: An Impression by Her Sister Irene Harrison*, with a Foreword by Mrs. V.L. Pandit (London: George Allen & Unwin, 1956). Some helpful specific details including her birth year are given in her obituaries in the *Times* (London), May 11, 1954, and the *Manchester Guardian*, May 11, 1954.

[78] Harrison, *Agatha Harrison* p. 27. A concise summary of the extraordinary career of Dr. Maude Royden who herself visited India in 1928 and 1934 is in her obituaries in the *Times* (London) and the *Manchester Guardian*, July 31, 1956.

[79] Harrison to Kamaladevi Chattopadhyaya, November 22, 1939, LSF, Harrison-ICG, Box 46, Folder 3.

[80] Harrison, *Agatha Harrison*, pp. 26-45. There is a brief analysis of her work in the broader context of the general program of the YWCA in Alison R. Drucker, "The Role of the YWCA in the Development of the Chinese Women's Movement, 1890-1927," *Social Service Review* LIII 3 (September, 1979), pp. 432-433.

[81] Quoted in Harrison, *Agatha Harrison*, p. 46.

[82] *Ibid.*, pp. 62-65.

[83] *Ibid.*, p. 57.

[84] *Ibid.*

[85] *Ibid.*, p. 67. It is presently impossible to determine if Mrs. Alexander Whyte was the widow of the Presbyterian minister or the wife of the former president of the Indian Legislative Assembly but the evidence seems to indicate that it was most probably the older woman. The principal source on the relationship batween Harrison and Andrews is Hugh Tinker, *The Ordeal of Love: C.F. Andrews and India* (Delhi: Oxford University Press, 1979).

[86] Quoted in Harrison, *Agatha Harrison*. p. 71.

[87] Tinker, *Ordeal of Love*, p. 259.

[88] *Ibid.*, p. 261.

[89] An overview is in Hugh Tinker, "The India Conciliation Group, 1931-50: Dilemmas of the Mediator," *Journal of Commonwealth and Comparative Politics* XIV, 3 (November, 1976), pp. 224-241.

[90] Harrison to Irwin, December 6, 1931, LSF, Harrison-ICG, Box 47, Halifax File.

[91] Harrison to Rathbone, December 20, 1932, *Ibid.*, Box 47, Rathbone File.

[92] Harrison to Rathbone, February 24, 1935, about Mehta, *Ibid.*, and Harrison to Rathbone, July 4, 1935, about Birla, *Ibid.*, Box 46 Folder 2.

[93] Lord Allen to Harrison, January 27, 1933, *Ibid.*, Box 47, Allen Folder.

[94] Interview with Horace Alexander, June 7, 1977, in Swarthmore, Pennsylvania.

[95] Lionel Fielden is typical in his comment that "I fancy that only England produces Agatha Harrisons. What her exact position was I never, though I knew and loved her for a long time, was able to dis-

cover...Where an Indian problem was, there was Agatha Harrison. But not, mind you, so that you'd notice her." Harrison, *Agatha Harrison*, p. 133.

[96]Harrison in Simla to Carl Heath, May 13, 1934, and Harrison in Calcutta to Heath, May 28, 1934, LSF, Harrison-ICG, Box 45, Folder 2.

[97]Harrison to Heath, May 13, 1934, *Ibid*.

[98]Harrison to Mahatma Gandhi, December 20, 1942, Nicholas Mansergh, Editor-in-Chief, E.W.R. Lumby, Assistant Editor, *The Transfer of Power, 1942-7*, Volume III (London: Her Majesty's Stationery Office, 1971), pp. 413-415, and Harrison to Gandhi, December 2, 1943, *Ibid*., Volume IV (London; Her Majesty's Stationery Office, 1973), pp. 510-513.

[99]Harrison to Alexander, Spring 1932, NMML, Alexander Papers.

[100]Harrison to Irwin then Halifax, September 1, 1935, LSF, Harrison-ICG, Box 46, Folder 14; Harrison to Indira Nehru, September 1, 1935, *Ibid*; Harrison to Henry Polak, September 4, 1935, *Ibid*; Harrison to Gandhi, September 13, 1935, *Ibid*.

[101]Jawaharlal Nehru to Harrison, July 15, 1936, August 6, 1936; September 20, 1939; October 21, 1939; November 16, 1929; May 4, 1940; January 10, 1941; NMML, Jawaharlal Nehru Papers, Part I, Vol. 31.

[102]J. Nehru to Harrison, November 4, 1937, *Ibid*.

[103]Harrison, *Agatha Harrison*, p. 80.

[104]Harrison to her family, April 18, 1934, LSF, Harrison-ICG, Box 45.

[105]Rathbone early conceded that "the English women's societies which have interested themselves in India are just as much divided as Indian women themselves...Several of them, such as the Open Door Council and St. Joan's Social and Political Alliance, expressed themselves in favour of the views of Mrs. Naidu and Begum Shah Nawaz regarding no special privileges for women." Rathbone to Subbarayan, FL, Rathbone, B 93, F 5, No. 7. Sarala Ray urged Sushama Sen to give evidence before the Joint Parliamentary Committee, Ray to Rathbone, *Ibid*., B 93, F 9, No. 21. Harrison nowhere stated her firm support for the AIWC position on universal suffrage but the very warm reception which the AIWC gave her during her 1934 visit to India is ample evidence of her agreement with that group, LSF, Harrison-ICG, Box 45.

[106]Harrison to G.D. Birla, August 12, 1933, *Ibid*., Box 46, Folder 2.

[107]*Ibid*. Rajkumari Amrit Kaur organized this campaign to obtain representative Indian women on groups appointed by the League of Nations. Many British women's organizations supported her efforts, including the Women's Freedom League, the St. Joan's Social and Political Alliance, the Women's International League, and the British Commonwealth League, in NMML, Rajkumari Amrit Kaur Papers.

[108]Harrison to Alexander, June 7, 1945, NMML, Alexander Papers:

Harrison to J. Nehru, August 6, 1945, NMML, Nehru Papers, Part I, Vol. 31.

[109] Harrison to Amrit Kaur, October 6, 1933, NMML, Amrit Kaur Papers.

[110] Rathbone to Wedgwood Benn, April 16, 1931, FL. Rathbone, B 92, F 2. Rathbone was more discreet in writing to Radhabai Subbarayan when she commented that Naidu was "a poet and orator, but not a practical politician, nor, I think, genuinely keen about women." May 15, 1931, *Ibid.*, B 93, F 5, No. 7.

[111] Harrison, *Agatha Harrison*, p. 124.

[112] Rathbone to Reddi, March 12, 1931, FL, Rathbone, B 92, F 1. She also frequently justified the need to compromise as in *The Harvest of the Women's Movement*, Fawcett Lecture, given at Bedford College, London, on November 29, 1935, and quoted in Stokes, *Eleanor Rathbone* p. 113.

[113] This chance remark was made in a conversation with Muhammad Ali Jinnah. He had commented that he had known both the Pethick-Lawrences since he had spoken for the suffrage movement during his early years in London. Agatha Harrison to Carl Heath, April 2, 1946, LSF, Harrison-ICG, Box 45.

[114] Cousins and Cousins, *We Two Together*, p. 331.

6
Kinship, Women, and Politics in Twentieth Century Punjab

DAVID GILMARTIN

Women have long served as the cement of the social structure of Indian society. Innumerable anthropological and sociological studies have shown the importance of women—or more particularly, of the kinship structures in which women have provided the critical links—in structuring local social and political organization. Assessments of the role of women in the political development of twentieth-century Indian society, however, have often lost sight of the central importance of women in kinship structure, and more important, of kinship structure in Indian politics. In this paper, I will try to show the symbolic role which issues of women's rights played in Muslim politics in twentieth-century Punjab, not because such issues were important for their own sake, but because such issues were tied to important questions concerning the role of kinship in ordering the political system. I can only hint at the significance of these controversies in affecting the social position of women themselves, for this is a subject which requires considerably more research. Nevertheless, any assessment of the role of women's issues in twentieth-century Punjabi politics depends ultimately on a general assessment of the changing political role of kinship in Punjab's political system.

The British and Customary Law: Kinship and the Ideology of the State

To understand the symbolic role of women's rights in

twentieth-century Punjab, it is necessary to understand first the relationship between kinship organization and the political order under the British. The attitudes of the British toward Punjabi society grew largely out of their peculiar position as colonialists. That the British, as alien rulers in India, had to rely on the cooperation of local indigenous political intermediaries has often been remarked. Less frequently noted is the development of a close association between the organization of British rule in the Punjab and the pattern of kin-based political organization in the countryside.

The framework of British administration in the Punjab was closely tied, almost from its inception, to local units of rural administration, demarcated on the basis of extended kinship ties, "tribes." The British use of the term "tribe" in the Punjab was in many ways idiosyncratic, for Punjabi village society bore little resemblance to "tribal" society in other parts of India. The "tribes" of Punjab, such as Jats, Rajputs, and Arains, though often Muslim, looked very much like the "castes" of other provinces. British emphasis on the importance of "tribe" in the Punjab, however, reflected their own appreciation of the importance of extensive, supra-village kinship ties in supplying the secular bonds holding Punjabi village society together. As the Lieutenant-Governor, Sir Robert Egerton, observed in 1878, "... the most fundamental basis for the division of the population in this part of India is tribal rather than religious, and should rest, not upon community of belief or ceremonial practice, but upon ancestral community of race, in which, whether it be genuine or only suppositious the claimants of a common origin equally believe."[1]

As the British developed their administration, such "tribal" ties provided the foundations on which they built administrative structures for controlling the countryside. In the last half of the nineteenth century, the British divided almost all Punjab districts into administrative units called *zails*—units varying in size from about ten to forty villages and intended by the British to encapsulate "tribal" organization within their administration.[2] This effort did not always reflect a deep British understanding of the varied and often ambiguous character of rural kinship organization in the Punjab, as indicated by the often fuzzy British use of kinship terminology.[3] In choosing *zail* leaders, or *zaildars*, for example, the British sometimes paid slight attention to existing traditions of lineage or *baradari* leadership, or to the character of village kinship, seeking instead to create "tribal" or "clan" leaders in the zails who would support their regime. As the system developed, therefore, *zaildars* often emerged not only as "the leading men of a particular tribe or section of the country,"[4] but also, and more important politically for the British, as "the representative [s] of Govenment" in the *zails*.[5] As a result, the structure of "tribal" leadership recognized by the British was in many ways artificial, adapted to serve the administrative needs of the British as much as to reflect "tribal" solidarity. But this did not, in the end, alter the important place that kin-based organization had assumed in the British system. Adapted to a system of colonial domination, the structure of kinship supplied the foundations of the administrative system.

The theoretical implications of this for the maintenance of the colonial system were most clearly explicated in British efforts to expound a system of "tribal" or "customary" law as the foundation of the Punjab's legal system. Of all the institutions underlying British authority, the law revealed most clearly the indigenous principles of legitimacy to which the British sought to tie their regime. Significantly, the legal system in Punjab was also adapted to the structure of "tribal" kinship in the late nineteenth century. With the passage of the Punjab Laws Act of 1872, the personal law of the the Punjab was linked, not to the law of Hinduism or Islam as in most other provinces, but to a system of customary law based primarily on "tribal" custom. A prominent British official, C. L. Tupper, subsequently expounded the importance of relying on the customary law as a means of grounding British rule firmly in the indigenous "tribal" structure of Punjabi society. As Tupper saw it, British association with Punjab's indigenous kinship structure was critically significant in legitimating British rule. "Native society will . . ." he insisted, "be the happier, so long as it can be held together by the bonds of consanguinity."[6] By supporting a system of law which tended to preserve the "tribal" structure of society, the British were thus not only justifying their rule in native eyes, but also assuring themselves a contented population.

The development of nineteenth-century customary law was tied empirically to the extensive recording of local "tribal" customs,[7] but it nevertheless rested, in Tupper's view, on fundamental principles of kin-based cohesion. Tupper himself, in his 1881 compendium of customary law, outlined these principles by focusing on the customs underlying the disposition of landed property within Punjab's kinship system. Though kinship in general was "the paramount influence in regulating property obligations,"[8] the key to the system of customary law lay in the balancing of property rights in order to maintain the extensive, "tribal" system of kinship—a system with many levels of kin association. In his search for general principles underlying custom, Tupper pointed in particular to those principles of landed inheritance which tended to preserve the integrity of groups at various levels of the kinship system, including both the cultivating family in the village and the more politically salient "clan" or "tribal" unit. Whatever inheritance practices tended "to preserve tribal cohesion, community of interest in the village, and the integrity of the family" could normally be presumed to "have the weight of past custom in [their] favour ..."[9] Custom could thus be seen as part of a single widespread system of property obligations which supported the fabric of Punjab's "tribal" kinship system. "Kinship and the land," he wrote, "combine to determine and regulate the form and practice of our communities."[10]

Most important for our purposes here, the identification of such principles of custom pointed clearly to the importance of women in the maintenance of Punjab's rural "tribal" fabric. Women provided the cement of the whole kinship system because, as Tupper pointed out, it was the character of marriage which gave the kinship system its basic structure and which determined the nature of inheritance patterns among the "tribes." What accounted for underlying similarities in custom, in spite of wide variations in detail, was the predominance of a pattern of marriage which fostered geographically widespread kinship linkages. This was the system of clan exogamy so common throughout northern India. Daughters in this system were married "outside the closely drawn limits of the clan, but within the looser, but still remembered, circle of the tribe or race of origin."[11] Marriage had thus become a means of keeping alive "the sense that the clan had expanded from the family of a common ancestor,"[12] and it was thus the key to the preservation of the whole social fabric of rural society. Since it gave the kinship system its extensive character, the structure of marriage also, indirectly, gave the kinship system its administrative and political significance for the British.

In such circumstances, the legal constraints which defined the woman's position as a link within this kinship system were of vital importance from the British perspective. Local custom, as Tupper and later British jurists analyzed it, was almost universal in denying a regular share in landed inheritance to daughters, since daughters normally passed by marriage out of their clan of origin. For land to be maintained within the immediate kinship group, it was thus theoretically essential that daughters be denied any share in their fathers' inheritance. This did not mean, of course, that daughters were left without provision, either through dowry, or maintenance if they were left unmarried or widowed.[13] But it remained a basic principle of the system that land could not pass to women unfettered, to be passed on to their heirs. ". . . The tutelage of women," Tupper declared, would in the ideal situation "be perpetual." Women would, as a result of the structure of the kinship system, always be "under the guardianship either of their husbands; or, failing these, of the nearest agnates by blood or marriage."[14] Such strictures did not imply that women would be socially isolated from their clan of origin after marriage, for social relations with their clan of birth would continue. But in matters of inheritance, which in a landed society defined the structure of kinship, these relations would, of necessity, have to be ignored.[15] Punjab custom was thus, in the eyes of the British, founded on the basic assumption that "as a rule, daughters and their sons, as well as sisters and their sons, are excluded by near male collaterals."[16]

As a presumption underlying inheritance, this "principle" of customary law was formulated by Tupper and others only after extensive observation of Punjabi custom. But significantly, and most important for understanding the subsequent evolution of custom, it was not merely the concern to record and categorize custom which prompted the search for such underlying presumptions. Tupper's aim in his analysis of customary law was not merely to place local variations in custom within a unifying framework; his object was to tie the whole subject to a single theory of Punjabi kinship—a theory which could provide a theoretical base for the structure of British rule. Such a social theory of indigenous society was essential if the British, as aliens, were to rule effectively. "It is difficult for a civilized foreign Government always to keep vividly present before it the breadth and depth of the gulf by which it may be severed from its subjects . . .," Tupper wrote, but "this is a difficulty which an improved theory of social history will obviously go far to remove."[17] Tupper's theory of custom was thus developed with clear political purposes in mind. " . . . Indeed," he wrote, "it necessarily happened that the view I had been led to form of the character of customary law in great part suggested to me the feasibility of using it for public or political ends."[18]

The significance of this for the evolution of inheritance law as it affected women cannot be overemphasized. Tupper himself identified the denial of inheritance to women as a key principle underlying his theory of kinship organization. The foundations were thus laid for the translation of this principle from a description of popular practice into a normative formula supporting the "tribal" system of kinship underlying the British administration. The exclusion of women from inheritance had become implicitly a political issue—a critical legal link in the maintenace of the British structure of authority.

The normative implications of Tupper's theorizing were by no means accepted immediately by all British administrators in Punjab, particularly since, in the late nineteenth-century, there was no universally accepted understanding of the nature of the legitimizing principles underlying their rule. British uncertainty about the relationship between their own authority as a centralizing bureaucratic force and the local authority embodied in kinship networks was reflected in the discussion over the question of codification of the customary law. Though Tupper had committed himself on political grounds to the principle of codification, even he had been wary of pushing codification too strongly in the face of considerable diversity in customary practice. In his 1881 compilation, he had thus recommended only the gradual introduction of declarations on custom for guiding the courts. These declarations would outline "general custom," or "such particular custom as it may be politically desirable to maintain or extend," but would only be "presumed to represent the fact in the absence of proof to the contrary."[19] This was a far cry from translating his principles of customary law directly into practice, but even this was opposed by critics such as the Lieutenant-Governor, Sir Robert Egerton who opposed any effort at all to freeze custom through legislative enactment. Egerton was convinced of the "tribal" character of rural Punjabi society, but saw greater political danger for the British in the codification of customary law than in allowing it to develop piecemeal. In his view, the inevitable tendency of the British administration was to erode "tribal" ties —"to dissolve the tribal bond and to give free scope to individual energy." Though Egerton had no desire to accelerate this trend, he felt any official legistative codification could only be politically dangerous, tending in the face of gradual social change to leave "the Legislature in the lurch."[20]

The question of codification of the customary law was shelved in the 1880s, and though later much discussed, never carried out.[21] The political considerations which had motivated Tupper's attempt to define general principles of custom, however, were subsequently to play a central role in the evolution of the law. The increasingly overt efforts of the British at the turn of the century to define the "tribal" political bases of their rule were exemplified most clearly by the passage of the Alienation of Land Act in 1900. This Act openly identified the stability of British rule in Punjab with the stability of Punjab's statutorily defined "agricultural tribes."[22] Similarly, the Pre-emption Act of 1906, like the Land Alienation Act, indicated the subordination in British thinking of the concern for allowing "free scope to individual energy" to the concern for maintaining a politically solid "tribal" base.[23]

Most important in relation to the rights of women, however, was the increasing tendency of the courts to seek uniform "tribal" standards of customary succession in their decisions, despite the lack of a formal customary law code. This trend was encouraged by the publication of W. H. Rattigan's *Digest of the Civil Law for the Punjab* in 1880, which ran eventually to thirteen editions and "considerably unified the customary law of the Punjab."[24] In addition, a number of important judges, such as Sir Meredyth Plowden and Sir Charles Roe, tended to rely on an "agnatic theory" of customary succession in their judicial decisions, a theory which apparently owed much to the theorizing of Tupper. Though an extensive study of cases would be necessary to determine the actual effects of the application of this theory, its formulation appears to reflect the growing belief in the late nineteenth century that even in the absence of positive evidence of custom, exclusion of daughters in favor of male collaterals could be taken as a basic judicial presumption. Though by no means invariably endorsed in law, the exclusion of daughters from landed inheritance had thus come to play an important role in British judicial thinking in spite of the failure to codify custom. This normative presumption reflected clearly the dominant trend in British political thinking at the time.

Not all British officials and judges accepted this view, even after the passage of the Land Alienation Act, and many criticized the assumptions implicit in the "agnatic theory." On one level, criticism focused on the anomaly inherent in the process of attempting to apply general theory to the interpretation of specific local and "tribal" custom. As Lahore High Court Justice LeRossignol noted, the Privy Council had, in its own definition of custom, declared that custom was "whatever is *proved* to be the active custom." And yet the Chief Court of Punjab had, by using general theory and the logic of analogy, extended the scope of custom not through the collection of examples, but by "logical process." "To call 'custom' a rule which is not proved to have ever been applied, but which can only be deduced logically," he declared, "is a contradiction in terms and misuse of language."[25] The extent to which this process had operated to produce standards of law for female inheritance which altogether transcended local custom was criticized by some Punjabi agriculturalist leaders themselves. As Mian Muhammad Shafi pointed out, under the "agnatic theory," daughters had sometimes been excluded from inheritance by male collaterals whose relationship was so distant that it was beyond the range of Punjabi kinship terminology. "Being an agriculturalist and a lawyer" himself, Shafi said in 1915, he felt "that the theory of agnatic succession had been carried too far by Sir Meredyth Plowden and Sir Charles Roe. The fact that there is no Punjabi word for an ancestor beyond a great-great-grandfather," was significant. It was an indication, in Shafi's view, of the limits beyond which the "agnatic theory" could not be pressed.[26]

The most critical challenge to the "agnatic theory," however, was based on concerns which were at root political, and which were tied to basic British perceptions about the nature of their role in Punjabi society. The most basic objection after 1900 came from British officials who believed that social change, brought about by the British themselves, had made any attempt to apply a sterotypical "agnatic" interpretation of customary law increasingly unrealistic. The Montgomery Sessions Judge, L.H. Leslie-Jones, echoing the earlier comments of Egerton, declared, "there are many influences, among which may be included the security of life and property, at work to dissipate the force of [the] agnatic bond and to disintegrate the village community, and we must anticipate the day when the desire for greater individual freedom of disposition and liberality towards females will cause men to look askance at the customs which served their purpose well enough in times of insecurity and unrest."[27] Faced with such influences, many felt that any unduly rigid interpretation of custom could only be counterproductive. As High Court Justice Sir Frederick Robertson put it in 1907, "the rights of women" had, "in the opinion of many... suffered unduly of late years under the too universal application of the 'agnatic theory'."[28]

But such a concern for social "progress" did not provide an answer to the political concerns which had first pushed men like Tupper toward social theorizing. The freezing of custom could indeed be politically dangerous, as many British officers realized, but this did not lessen their underlying need for indigenous legitimizing principles for the administration. These principles had, particularly since the passage of the Land Alienation Act, become closely associated with the maintenance of Punjab's "tribal" kinship structure. The "agnatic theory" of succession, whatever its impact on the position of women, was, for many British officers, of a fundamental political significance which transcended the less well-defined concern for social progress. As W.H. Rattigan expressed it, "it may be true that there are internal silently operating powers which in all societies make for change and for the transmutation of a set of ideas, based upon tribal or family ownership, into another and a totally different conception of the rights of property based upon individualistic theories. But, unless I am egregiously mistaken, it is not the policy of our administration to further or hasten this change... Although we may not be able to stop altogether this current of individualistic thought from slowly undermining the foundation on which village property is based, it it within our power to retard and weaken this destructive process."[29]

Rattigan's statement, though certainly not accepted by all, captured well the dominant judicial view during the period when the Punjab's system of customary law was being forged. The maintenance of a system of extended "tribal" kinship had come to be seen as central to the stability and legitimacy of British rule in the Punjab, and the system of customary law developed as a judicial reflection of this basic political fact. The result was that the inheritance rights of women were mortgaged, in theory, to wider political concerns underlying the development of the legal system of the Punjab. The denial of inheritance rights to women, in fact, became symbolic of the solidity of the kin-based political foundations of the British colonial state.

Custom vs. Shariat : The Law, Women and Politics

For the British, kinship structure had become more than a curiosity for amateur ethnographers; it provided a political and ideological foundation for their rule. As far as the rights of women were concerned, this proved to be of signal importance. Though in practice inheritance patterns affecting women continued to vary considerably,[30] the legal system in the late nineteenth and early twentieth centuries increasingly denied women the right to inherit property, not just because local custom in many parts of the Punjab traditionally denied them this right, but because this denial had become an element of ideological importance to many British jurists and administrators.

In succeeding years, British rule in the Punjab came under increasing challenge from various sides. Prominent among the challengers of the colonial system were many urban Punjabi Muslims, whose criticism was directed not just at the presence of the British as alien colonial rulers, but more fundamentally, at the rural, "tribal" structure of authority which supported the British regime. Central to the concerns of these critics was the definition of a transcendent religious basis for political solidarity, which would transcend the ties of kinship. It was, in fact, no accident that these Muslim critics of British rule were concentrated in the cities, where the political influence of kinship had weakened under the British, and where "individualism" was strongest. Their criticism of the British regime reflected not just the rise of the increasing "individualism" that many British officials themselves had foreseen, but also a new political view of society and the state based on an ideological commitment to Islam rather than on the ties of kinship and "tribe." Such a view was perhaps most eloquently expressed by Sir Muhammad Iqbal. "As a cultural movement Islam rejects the old static view of the universe," he wrote, "and reaches a dynamic view. As an emotional system of unification it recognizes the worth of the individual as such, and rejects blood-relationship as a basis of human unity. Blood-relationship is earth-rootedness," he declared. Transcending kinship, Islam sought ideally to provide "a purely psychological foundation of human unity..."[31]

The implications of such a view for the position of women can be seen clearly in the contrast between the shariat, the Muslim law, and the principles of customary law as applied by the British. Muslim reformers, who were critical of the structure of "tribal" authority under the British, saw nothing as more central to the definition of a collective Muslim identity than the spread of adherence to the shariat, which was symbolic of a primary commitment to Muslim community. As a legal system supporting a distinctively conceived social and political order, the shariat was "in direct uncompromising conflict" with the customary law.[32] So far as women were concerned, the rules of shariat were very different from those of the customary law, and nowhere more so than in the matter of female inheritance. In sharp contrast to their position under customary law, daughters were, under the shariat, guaranteed a share in landed inheritance (though a lesser share than sons). For those attacking the colonial regime from an Islamic perspective, the question of female inheritance was thus an ideological issue of first importance.

This was expressed in the early twentieth century in widespread criticism of the inheritance rules of customary law. As the *Paisa Akhbar* admitted in 1915, "it is undoubtedly true that many Muhammadan agriculturalists and landlords do not, through ignorance, leave land to their daughters."[33] But acceptance of this as the basis of an officially recognized system of law was, the newspaper declared, totally unacceptable and a betrayal of the normative order of Islam itself. ". . .Religious law is so complete in its treatment of questions of inheritance," the *Vakil* of Amritsar editorialized, "that no secular law could replace it."[34] As a political issue, the question of guaranteeing a share of inheritance to daughters was for many reformers central to the formation of Muslim solidarity. As a pamphlet asked of Muslims in 1916, "When you consider the command of your Prophet as nothing as compared with usages and customs and you utter blasphemy even before the court and say that you are bound by custom and that you have no faith in shariat, how can you expect intercession from your Prophet?"[35]

The difference between custom and shariat was thus perceived by many reformers as a moral issue closely related to the basic foundations of the political system. In practical social terms, however, one should not press the contrast between custom and shariat for the individual Muslim too far. Though the preservation of a political order based on networks of kinship was not, as in the case of customary law, at the theoretical root of the shariat, the rules of inheritance under the shariat were nevertheless also affected by a concern for the vitality and cohesion of kinship groups. The shariat itself had grown out of the agnatic system of tribal inheritance in pre-Islamic Arabia, and though this had been "radically modified by the Sunnis as a result of the revelations of early Islam,"[36] considerations of kin-based solidarity continued to play an important part in its actual workings. Though daughters were guaranteed a share in inheritance, therefore, this by no means represented a complete rejection of the political view of women as links in kinship organization. Such a view was embodied, for example, in the law of pre-emption, which was as much a part of Muslim law as it was of Punjab custom, and was intended to insure the social integrity of local kinship groups. One urban Muslim notable observed at the beginning of the twentieth century that the law of pre-emption was "one of the most important institutions of Islam, established by social, religious and political necessities of the country," and much needed "in a country in which different creeds and races abound..."[37] Considerations of the rights of the individual, whether male or female, were in such legal constructs clearly subordinated to the practical requirements of maintaining the integrity of local kinship groups.[38]

In social terms, the significant contrast between customary law and the shariat was not between a system which recognized the importance of kinship and one which did not. In so far as the character of kinship was at the root of the contrast, it was a contrast between two different types of kin-based solidarity, which were associated with two different patterns of marriage in Punjab, and which had very different political implications. C.L. Tupper had observed in his original attempt at formulating the principles of customary law that the whole structure of the "tribal" system in Punjab was based on extensive patterns of marriage which bound large numbers of Punjabis together in "tribal" categories which often transcended the bounds of immediately traceable kinship. It was, in fact, this system which gave central theoretical significance to the common denial of inheritance to women, for such a denial was essential in an extensive marriage system in order to preserve the integrity of family and village property. The rules of inheritance under the shariat were associated, however, with a pattern of marriage based on preferred parallel cousin endogamy. This pattern kept property, even when inherited by daughters, within the localized kinship group. In political terms, the extensive kin-based political ties of the "tribal" system which were so important in the British administration were replaced in the ideal Islamic system by more powerful, yet more narrowly localized kinship bonds. In such a system it was, in theory, the ideological bonds of Islam, rather than kinship, which provided the foundations for the integration of society.

Though little research has been done on the actual extent of such marriage patterns in the Punjab in the nineteenth and twentieth centuries, the available evidence suggests that these patterns were of some importance in parts of West Punjab in the late nineteenth century, and may have become more important in the twentieth. Tupper himself, in spite of his insistence on the theoretical importance of extensive "tribally"-based marriage patterns, published evidence in his customary law treatise indicating that among such prominent central Punjabi Jat clans as the Chattah and Tarar, Muslims were "much addicted to marriages of close affinity within the clan."[39] Later evidence collected in a sample survey at the time of the 1921 census showed that the incidence of cousin marriage in the Punjab ranged from as high as 60% among Muslims surveyed in Attock District to 11% among the Muslims sampled in Delhi.[40] Though such evidence hardly provides an empirical foundation for challenging the predominance of the extensive marriage patterns emphasized by Tupper, it does suggest that social foundations may already have existed in the Punjab for an interpretation of inheritance far different from the "agnatic theory" of customary law propounded in the late nineteenth century by the British courts. In such a light, one might interpret the movement toward the shariat not as a rejection of the political importance of kinship, but as just one manifestation of an indigenous reaction against the attempt to elaborate customary law within a single theoretical mold.

Whatever the validity of such an interpretation, however, it can only hint at the critical political implications of the challenge to custom in twentieth century Punjab. The greatest significance of this challenge derived not from the social origins of the law, but rather from its relationship to the ideology of the state. Kinship patterns were an element in structuring the inheritance law of the shariat, but the moral imperative of the shariat did not derive from its support for a particular form of kinship. Rather, the significance of the shariat grew from the ideological commitment it implied to a type of political solidarity which, as Iqbal had put it, explicitly transcended kinship. Support for the shariat was thus symbolically important in Muslim Punjab as a call for a new political order, a new foundation for the state to replace the colonial ideology of the British. For women, the importance of the shariat lay less in the specific provisions of Muslim law than in the rejection of the normative order based on "tribal"solidarity.

The political implications of this issue can best be seen in the context of the political conflict during the 1920s and 1930s between opposing Punjabi groups whose positions reflected the two political alternatives. On one side was the pro-British Unionist Party, which was organized in the Punjab Legislative Council in the early 1920s and which was the inheritor of the British administrative tradition. It was a party primarily of Muslim rural leaders, whose power lay in "tribal" structures of authority and who supported both the Land Alienation Act and the "tribal" ideology which had found judicial expression in the "agnatic theory" of customary law. Opposed to the Unionists were numerous critics. These included not only Hindus and Sikhs who were opposed to Muslm domination, but also, and most important for the analysis here, Muslim supporters of the shariat. These Muslims wished to free India from British domination, and in addition, to transform the indigenous political system—to establish a moral political order based on Islam which would transcend the bonds of kinship.

Not surprisingly, conflict over the foundations of the law proved to be of basic importance as the opposition between these groups developed, and the legal position of women emerged in this context as a significant symbolic issue. By the 1920s, some urban, well-educated Muslim women had already begun to agitate for improvements in female inheritance law.[41] But the more general, politically-motivated pressure for legal reform soon proved far more important in drawing attention to the issue. This was underscored in the early 1930s when Malik Muhammad Din, a member of the Punjab Legislative Council from Lahore, introduced a bill in the Council which called explicitly for the supercession of custom by Muslim personal law. Though Malik Muhammad Din pointed to the need for improved female inheritance rights as a major justification for the bill, the specific circumstances of the bill's introduction indicated the political conflicts underlying the issue. Malik Muhammad Din proposed the bill largely in response to the passage in 1931 of a Unionist-backed bill which gave legislative sanction to the local inheritance customs of the powerful, pro-Unionist Tiwana family of Kalra, in spite of the conflict between those customs and the shariat.[42] Malik

Muhammad Din's bill, therefore, sought to challenge the very foundation of Unionist power by seeking legislative affirmation of the moral supremacy of the shariat.

The political nature of the conflict between custom and shariat and the central place of female inheritance within this conflict were subsequently analyzed in the Punjab government's discussion of the bill. Under customary law, the government's Legal Remembrancer observed, women had been viewed only as conduits for land to pass from generation to generation, not as actual owners of land, the theoretical disposition of which vested in the "tribe".[43] Under the shariat, however, the assumptions affecting the disposition of land were to be changed drastically, with potentially sweeping impact on the structure of rural society. As the British discovered when they circulated the bill for opinions from the districts, many rural Punjabi Muslims viewed the establishment of female inheritance rights under the shariat as a threat to the entire structure of rural, "tribal" authority. The Muslim Tehsildar of Kharian Tehsil declared that "to abrogate the tribal law altogether by one stroke of the pen and thereby substitute the Muhammadan Law instead would not only be impracticable under the circumstances but would completely disintegrate the homogeneity of the agricultural tribe."[44] This view was echoed by other rural Muslim leaders Daughters could be provided for through dowry, a Jat leader of Gujrat District declared, but if they were guaranteed shares in the land according to shariat, then the Land Alienation Act would be undermined and the agriculturalists would be ruined.[45]

Not all rural Muslims opposed the bill, of course, for few Muslims were willing to oppose openly the holy law of Islam. Some pointed to an already increasing tendency toward adherence to the shariat, both among the better-educated and among those Muslims who adhered to preferred parallel cousin patterns of endogamy. One leading Muslim observed that the bill in itself served as a potential incentive to encourage closer degrees of endogamy, a warning to Muslims "to be cautious in marrying their daughters."[46] But among Muslims offering opinions of the bill, such considerations were secondary to the overall political implications of the measure. The leaders of the Unionist Party opposed the bill on grounds which reflected their own concern for maintaining the "tribal" system underlying their authority. This concern was also reflected in the comments of the provincial government: "The Governor in Council considers that the bill is dangerous to the general economic structure of the province as a whole, and to the interests of the rural Muslim community in particular."[47]

Malik Muhammad Din's bill was quietly blocked by the Unionists and never allowed to reach a division in the Punjab Council, but the issues which the bill brought to the fore nevertheless continued to agitate Muslim politics. After 1935, the newly rejuvenated Muslim League increasingly provided leadership for community-minded Muslims who supported adherence to the shariat, and in 1937, the League's all-India leader, Muhammad Ali Jinnah, carried the fight for the supremacy of the shariat in matters of personal law into the Central Legislative Assembly.[48] Once again, as in the debate in Punjab, the question of women's rights played an important part in the call for support of the shariat, but the issue remained, even in the Central Assembly, largely symbolic. Though well-educated women remained active in the fight for inheritance rights at the all-India level,[49] the key issues in the fight for the shariat centered on the challenge to the structure of political authority posed by the adoption of Muslim law in provinces such as the Punjab where customary law was important. It was, in fact, with regard to the Punjab that the controversy was greatest. Lahore High Court Justice Din Muhammad noted that many rural leaders in the Punjab continued to be wary of the shariat because they feared that in allowing an inheritance share to daughters, the shariat would "... cut at the root of the system under which they were living ... "[50]

Showing the political skill which was his trademark, Jinnah was able to steer the bill successfully through the Assembly in spite of this opposition, thus enacting the first Shariat Act covering all India's Muslims.[51] But the compromises he had to make to secure the bill's passage dramatized the continuing contradictions inherent in the issue. For Jinnah, the passage of an all-India Shariat Act was of immense symbolic importance, for it demonstrated legislatively the commitment of all India's Muslims to an Islamic moral system. But with political power in the Punjab still tied to the "tribal" structure of the

British administration, even Jinnah could not in practice challenge directly the power of Punjab's rural magnates. Jinnah's success in securing passage of the bill was achieved only with extensive compromises on precisely those aspects of Muslim law which appeared to threaten the power of the Unionists and the British. On the critical question of the inheritance of agricultural land the bill was altogether silent, for this was a subject reserved for legislation by provincial governments and was thus beyond the scope of the bill in the Central Assembly. Even with regard to those issues covered by the bill, however, Jinnah by no means pushed the shariat to its logical conclusion. Adherence to the shariat in matters of adoption, wills, and legacies was left by Jinnah's compromises wholly to the option of individual Muslims, in spite of the vigorous objections raised by scholars in the religious law.[52] Whatever the symbolic value of the shariat, therefore, Jinnah could not hope in 1937 to push through a bill which would transform the legal system entirely, at least as long as the structure of political authority in provinces like the Punjab remained rooted in the "tribal" colonial administration.

The effects of the 1937 Shariat Application Act were thus extremely limited. Punjabi reformers who were explicitly concerned with women's rights, such as K.L. Gauba and Baji Rashida Latif, pressed repeatedly in the late 1930s and early 1940s for provincial legislation to extend the scope of the Shariat Act and to guarantee female rights of inheritance. Such legislation stood little chance in an assembly which continued to be dominated by the Unionist Party. As one British official noted of a bill to extend the coverage of the shariat to include succession to agricultural property, "It seems certain that a Bill of this type is not really wanted by the vast majority of Muslims in the Punjab. The Muslim Personal Law (Shariat) Application Act, 1937, goes far enough—some people would probably think too far."[53] Whether "the vast majority of Muslims" really opposed the extension of the shariat is impossible to say, but it is clear from such attitudes that any substantive change in inheritance law as it affected women was impossible as long as the colonial structure of authority endured.

Only with the emergence of Pakistan as an independent

state did the transformation prefigured by the Shariat Application Act of 1937 actually begin to occur. With the Muslim League's defeat of the Unionist Party in the elections of 1946 and the departure of the British in 1947, the old colonial system in the Punjab finally collapsed. This signaled a revolution in the nature of authority—a revolution not primarily in the structure of the administration, but in the moral foundations of the state. Though the "tribal" structure of rural authority remained intact in many areas, the end of British rule brought an immediate and dramatic change in the relationship between kinship and the state. This change provided the foundation for the substantive changes in the legal system that reformers had long advocated. By the West Punjab Muslim Personal Law (Shariat) Application Act of 1948, the system of customary law which the British had developed over a century was, at a stroke, almost wholly superceded. The act declared "in all questions regarding succession (including succession to agricultural land) ... the rule of decision in cases where the parties are Muslims shall be the Muslim Personal Law (Shariat)."[54]

For women, the emergence of Pakistan thus finally opened new possibilties regarding landed inheritance. But to understand the nature of the transformation which had taken place, it is necessary to see it within the context of the political changes accompanying the emergence of a new state. The significance of the emergence of Pakistan for women lay not in the commitment of the founders of Pakistan to women's rights, or even to the shariat as such, but rather in their commitment to the establishment of a state based upon an ideology of Islamic solidarity rather than upon indigenous "tribal" kinship structures. In practical terms, the inheritance rights of women continued to be limited by many complex issues, but changes in the nature of the state had brought basic changes in the way women were legally viewed. Freed from the political necessity of maintaining the solidity of the "agricultural tribes," inheritance laws for women could begin to evolve in ways which reflected not only the dictates of the shariat, but a concern for individual equity as well.

NOTES

[1] Letter from Sec. to Govt., Punjab to Sec. to Govt. of India, Dept. of Revenue, Agriculture and Commerce, August 24, 1878, Printed in C.L. Tupper, *Punjab Customary Law* (Calcutta: Government of India, 1881), Vol. I, pp. 225-226.

[2] The division of Punjab into *zails* is discussed for various districts in Punjab Board of Revenue, hereafter cited as PBR, File 61/142.

[3] Terms such as "tribe", "race", and "clan" were often used with little appreciation of their Punjabi or Urdu equivalents. The attempt to relate these terms to native terminology could generate considerable confusion, as indicated in Tupper, *Punjab Customary Law*, Vol. III, p. 4.

[4] Letter from E.A. Prinsep, Settlement Commissioner, Punjab, to Sec. to Financial Commissioner, June 27, 1871, PBR, File 61/142.

[5] Proceedings of the Lieutenant-Governor, February 29, 1872, PBR, File 61/142.

[6] Tupper, *Punjab Customary Law*, Vol. I, p. 17.

[7] Records of custom were originally collected from each village in the Punjab as a part of settlement operations. After 1873, however, local notables were called together in various parts of the district by the settlement officer and asked a set of questions concerning custom. The new procedure appears to have reflected a view of custom as more distinctly "tribal". For a brief account of the evolution of custom, see Alan Gledhill, "The compilation of customary law in the Punjab in the nineteenth century," in John Gilissen, ed., *La rédaction des coutumes dans le passé et dans le présent* (Brussels: Institut de Sociologie de l'Université Libre de Bruxelles, 1962).

[8] Tupper, *Punjab Customary Law*, Vol. II, p. 84.

[9] *Ibid.*, p. 78.

[10] *Ibid.*

[11] *Ibid.*, p. 70.

[12] *Ibid.*

[13] *Ibid.*, p. 73.

[14] *Ibid.*, pp. 76, 71.

[15] *Ibid.*, p. 73.

[16] J. Boulnois and W.H. Rattigan, *Notes on the Customary Laws of the Punjab* (1867), quoted in *Ibid.*, p. 80.

[17] *Ibid.*, p. 98. "A sound theory," Tupper added, "Would not merely inculcate moderation in the present; it would be a standing guide to continuous progress."

[18] *Ibid.*, Vol. I, p. 22

[19] *Ibid.*, p. 23

[20] Letter from W.M. Young, Sec. to Govt., Punjab to Officiating Sec. to Govt. of India, Home Revenue and Agriculture Dept., February 10, 1881, Printed in *Ibid.*, p. 221.

[21] The history of the debate on the codification issue up to 1915 is

covered in Notes by Messrs. H.D. Watson and G. Worsley, Under-Secretaries to Govt., printed in *Report on the Punjab Codification of Customary Law Conference (September 1915)* (Lahore: Govt. Printing, 1915), pp. 51-59.

[22] The overt concern of the Land Alienation Act was to prevent land from passing into the hands of non-agriculturalist moneylenders, but the Act was structured so as to make the preservation of land in the hands of "agricultural tribes" its primary purpose. For a detailed discussion of the administrative controversies leading up to the passage of the act, see P.H.M. van den Dungen, *The Punjab Tradition* (London: George Allen and Unwin, 1972).

[23] The passage of the Pre-emption Act was, in fact, seen by some as a first step in the codification of customary law. Note by G. Worsley Under-Secretary to Govt., Punjab, Revenue Dept., February 18, 1915, printed in *Report. . .of Customary Law Conference*, pp. 58-59.

[24] Alan Gledhill, "The compilation of customary law. . .," p. 140. Rattigan himself saw the *Digest* as the forerunner of a future customary law code, W.H. Rattigan, *A Digest of Civil Law for the Punjab* (13th ed. Allahabad: University Book Agency, 1953), pp. xiv-xvi.

[25] Note by the Hon'ble Mr. Justice W.A. LeRossignol, September 16, 1915, printed in *Report. . .of Customary Law Conference*, p. 39.

[26] *Report. . .of Customary Law Conference*, p. 19. Shafi's concern was subsequently legislatively recognized with the passage of the Punjab Custom (Power of Contest) Act of 1920, which barred suits to block alienations by any agnate not descended at minimum from a common great-great-grandfather. A.A.K. Lodhi, *Customary Law of the Punjab* (Lahore: Caravan Book House, 1963), pp. 84-85.

[27] Note by Mr. L.H. Leslie-Jones, printed in *Report. . .of Customary Law Conference*, p. 36.

[28] Note by the Hon'ble Mr. F. Robertson entitled, "Suggestions Regarding Codification of Customary Law," April 11, 1907, printed in *Report. . .of Customary Law Conference*, p. 86.

[29] Note by Sir William Rattigan, December 26, 1897, printed in *Report. . .of Customary Law Conference*, p. 72.

[30] Though the British themselves were aware of wide variations in custom, this did not stop their frequent efforts to analyze customs in terms of general principles. A good example is provided by the case of N. Hancock Prenter, who undertook a survery of custom in central Punjab in 1920. "At first sight," he wrote, "it would appear. . .that the proverbial attachment to tribal custom is a myth, and that no people in the world show such disregard for custom as the Punjab agriculturalists. It appears to a superficial examiner of the material collected that our thousands of instances are nearly all exceptions to the apparently established rule of agnatic succession. . ." Such observations, however, did not prevent Prenter from generalizing that "the principles on which the customs are based are more or less common to all the agriculturalist tribes of the block". Punjab Civil Secretariat Archives, hereafter cited as PCSA, B procs., Home (Judicial), File 262, 1923.

[31] Allama Muhammad Iqbal, *The Reconstruction of Religious Thought in Islam* (Lahore: Sh. Muhammad Ashraf, 1971), p. 146.

[32] Statement of M. Ahmed Khan, Tehsildar of Kharian Tehsil. PCSA, Home (Judicial), File 20, October 1936.

[33] *Paisa Akhbar* (Lahore), September 18, 1915. Report on Newspapers and Periodicals in the Punjab, 1915, no. 38.

[34] *Vakil* (Amritsar), October 23, 1915. Report on Newspapers. . ., 1915, no. 43.

[35] *Lamaat* (Lahore), April 2-3, 1916. Report of Newspapers. . . 1916, no. 15.

[36] J.N.D. Anderson, "The Eclipse of the Patriarchal Family in Contemporary Islamic Law," in J.N.D. Anderson, ed., *Family Law in Asia and Africa* (New York: Praeger, 1967), p. 222.

[37] Note by Nasir Ali, Honorary Magistrate, Delhi, October 1, 1910, PBR, File 441/212 B.

[38] As several authors point out, pre-emption in rural Punjab was more strictly a "village" than a "tribal" institution. See, for example, Rattigan, *Digest of Civil Law*. . . p. 921. Its intent, however, like the 'agnatic theory' of customary succession, was to prevent land from passing out of a corporate group to strangers.

[39] Tupper, *Punjab Customary Law*, Vol. II, p. 200.

[40] For first cousins only, the respective percentages for Attock and Delhi were 42% and 7%. *Census of India*, 1921, Vol. XV (Punjab and Delhi), p. 260. The political importance of changing patterns of parallel cousin marriage among rural notables in twentieth century Punjab is analyzed in Emily Hodges, "The Pir, the Faqir and the Industrialist," paper presented to the Association for Asian Studies, Chicago, March 1978.

[41] The concern of educated Muslim women with inheritance rights under the shariat is suggested in Gail Minault, "Sisterhood or Separatism: The All-India Muslim Ladies' Conference and the Nationalist Movement," above.

[42] Shortly before the drafting of Malik Muhammad Din's bill, Sir Umar Hyat Khan Tiwana had arranged the passage in the Council of a bill, the Kalra Impartible Estate Bill, establishing the succession to the Kalra estate by primogeniture. *Punjab Legislative Council Debates*, Vol. 19 (1931), pp. 788-792: Vol. 20 (1931), pp. 61-78, 120-133, 183-205.

[43] "Custom" he wrote, "is not uniform, but in the great majority of families, it is founded on the axiom that the real owner of the land is a tribe, so that finally the land passes to the reversioners, who have power to control the disposition of the land by the member of the tribe in possession. . ." PCSA, Home (Judicial), File 20, October 1936.

[44] Statement of M. Ahmed Khan, Tehsildar of Kharian Tehsil, PCSA, Home (Judicial), File 20, October 1936.

[45] Statement of Chaudhri Bahawal Bakhsh, president, Zamindara League, Gujrat. PCSA, Home (Judicial) File 20, October 1936.

[46] Statement of K.B. Nawab Umardraz Ali Khan of Karnal, PCSA, Home (Judicial), File 20, October 1936.

[47]Note by S.L. Sale, Sec. to Govt., Punjab Legislative Dept., PCSA, Home (Judicial), File 20, October 1936.

[48]The original impetus for a central Shariat Bill did not come from Jinnah, but from Muslim reformist religious leaders of the Punjab. The bill was originally introduced in the Central Legislature by Hafiz Abdullah of Lyallpur and had the support of the Jamiat-i-Ulama-i-Hind. Jinnah, however, took over the legislative leadership of the fight for the bill in 1937. Tahir Mahmood, *Muslim Personal Law* (New Delhi: Vikas Publishing House, 1977), p. 29.

[49]Tahir Mahmood, *Muslim Personal Law*, pp. 29-30.

[50]Opinion of Justice Din Mohammad, NAI, Home (Judicial), File 36/17/35/Judl.

[51]Jinnah's parliamentary role in securing passage of this act is detailed in Mohammad Jafar, I.A. Rehman and Ghani Jafar, eds., *Jinnah as a Parliamentarian* (Islamabad: Azfar Associates, 1977) pp. 229-331.

[52]Tahir Mahmood, *Muslim Personal Law*, pp. 31-32.

[53]View of A.V. Askwith, PCSA, B. Procs., Home (Judicial), File 499, 1939.

[54]Lodhi, *Customary Law of the Punjab*, p. 90.

7

Nationalism, Universalization and the Extended Female Space

GAIL PEARSON

AT THE AZAD MAIDAN

> The Azad Maidan was a glorious great sight,
> Where women in orange, and women in white
> Assembled in thousands to bless the great Sage
> Who taught them to write for new history a page.
> Like soldiers of peace worked the orange-brigade,
> With disciplined method their part they well played.
> Encircling the others of lily-white heart,
> While sang they their mantram of women's great art.
> And men who but lately belittled their state,
> Now learn from the women how they can be great;
> So nobly the women do answer the call,
> That India's new life is the wonder of all.
> Their sufferings tune in with courage and faith,
> Their service exhales a life-giving sweet breath,
> Their sacrifice sings of a fear of God,
> A mother's a mother, at home or abroad. Oh great is the work of the orange-brigade,
> The whole world so wonders at women arrayed
> To play with great glory a unique new game
> With peace to endow the strifeladen world's shame.
>
> —*SEVIKA*

Indian nationalism remains an entrancing story. It is the story of flamboyant personalities, and of quiet national workers. It is the story of the evolution of a new state structure, of complex nagotiation and bargaining between colony and metropolis, between different parties in each, and between the various factions and interest groups. It is the story of dramatic acts of courage and of quite persistent work. It included the extraordinary mobilization of peoples to achieve a single objective, and the retention of real power in the hands of the few. Perhaps one of the major characteristics of the national movement was its cohesiveness both in times of crisis and in times of negotiation, despite the big differences in perspective of many of its constituent parts.

In all of this, the situation of women has received little attention. At best the exploits of "nationalist" heroines from Laxmi, the Rani of Jhansi of 1857 fame, to Usha Mehta of 1942 have been uncritically lauded.[1] At worst, the contribution of women has been ignored altogether, in order to facilitate data collection and analysis.[2] Yet, if we examine the female role, it is clear that the participation of women in the nationalist movement was crucial in molding the character of a social movement that could draw on the contribution of competing classes and social groups, yet maintain its essential unity. In a symbolic fashion, women provided the cohesive force which enabled the men of those class interests which dominated the Indian National Congress to present the nationalist movement to the people of India as a social movement which represented the aspirations of all social groups. The role of female participants was to provide the basis for the universalization of the whole movement. The eventual success of the Congress-led bourgeois nationalist movement rested on the success of this universalization. Thus the participation of women in the nationalist struggle was crucial to its success.

The transformation of the nationalist movement in the twentieth century into a mass movement required the support of diverse categories of individuals, classes, and social institutions.[3] Women, a category that was as yet undifferentiated in public consciousness, was the sole universal category which cut through social divisions and could mean all things to all persons. The use of such a universal category by male nationalists to describe the nationalist movement, as evidenced in exaggerated newspaper reports and Congress accounts of its own activities,[4] could defuse any argument that the movement in its mass agitationist phase was the preserve of any particular group. It could be argued that if one woman was participating then all women were participating. Woman was a category distinct from that of caste or class, hence she could be symbolic of the participation of a united social universe.[5]

Tied with the universalization of the movement through female participation was the importance of demonstrating that the movement was successful. A failed movement would not constitute a universal movement. Here again women were crucial. For surely, it was argued, if even sacred Indian womanhood participated, then the movement could not fail.[6]

To be universal and successful the movement needed a worthwhile protagonist. In a social movement where mobilization was all-important, lengthy treatises on imperial economic exploitation, on the manipulation of trade relations, or on the nature of the imperial state and polity were of little use. What was needed was tangible demonstration that the British masters were wicked and untrustworthy and should thus be resisted. Here again, women were crucial to the public demonstration of this aspect of imperial rule. Through putting women in the forefront of processions, giving as wide as possible coverage to their arrest, and reporting the maltreatment of women by the police, it was easy for nationalists to arouse the anger of the people against imperial rule and their sympathy for those who opposed it. Outraged Indian womanhood was the theme of numerous articles, pamphlets, and speeches.[7]

Through decades of struggle, it was important for the maintenance of unity to present the picture of a movement which was progressing towards the achievement of its objectives. In the ebb and flow of the mass agitation, it must have been difficult to maintain the appearance of constant progress, and certainly difficult to maintain the fervor of civil disobedience twenty-four hours a day, seven days a week. During this phase, as the issue of foreign cloth had long been important as the symbol of all foreign domination, so the maintenance of the cloth boycott was important as the symbol of all resistance. The importance of women to the boycott, in Bombay particularly, cannot be overemphasized. At many stages they were the only ones picketing in the cloth markets. They were far more effective than male volunteers, for what cloth merchant would keep his shop open if he felt that he would be responsible for the arrest and outraged modesty of Indian womanhood?

All of these aspects of the importance of women to the nationalist movement—its universalization, the demonstration of the repressive nature of government, and the necessity for all to support nationalist activities—required the participation of a certain kind of woman: the woman of traditional values, fears, and prejudices. The appearance of women of the female intelligentsia in leadership roles, both in times of negotiation and times of confrontation, facilitated the process of universalization.[8] It would have been very easy, however, to dismiss the participation of a few university-educated and well-traveled women as the sometime contribution of a few idiosyncratic ladies.

By the twentieth century, mediating structures between the separate world of the household and the public world of affairs had been created in Bombay. The extended space of the female world comprised such institutions as the girls' school or women's organization, and was characterized by a lesser degree of segregation than that of the household, and adherence to the concepts of middle-class social reform. The participation of women from this extended female space was essential to the process of universalization of the nationalist movement. Unlike the female intelligentsia, the women of the extended female space had simply a few years learning in a formal educational institution, or training in a less-structured women's association, and were still essentially of the separate female world. These women were still closely tied to that world which, in one sense, was all-powerful, but which in another required protection. Yet, they were familiar enough with the values of social reform and national uplift to have no hesitation at moving from the traditional household to the rough and tumble of street politics in times of national crisis.

The links which the women of this extended female space retained with the traditional power of women in the segregated household did not hinder the process of their politicization. This process was uniquely suited to their situation in an intermediate social space between the household and the public world. It rested on the mediating role of the female intelligentsia who brought the ideas of world of affairs to the extended female space, and on the genius of Gandhi who both captured the loyalty of the members of this mediating female intelligentsia and who addressed himself to women of the extended female space in terms they could understand, with a program they could implement.

Even before the advent of Gandhi, the process of politicization within the extended female space was clearly linked with nationalist ideology. When members of the Gujarati Hindu Stree Mandal celebrated Dadabhai Noroji's birthday to honor him as a promoter of female education, they also honored the father of the nation.[9] When Sarojini Naidu was present on such occasions, she talked directly of nationalism.[10]

When Gandhi first entered the arena in 1917 he addressed himself to his "educated sisters."[11] Within a short time, however, impressed by the extent of the associational networks in Bombay, and with an already shrewd assessment of the potential of women for hindering or supporting his program, he declared that educational attainments were of little relevance to national work. "It is not true that without such knowledge [of letters] one cannot take part in national work."[12] In Bombay, Gandhi addressed himself to Gujarati and Maharashtrian women, both through members of the female intelligentsia such as Avantikabai Gokhale and Jaijee Raijee, and directly through such organizations of the extended female space as the Bhagini Samaj, Gujarati Hindu Stree Mandal and Hind Mahila Samaj.[13] He preached a massage of national uplift, national strength, social reform, and the importance of women such as themselves to the task.

It was through spinning that Gandhi politicized women most readily, imbuing them with ideas of a unified nation and opposition to foreign rule, and providing them with tangible evidence of their own participation in a political process. Spinning was an activity that was eminently suited to the life of the woman within the segregated household and its extension in the ladies' associations. It could be undertaken individually or communally, by both educated and uneducated, by both rich and poor. Spinning linked women both with other sections of the nation and with anti-imperialism. The women of the extended female space could link themselves to the poor, remembering as they spun the story of Gandhi's discovery that in Bihar, in some village households, there were not enough saris to clothe all the women of the family.[14] Through an activity that brought them, if only in their imaginations, into contact with other classes and other provinces, middle-class housewives could envisage the nation as a corporate entity. The spinning and weaving of *khaddar* for clothing brought *swadeshi* right into the household. Through the issue of foreign cloth, the necessity of self-government and self-determination in economic matters became a reality for these women. Economic nationalism was an activity in which they participated.

The *swadeshi* movement was a universalizing movement *par excellence*. Not only did it take political activity into the heart of the nation's social structure, but it created the impression that each individual household might support the nationalist movement. The *swadeshi* vow to use Indian-made goods only had potential universal appeal. Such a strategy to create a universal idiom of nationalist politics centered on the household could not possibly have succeeded without the support of the *ranis* of the household who made the decisions regarding the purchase of commodities and clothing. Gandhi himself demonstrated that he was well aware of the absolute necessity of strong female support.

> The swadeshi vow cannot be kept fully if women do not help. Men alone will be able to do nothing in the matter... it is necessary that women should be fired with the spirit of swadeshi. So long as that does not happen, men will not be in a position to take the vow.[15]

While Gandhi urged women of the extended female space to spin on numerous occasions,[16] the process of linking the activities of associational women with nationalist ideology continued through the celebration of the birthdays of nationalist figures, the holding of meetings to listen to nationalist speeches, and the intertwining of religious celebration and political protest.[17] The process of politicization resulted in the acknowledgement by some associations of the extended female space that woman could in fact be a political being. In both the Gujarati Hindu Stree Mandal and the Bombay Presidency Women's Council it was decided that women could take part in political activities—in the one if the majority approved, in the other at an individual level, provided this did not interfere with the cohesion of the Council.[18]

This process also resulted in the establishment of specifically nationalist political organizations within the extended female space. A National Girls' School was established in Bombay in 1921.[19] In the same year three new associations for women were established: the All-India Ladies' Khilafat Committee which was short lived, the Shri Sarada Samaj of Dadar set up specifically for spinning, and the Rashtriya Stree Sabha which was to provide a focal point for many future nationalist activities among women.[20]

The upsurge in politicization associated with non-cooperation was not limited to ideas but was connected with new activities for women as well. First and foremost was the increase in the numbers of women following the constructive program through spinning. Various ladies' associations including the Hind Mahila Samaj, Shri Sarada Samaj, Saraswat Mahila Samaj, the Rashtriya Stree Sabha and a girls' spinning school at Pydhonie ran classes in spinning and embroidery on khaddar.[21] There were from two hundred to three hundred women involved in these group spinning activities, and no doubt more spun simply as individuals.[22] Despite exhortations to wear khaddar, there is little evidence of enthusiasm among women to do so, except among individual devotees.[23] Women also raised among themselves significant contributions to the Tilak Swaraj Fund and the Khilafat and Smyrna Funds.[24]

The fact that significant numbers of women supported non-cooperation and the constructive program no doubt facilitated public acceptance of Gandhian strategies and their viability. But these household activities by women were not the sole means of promoting the universalization of the nationalist movement. Two public events in which women of the extended female space participated had a great impact on public consciousness: A procession to oppose the visit of the Prince of Wales to Bombay in November, 1921 featured the participation of up to one thousand women. The procession received extensive publicity and was described as "unique."[25] The press also gave wide coverage to the participation of women in the public burning of foreign cloth in the mill areas at night.[26] These events helped further to underwrite the legitimacy of the nationalist struggle. While the men of various factions argued among themselves, the women remained aloof from such politicking and worked for an idealized notion of *swaraj* and national unity.

The nationalists maintained, and the associational women concurred, that the women of India should develop themselves in order better to contribute to the progress of the nation.[27] Sarojini Naidu had been one of the first persons to link the fate of women with the fate of the nation.

> It is well for us to remember that the success of the whole movement lies centred in what is known as the woman question. It is not you but we who are the true nation-builders.[28]

This identification of the regeneration of women with that of the nation rested on two complementary sources: the orientalist notion of the former golden age of Hindu polity, and the qualities of beneficence and self-abnegation of ancient heroines. The resurrection of the spirit of the past was to be joined with the ideology of self-sacrifice personified in the traditional Hindu wife. A wide range of nationalist leaders including Gandhi played up the theme of the revival of the spirit of sacrifice in devotion to their *dharma* by ideal women such as Sita, Draupadi, Damayanti, Savitri and Rajput *satis*.[29] This ideal woman was to devote herself to encouraging her brother, husband, and sons to support the rebuilding of the nation, and was to be prepared to sacrifice herself for that ideal. The new woman was asked to develop her social awareness not for self-knowledge, but to extend the ideal of sacrifice from encompassing only husband and family to include the nation. She was encouraged in this by both male and female nationalists, and Bombay women of the extended female space readily concurred with this ideal.

> I want to sacrifice myself in it (this Nation-building idea) like a moth in the lamp flame, with a song of hope on my

lips...as the funeral pyre was a step upward towards the perfection of a widow's soul in old times—so is this nation-building idea to a modern Indian woman.[30]

From the time of noncooperation until the resurgence of the nationalist movement in civil disobedience, the women of the extended female space remained faithful to the nationalist ideal but politically inactive. Nevertheless, girls' education expanded rapidly after the 1920s and women's associations continued to operate.[31] Within the extended female space this provided continually expanding numbers open to ideas of social reform and nationalist consciousness. A few women had perhaps continued to wear *khaddar*, and organized spinning activities had continued intermittently. The civil disobedience movement of the early 1930s, however, marked a radical change in the nature of participation by extended space women.

The civil disobedience period from March, 1930 until May, 1934 firmly stamped the nationalist movement in the mold of mass politics. The civil disobedience movement encompassed diverse sections of the population in presidency cities and *mofussil* towns, from rich merchants to poor peasants.[32] They supported the movement for differing reasons and made sectional demands in the course of the movement, yet overall they were moved by a nationalist sentiment which contained certain common elements, and for such diverse social groups, a surprising degree of coherence. The emphasis placed on female participation helped to preserve the cohesion of the nationalist struggle.

The main body of female participants in civil disobedience activities were not from the intelligentsia. English education or articulate ideas were not a prerequisite for participation. Most of the women came from the extended female space. We have no exact figures of the numbers of these women, although we can estimate that in Bombay city there were a few hundred women volunteers altogether.[33] Allowing for students and members of the female intelligentsia, probably over half of this number were women of the extended female space. Of those jailed, there were somewhat over one hundred in the first phase and about two hundred in the 1932-34 period.[34] Again we can estimate that over half were from the extended female space.

These figures do not account for the large numbers of women who marched in the occasional procession, attended the large public meetings, engaged in spinning activities at home or at their ladies' association, wore *khaddar* ocassionally, or fasted on days of national importance.

The women of many of the ladies' associations of the extended female space gave direct support to civil disobedience. Half the ordinary members of the Bhagini Samaj and most of its prominent members joined the civil disobedience movement.[35] Many of the women of the Gujarati Hindu Stree Mandal supported the movement as did ladies from the Women's Indian Association, Saraswat Mahila Samaj and Hind Mahila Samaj.[36] These were largely married women but also included widows. These women came largely from comfortable circumstances in either professional or business families. The predominant group was connected with business at many levels ranging from the wives of clerks to those of rich *shetias*. They were from a number of different communities, Muslim, Maharashtrian, Marwari, but the major groups were Gujarati. What distinguished these women from their compatriots was their level of education. In comparison with other women of their communities, these women had a higher degree of formal education, albeit simply to sixth standard in the vernacular.[37]

These women of the extended female space did not hesitate to accept leadership positions in the course of civil disobedience. Initially, such positions were taken by women of the intelligentsia who continued to predominate. Women of the extended female space, however, also became members of the War Council and addressed large public meetings, as well as serving as Congress volunteers or *desh sevikas*, and participating in the illegal manufacture of salt, in salt raids, and most importantly, in the picketing of foreign cloth shops.[38] The leaders and activists were backed by a wide-ranging support system of women who were involved in the constructive program and strongly backed the idea of *swadeshi*.

The objectives of the *swadeshi* program as a universalizing and unifying force, emanating quietly from the household, were not lost sight of in the dash and drama of civil disobedience. It was the associations of the extended female space which sustained and developed this program among the less venturesome but nonetheless staunchly nationalist women of the city, while the male and female politicians concentrated their attention on bolder activities. "Let each *chawl* be a Sangh, let each street be a Sabha"[39] declared the ladies of the Desh Sevika Sangh who, supported by the ladies of the Gujarati Hindu Stree Mandal, Saraswat Mahila Samaj, and Women's Indian Association went about forming residents' committees to promote *swadeshi* and spinning.[40] At least twenty-two classes to teach spinning were established in the city during this period catering to four to five hundred women.[41] This support from the heart of Indian society plus the dramatized public activities of women were crucial to the success of civil disobedience.

Salt was the issue around which Gandhi focused both the anti-imperialist struggle and the pragmatics of organizing supporters for this struggle. It was also the issue which confirmed the importance of extended space women to the universalization of the movement. Gandhi launched the salt *satyagraha* in March and then extended it to a mass campaign at the beginning of April, 1930. At this point, he wanted to arouse widespread popular indignation against the British and to recruit as many volunteers for future civil disobedience activities as possible. The support of women at this juncture, if widely demonstrated, would indicate the viability of a civil disobedience campaign and facilitate the recruitment of volunteers. Both the Congress socialists and Gandhi were well aware of the usefulness of female participation.[42] During this period, the role of peasant women in the earlier Bardoli struggle, the participation of women in civil disobedience in Gujarat, Gandhi's instructions to the female intelligentsia to organize other women, and the spontaneous activities of women in breaking the salt laws on the beach at Chowpatty all received publicity.[43] Female participation in the nationalist struggle was given front-page priority in the sympathetic press, and this coverage and accompanying photographs were clearly calculated to present the nascent movement as being as widespread as possible.

The press emphasized the fact that Bombay women spontaneously and without hesitation broke the salt law by manufacturing illegal salt from salt water in pans brought from their homes:

They celebrated...the occasion like a marriage festival. Filling their pots with sea water, they returned to their homes to manufacture salt.[44]

This made front-page news three weeks in a row. The nationalist press may have publicized the spontaneity of women, but their salt-centered activities were carefully organized. The first women to break the salt laws were Congress leaders who ceremoniously lighted *segrees* on the sands. They were followed by Congress volunteers, among whom were women who carefully carried salt water to the pans at Congress House.[45] Nevertheless, the 'spontaneity' of ordinary women captured the public imagination, and this created an overwhelming impression of female support and participation. It mattered little that the majority of participants in this and subsequent activities were predominantly Gujarati and almost without exception middle-class; they reached the Congress and public consciousness simply as women. This fact, in turn, helped foster the image of a universal social movement.

By the end of April, 1930 enthusiasm for civil disobedience was waning, but following Gandhi's arrest in May the movement intensified.[46] Again, the press noted the activities of women as proof that the movement was a continuing success with firm public support.[47] In the first half of May, women participated in salt raids, commenced picketing, and became involved in massive public meetings and processions. While the salt raids featured such members of the female intelligentsia as Sarojini Naidu and Lilavati Munshi as much-photographed front-page news, the women of the extended female space joined the Desh Sevika Sangh, the volunteer body of the Rashtriya Stree Sabha which underwrote the picketing of cloth shops and the propaganda processions. At the height of the movement, 250 women picketed, either by sitting inside the shops or else by standing outside to dissuade purchasers.[48] At the same time, ladies from a wide range of organizations within the extended female space marched in a procession of about a thousand to support the *swadeshi* campaign declaring:

It has fallen to the lot of men to do more difficult and strenuous work; and it behooves Indian women that they too should contribute their share in this National Struggle for Freedom.[49]

During July, organizational and political imperatives forced the Congress to court the working class population of the city more vigorously. The *swadeshi* program in the mill areas aimed at regenerating and recruiting workers through the anti-liquor campaign. Again, middle class women of the extended female space were called upon to demonstrate the efficacy of civil disobedience. In July also women picketed the auction of toddy shop licences so effectively that the auctions were postponed.[50]

Women again played a prominent role in reviving the campaign the following month, when the majority of the Congress Working Committee, who wanted peace, had been defeated by Vallabhbhai Patel, who was determined to continue the campaign. The Congress required a dramatic act to retain public support. Up until this time, most of those pursuing civil disobedience had not ventured into the Fort, the heart of British Bombay, the city's prime business and shopping area. One evening at the beginning of August, however, a procession of volunteers including forty-five women gathered together to celebrate Tilak Day. Led by Pandit Malaviya and Hansa Mehta, they contravened police orders and marched into the Fort, where they squatted on the road all night and were arrested in the morning. This event, when women stayed out all night with men in defiance of the Raj has stuck in the minds of many who remember the civil disobedience days.[51]

By October of 1930, public enthusiasm for civil disobedience had once again waned, and the Congress was valiantly attempting "to make every house a Congress house." Women who had remained staunchly behind the Congress once again came to the fore, more and more taking prominent roles. At a meeting at the renamed Azad Maidan, Mrs. Kamlabai Prabhu declared that if even all men were removed from the fighting line by the police, Indian women would continue to fight and win India's freedom.[52] During the ensuing period, a succession of women members of the War Council offered themselves for arrest in the city and suburbs, and made front-page news.[53] While these women were from the intelligentsia, their sisters who took over from the male volunteers the job of picketing foreign cloth shops, going so far as to stage hunger strikes in front of the shops, were largely from the extended female space.[54]

The Bhandup incident, when the police took a number of those women volunteers in a van and dropped them outside the city limits as an alternative to arrest, excited public opinion through tales of defenseless women "dropped in the jungle" by the agents of an oppressive foreign power.[55] This and subsequent reports of outrages upon the honor of Indian women were used to demonstrate the insult which British domination signified for India at its deepest psychological level. At public meetings, women themselves called for the defense of their honor and the defense of all that was Indian through support of the civil disobedience movement.[56] Women were willing to act as volunteers when others were less enthusiastic, offer themselves for arrest, and provide a symbol of all-Indian resistance. These themes were reiterated until civil disobedience itself was suspended, and were continued in a more muted fashion in the second phase of civil disobedience, earning for women the congratulations of the Mahatma—the architect of their participation.

Independence was still many years off when civil disobedience was withdrawn in 1934. The nationalist movement underwent many transformations thereafter, drawing in still other sections of the population. The universalization of the nationalist movement created the illusion that, since the whole society had participated in the struggle for freedom, then *ipso facto* all its members participated equally in the new nation. Universalization helped to obscure gross hierarchy, inequality, and even for some time, political differences.

On the basis of their mediating role in a segregated society, the women of the intelligentsia were able to negotiate participatory rights in the emergent state structure.[58] As a result of the 1935 constitutional provisions which conferred the right to vote on those women who were literate or married to men of property, the Bombay women of the extended female space were also able to participate in the political process.[59] However, the notion that all women would in time participate did not alter India society's concept of women. The universalization of female participation, and thus of the nationalist movement as a whole, had been based on the image of the sanctified participation of the sacrificing woman associated with traditional values. The political role offered to women in the nationalist movement and the new state did not contradict those values. "Free India means free womanhood," the women of Bombay had chanted in a nationalist procession.[60] The women of the extended female space were free—free to continue the round of meetings and lectures in ladies' associations, free to promote female education, free to advocate limited social reform within marriage, and free to vote in the occasional election. Women had been of utmost importance to the nationalist struggle and the emergent state. Those on whom this universalization had been based, the women of the extended female space, gained little from this process. Other women—factory workers, itinerant peddlers, farm laborers, subsumed by the term "traditional womanhood," gained less.

NOTES

[1] See for instance Manmohan Kaur, *Role of Women in the Freedom Movement, 1857-1947* (Delhi: Sterling, 1968).

[2] One searches in vain for an analysis of the female contribution in recent additions to nationalist historiography, for example: C.J. Baker, *The Politics of South India, 1920-1937* (New Delhi: Vikas, 1976); B. .R Tomlinson, *The Indian National Congress and the Raj, 1929-1942* (London: Macmillan, 1976); D.A. Low, ed., *The Congress and the Raj* (London: Heineman, 1977); G. Pandey, *The Ascendancy of the Congress Pradesh, 1926-1934* (Delhi: Oxford University Press, 1978).

[3] Pandey refers to the "Congress's 'umbrella' approach to all and sundry." Pandey, *Ascendancy of the Congress*, p. 106.

[4] Syed Mahmud, Jairamdas Doulatram, Jawaharlal Nehru, "Report of the Congress Activities, 1930," October, 1931. AICC Papers, File G2, 1931, NMML. There are significant differences in numbers of participants consistently reported in the *Bombay Chronicle* and in the daily letter of the Police Commissioner, Bombay.

[5] That this concept of undifferentiated woman was essentially an upper caste concept attests to the ideological dominance of those groups.

[6] CID Police to Govt., 750/H/3717, February 5, 1931, Bombay Police Commissioner's Office [BPCO].

[7] For example, "If you want to save your sisters from being trampled under the hoofs of horses or save their skulls from being cracked

by lathi take oath from today not to use British goods," from a handbill. Purshotamdas Thakurdas Papers, File 101, 1930, NMML.

[8]On the female intelligentsia and the creation of the extended female space, see G.O. Pearson, "The Female Intelligentsia in a Segregated Society—Bombay, A Case Study," in M. Allen and S.N. Mukherjee, eds, *Women of India and Nepal* (Canberra: Australian National University Monographs on South Asia, forthcoming), pp. 135-153.

[9]*The Gujarati Hindu Stree Mandal, Bombay—A Short Account* (Bombay: K.B. Maniar, 1936), p. 22; *Gujarati Hindu Stree Mandal, 1915-1917* (Bombay: 1917), p. 11, Office of GHSM, Bombay.

[10]*Gujarati Hindu Stree Mandal, 1915-1917*, p. 11.

[11]Gandhi's Message to Gujarati Hindu Stri Mandal on or before November 14, 1917 (tr. from Gujarati), *Gijarati*, December 2, 1917, in *Collected Works of Mahatma Gandhi* [CWMG], XIV, p. 86.

[12]Speech at Women's Meeting, Bombay, May 8, 1919 (tr. from Gujarati), *Kheda Vartaman*, May 21, 1919, *CWMG*, XV, p. 291.

[13]*Gujarati Hindu Stree Mandal, 1913-1915* (Bombay: 1915), pp. 13, 17; Gandhi, "Message of Gokhale's Life," dated before February 4, 1917, original published in *Bhagini Samaj Patrika*, *CWMG*, XIII, p. 202; *Hind Mahila Samaj: 50th Anniversary Souvenir, 1918-1968* (Bombay: 1968); *Hind Mahila Samaj: 50th Anniversary Report, 1918-1968* (Bombay: 1968), Office of HMS, Bombay.

[14]Interview with Mrinalini Desai, April 12, 1976.

[15]Speech at Women's Meeting, Bombay, May 8, 1919, *CWMG*, XV, p. 291.

[16]For example, ". . . take the first lesson in the school of industry, namely spin cotton and weave." Gandhi's message to Gujarati Hindu Stri Mandal, November, 1917, *CWMG*, XIV, p. 87.

[17]For example, *Bombay Chronicle* [BC], November 17, 1921; January 6, 1922; September 1, 1923.

[18]*Gujarati Hindu Stree Mandal, 1921-1923* (Bombay: 1923), p. 1; Letter to Mrs. Houston, March 23, 1919, in Minutes Book of the Management Committee of the Bombay Presidency Women's Council, December 11, 1918—February 20, 1923, Office of Maharashtra State Women's Council, Central Library, Bombay.

[19]"History of the Non-Cooperation Movement in the City of Bombay," CID File 274/A, p. 13, BPCO; Secret Abstract of Intelligence, Bombay [SA] 1921, para. 548 (13), CID DIG Intelligence Office, Bombay [CDIO].

[20]*BC*, August 24, 1921; SA 1921, para. 461 (29); SA 1921, para 337 (26), CDIO.

[21]SA 1921, para. 523 (38); SA 1921, para 461 (29), CDIO; *Hind Mahila Samaj 50th Anniversary Report, 1918-1968*; "Fifty Years Tale of Growth," *Saraswat Mahila Samaj Annual Report* (Bombay: 1967), App. D, pp. 411-417.

[22]Estimated from membership of associations and occasional figures given of numbers spinning, e.g.: 100 at Pydhonie School, SA 1921, para. 603 (6) CDIO.

[23] SA 1922, para. 493 (11). CDIO.

[24] SA 1921, para. 548 (13); SA 1912, para, 548 (16), CDIO.

[25] SA 1921, para. 1275 (5), CDIO; *BC*, November 17, 1921.

[26] *BC*, November 18, 1921.

[27] *Gujarati Hindu Stree Mandal, 1915-1917*, p. 11; Gandhi, Speech at Women's Meeting, Bombay, May 8, 1919, *CWMG*, XV, p. 290.

[28] Lecture delivered at the Indian Social Conference, Calcutta, December, 1906, in Sarojini Naidu, *Speeches and Writings* (3rd edn. Madras: Natesan, 1925), p. 10.

[29] Speech at Bhagini Samaj, February 20, 1918, *CWMG*, XIV, p. 204; cf. Tilak addressing the Hind Mahila Samaj, *BC*, March 22, 1920.

[30] *BC*, January 20, 1922.

[31] Between 1920-21 and 1937-38, the number of girls under instruction in the Bombay Presidency increased by almost 100%, from 189, 814 to 347, 849. *Report on Public Instruction in the Bombay Presidency, 1937-38*, pp. 23, 103.

[32] For instance, Baker, *The Politics of South India*, pp. 211f; and Pandey, *The Ascendancy of the Congress*, pp. 95f; 156f.

[33] "Hindustan Seva Dal Report for 1930," in CID 18/INC/31 (11), 30, CDIO: *The Rashtriya Stree Sabha's Report of the Desh Sevika Sangh 1931-1931* (Bombay: 1931), p. 5. I am indebted to Miss Narju Dastur of Bombay for this report.

[34] CID Police to Govt., 4377/H/3717, September 9, 1931, BPCO; Home Special, 750 (22) 3, Maharashtra State Archives [MSA]. 1932-34 figures compiled from daily letter of the Police Commissioner, Bombay.

[35] *The Servants of India Society, Poona Report of Work, 12th June 1930 to 12th June 1931* (Poona: 1931), p. 13. SIS Office, Bombay.

[36] *Gujarati Hindu Stree Mandal, 1929-1931* (Bombay: 1931), pp. 13-14, GHSM office, Bombay; *Women's Indian Association Report, 1931-1932* (Madras: 1932), pp. 4,19, AIWC Library, Delhi.

[37] G.O. Pearson, "Women in Public Life in Bombay City with Special Reference to the Civil Disobedience Movement," (PhD. Thesis, Jawaharlal Nehru University, 1979), pp. 292-294, 296.

[38] Home Special, 750 (22)-B, MSA; *The Rashtriya Stree Sabha's Report of the Desh Sevika Sangh 1930-1931*, App. E.

[39] *BC*, October 15, 1930.

[40] *Gujarati Hindu Stree Mandal, 1929-1931*, pp. 13-14; *BC*, April 5, 1930; *Women's Indian Association Report, 1930-1931* (Madras: 1931), p. 4, AIWC Library, Delhi.

[41] *The Rashtriya Stree Sabha's Report of the Desh Sevika Sangh, 1930-1931*, App. B, pp. 24, 26.

[42] *BC*, March 24-25, 1930; Fortnightly Report, [FR], 2nd half of March, April 18, 1930, NAI.

[43] *BC*, March 13 and 24, April 8-12, 14-19, 21-22, 1930.

[44] *BC*, April 14, 1930.

[45] *BC*, April 12, 14, and 21, 1930.

[46] *FR*, 2nd half of April, May 18, 1930; FR, 1st half of May, June 18, 1930, NAI.

[47]*BC*, May 17 and 23, June 3, 1930.
[48]CID, 2123/H/3717, May 12, 1930, BPCO.
[49]*BC*, May 14, 1930.
[50]FR, 1st half of July, August 18, 1930, NAI; *BC*, July 22, 1930; CID Police to Govt., 3663/H/3717, July 21, 1930, BPCO.
[51]FR, 2nd half of July, August 18, 1930, NAI; *BC*, August 8, 1930; CID Police to Govt., 3884/H/3717, August 2, 1930, BPCO.
[52]*BC*, October 17, 1930.
[53]*BC*, October 22, 24-55, November 18, 22, and 27, 1930.
[54]*BC*, October 14, 1930; For a list of Desh Sevikas arrested while picketing, see *The Rashtriya Stree Sabha's Report of the Desh Sevika Sangh, 1930-1931*, App. E.
[55]*BC*, October 27, 1930. This tactic was also used in other provinces.
[56]*BC*, November 4, 1930,
[57]*BC*, March 12, 1931.
[58]G.O. Pearson, "The Female Intelligentsia in a Segregated Society, (forthcoming), pp. 143f.
[59]For the voting provisions see Government of Great Britain, *Joint Committee on Indian Constitutional Reform, Session 1933-1934, Report*, I (Pt. 1), p. 75.
[60]*BC*, October 4, 1930.

PART III

WOMEN'S RIGHTS AND POLITICAL PARTICIPATION IN CONTEMPORARY INDIA AND PAKISTAN

8

The Indian Women's Movement and National Development: An Overview

SHAHIDA LATEEF

Introduction

In developing countries, movements for the emancipation of women from the confines of their traditional roles have been the result of revolutionary political changes rather than evolutionary social changes. Such changes are frequently ahead of the absorptive capacity of their social structures. The presence of western colonial powers in these countries accelerated the pace of political, social, and economic development. Of these the political system was most readily adopted by leaders motivated by the necessity of organizing themselves to deal with the colonial power. The need for this political organization was, in part, due to nationalism but primarily due to increasing economic pressures, as traditional occupations and crafts were disrupted by colonial restructuring of the economy. Social structures reacted to these economic and political changes, and the leadership came under pressure to model social changes on ideology current in the west and evolved for western needs. Since social structures had remained stultified as a result of political upheavals over long periods in such societies, reform movements quickly developed to remedy some of the more obvious disabilities of society in general and women in particular. The tendency was to force the pace of social change through legislation. In India, these efforts on behalf of women were concentrated primarily in urban areas, and espoused by westernized sections of society. They overlooked the economic and social disabilities of vast numbers of women who lived in the rural and more traditional sections of urban areas.

Most nationalist movements have been important vehicles for social reform and modification in women's status and roles. Women were considered important to the national effort, since they could carry forward the aims of the national movement and help in the implemention of its ideology. This broad coalition subsumed, for a time, regional and other differences, and resulted in successful independence movements and in favorable legislation for women in many developing countries. It provided the infrastructure of rights for women and created an awareness of their importance and necessary involvement in modern political and economic structures. It was left to later women leaders to deal with the problems created by political and economic restructuring and to evolve a new ideology to meet the post-independence requirements of their constituents.[1]

The process of adjusting to new requirements and evolving an ideology to meet this need has made the present Indian women's movement unrecognizable in western terms. It has neither the ideology, organization nor tactics of a pressure group which characterize the movement in the United States. While this means that women's issues are considered marginal in economic and political decision-making, this is a necessary phase through which the movement has to pass, in order to shed its earlier western orientation and address itself to issues which are specific to Indian political, economic, and social realities. However, this new direction in the Indian women's movement has only been possible because of the success of the earlier western-inspired movement, since it provided the infrastructure which enabled the present leadership to respond to the current needs of Indian women. These needs stem from political, economic, and social changes which have been underway over the century, but particularly since independence, when economic development became a national priority.

Development in India is a planned attempt at political

and economic changes considered necessary to extend the benefits of economic growth to all sections of society. Structural economic change brought about in this way has indeed altered the income base in urban and rural areas. But while development has shifted the traditional balance, its effects have not always favored the poor or women, neither of whom have been able to take advantage of change. Both groups have, as a result, lost ground. Development has not resulted in redistribution, since entrenched political interests and social structures have continued to work against it. The development process, therefore, has not been able to benefit women or the poorest sections of Indian society as intended.

Recent social science literature reflects the re-evaluation taking place both of the effects of development and its impact on the status and role of women.[2] This is necessary, since it is questionable whether either economic development or legislative changes act as equalizers, when customs and practices sanctified by religion are deeply embedded in traditional societies. In such societies 'equality' itself is contextually difficult to define, since an untouchable woman's equality with her male counterpart hardly constitutes equality with men as generally understood in the West. The indices to be used for measuring the status of Indian women, therefore, have to take into account the existence of 'accepted inequalities' between castes, religions, regions, and classes. This makes it analytically necessary to differentiate between ascribed and achieved status. While status refers to the degree to which individuals have authority or power in the public or private domains,[3] ascribed status refers to attributes an individual possesses as a factor of birth, i.e., community, religion, and language.[4] Citizenship conferred at birth may also imply certain economic and political rights legislatively gained. Achieved status refers to individual achievements in terms of educational, political, and economic attainments. Within this framework, control over decisions that effect one's life, particularly in the social and economic domains would enhance status.

This paper examines the Indian women's movement in the context of economic development and social and political change in India. The period before independence will be reviewed, highlighting those factors which have had an enduring effect on the women's movement. The review puts the contemporary women's movement in perspective, since it has a bearing on its direction and content.

Evaluating the Transition

The women's movement in India had had three distinct phases. The first, in the nineteenth century, was directed at improving women's status and increasing their role beyond the purely domestic. This was an effort initiated and directed primarily by men. The second phase constituted the women's take-over of the first movement. The involvement of western women and of men in the earlier phase meant that the direction of the movement and the collaborative effort with men had already been established, and the new Indian women leaders were able to use the national movement, which sought their cooperation, to wring concessions and promises of support for legislative changes in their favor. The success of this phase culminated in the equality of citizenship granted by the constitution, which was followed by legislative equality with men in all social matters. Once the drive towards legislation which had sustained the momentum of the movement subsided, however, this phase of the women's movement waned. What should have been a period of consolidation of rights legislatively gained saw instead the movement lapse into complacency and become institutionalized. This was in fact due to the elite orientation of the movement, which had not taken into consideration the expectations and requirements of women at other economic and social levels.

Over the last decade, however, there have been definite signs of the realization that there can be no broad alliance of Indian women without the involvement of women from all economic and social strata and that such an involvement can only come about if their problems are addressed, not at the abstract level of legislative or constitutional equality, but directly at the economic and social levels. This can only be achieved if the movement addresses itself directly to all women by becoming a horizontal movement rather than the vertical movement from upper to lower that it had been previously. This then is the third phase of the movement: An acknowledgement that many issues such as seclusion, education, and legislative rights were meaningless to the large majority of women since their primary concerns were at a more basic level. These women were unable, within the parameters of their disabilities, to take advantage of legislative rights for women. There has been an instinctive realization on the part of new women leaders that the Indian women's movement cannot advance, and women become a pressure group, without the involvement of women at all economic and social levels. Since the major concerns of women from rural and most sections of urban life are economic, the new direction is to provide women with support organizations which can represent them in their struggle for improved employment conditions, child care, and credit.

The emergence of a women's movement in India was the result of the interaction between traditional Indian society and the British colonial power. In the nineteenth century, as the British moved to consolidate their power, the ability of Indian leaders to control economic and political change became increasingly difficult. This led them to turn their attention to social change, as necessary to overcome the natural divisions within Indian society, to counteract the effects if not the fact of foreign occupation. It became a perception of the time that structural social change would strengthen and consolidate Indian society, without which no real resistance to political and economic domination would be effective. These efforts at social change focused as much on women as they did on the iniquitous caste divisions in Indian society. The glaring disabilities of Indian women of the time included sati or widow immolation, infant marriages, and lack of widow remarriage or inheritance rights. This subjugation was enforced by confining women to specific domestic roles. Their options were limited by early marriage, seclusion, and lack of education. While this pattern was not always consistently followed—custom and tradition differed from region to region—the attitude that women and their honor were the bases of family honor was more or less universal. Even in those regions which were and continue to be matriarchal, the power and authority exercized by women was tempered by social attitudes toward modesty which precluded their participation in the public domain.

The status of an Indian woman had traditionally been adjudged indirectly, through the status of her maternal family and when she married, through the status of her husband's family. The family's status was derived from their caste or occupational ranking and monetary standing. A woman's status within the family was a reflection of her husband's position in the family hierarchy and of her own rise through defined avenues such as child bearing and maturity to a position of influence within the family.[5] The cultural value assigned to women's roles and status were significantly below those of men. The socialization process of women emphasized the supportive aspects of their role, any improvement in their position was related to their child-bearing capabilities and their increasing seniority.

The movement for the emancipation of women from their traditional cycle of infant marriage and its inevitable sequence was the result of the catalytic presence of European powers in India, which was directly related to changing political and economic structures in the nineteenth century. Indian social reformers, provoked by the collapse of traditional Indian society and by the strictures of foreign missionaries on their social habits and values, particularly as they related to women, sought to relieve women of the burden of widowhood and economic dependence through education and widening roles outside the family.

The first phase, therefore, was to remove women's vulnerability to *sati*, infant marriage, and widowhood, and to create the climate in which they could participate in certain public spheres. This movement, led primarily by male social reformers, was aimed at providing women with options, based on the needs of certain urban castes and classes to whom many of the restrictions applied. Women of other castes, classes, and in rural areas were of necessity less protected and therefore less constrained, even though normative codes of behavior remained similar to those of the protected upper-caste women.

By the end of the nineteenth century, in urban areas, women liberated by the earlier movement were able to organize into groups to represent their point of view before government and the public. Working within existing limitations, these groups sought to improve the status of women within the family by urging support for raising the age of marriage, for women's education, and widow remarriage. This movement provided a platform for women leaders and a number of women rose to prominence. These women were inevitably members of families already involved or influenced by the reform movement and the burgeoning national movement. This strengthened the ability of women's groups to obtain the support they needed. The second phase was, therefore, able to consolidate the gains already made.

By organizing their efforts, women were able to orchestrate their demands effectively, making them by degrees the minimum acceptable. They were also able to take advantage of certain 'protected' careers which became available as the movement gained ground. These included medicine and teaching, which due to the practice of seclusion, were services only women could provide for other women. As the base of the women's movement widened, a national conference on women's education was organized. This led to the setting up of an all-India women's organization, the All-India Women's Conference in 1927. This organization was expected to coordinate the efforts of all women's groups and to formulate policy on women's issues. While this organization remained apolitical and dedicated to furthering specific interests, it supported and had the support of many leaders of the national movement. Many of its members were members of political parties and used this connection to gain the support of different political parties for their cause.[6]

The rhetoric of women leaders and their demands were in marked contrast to their own life experiences and to the expectation of the majority of Indian women whose lives remained untouched by these efforts. At best, the movement remained confined to a small group of women who had the support and encouragement of their families to participate in the movement and attend meetings all over the country. It is safe to assume that the women so involved were members of families already economically and socially established. This was unlike the national movement which attracted all categories of persons. This orientation of the women's movement was reflected in the issues with which the women concerned themselves, concentrating on the problems of urban middle-class women, since the emphasis was on legislative rights, rather than on economic opportunities and regulations for wage-earning women. The preoccupation with legislative rights and lack of emphasis on economic rights was a reflection of the times, when marriage was considered universal; there was little need, therefore, for special attention to women's employment. The result was that while women acquired certain basic legal rights, it took them longer to exercise them and to establish their requirements beyond those rights, and in many ways these requirements still need to be fully understood and accepted.

The emphasis before independence, therefore, was on providing Indian women with better economic and social options, but within the framework of the family and its economic situation, not as independent individuals. The position of women, it was felt, could be safeguarded and improved through inheritance and remarriage rights and by increasing their roles beyond those of wife and mother. This emphasis primarily benefitted urban women. In rural areas, women were already involved in working outside the home and played an important part in production, although women's labor was associated with lower caste and economic status. The ideal remained the protection and seclusion of women as practiced by upper castes and the rich. There was consequently no pride in, or open acknowledgement of, women's economic participation. This detracted attention from women who were producers and heads of their own households, and meant that they received no government aid for their specific requirements. The lack of acknowledgement of female economic participation also meant that their labor remained under-enumerated and unrecognized as vital to agricultural production. This lack of acknowledgement and under-enumeration in an era of planned development meant that no specific efforts were made to train or help women to utilize the new economic opportunities being made available.

It took time for the third phase of the movement to crystallize and for the next generation of women leaders to emerge, better trained and attuned to the problems confronting women. They are better able to identify factors which were and are arresting the progress of women at lower socio-economic levels and are evolving a broad alliance of women at all levels to give the dormant movement new direction and dynamism. This new movement in some ways resembles the 'social work' element of the second phase, but unlike that phase, in which there was only a vertical movement of ideas and efforts, now there is a greater horizontal movement, permitting a free flow of ideas and effort between women leaders and their constituents.

Three examples of this horizontal movement illustrate the problems women face, the willingness and capacity of emerging women leaders to find solutions to them, and the susceptibility of Indian political and economic structures to manipulation for women's advantage. These experiments prove that social and governmental indifference to women's specific economic and social problems can be overcome by sensitive women leaders even when this leadership remains above their constituents in caste and class position. Coordinating their efforts to overcome problems, however, requires an exchange of ideas and mutual assistance illustrated by the horizontal movement in the three experiments discussed.

In Delhi, an organization called the Mobile Crêches has directed its efforts toward improving the condition of female construction workers and their children. While the impetus for the organization was provided by the new breed of women leaders, its structure and the ideology evolved as a result of the interaction between the female construction laborers and the women leaders. An unsentimental appeal was made to the management of large construction firms to provide funds for the project so that the productivity of their workers could be improved. The expansion and success of the Crêches, now operative in a number of states, is a testimony to the responsiveness of business firms when women's problems are related to general economic concerns.

In Ahmedabad, the Self-Employed Women's Assocation was the result of a survey done by women leaders to ascertain the problems and requirements of women laborers. It subsequently developed into a cooperative of women laborers which operates its own bank and provides other services for its members. This cooperative, based on the specific requirements of women laborers, developed through the involvement of women leaders and women laborers to the point where women laborers are assuming managerial positions in the organization. The cooperative has had many beneficial social and economic effects. On the economic side, it demonstrated that nationalized banks can be used effectively to promote women's interests, and that a cooperative can strengthen the credit rating and the bargaining power of its members with other institutions. On the social side, members have gained status within their families and the community due to the economic benefits resulting from their membership, and the support of the organization in times of family or community trouble.

In rural Maharashtra the Bazm-e-Niswan has been active in education and training. Women leaders have sought to involve women in the rural areas in providing services needed by the community. The organization provides an outlet for rural women to participate in group activities and serves as a basis for the development of future women leaders. The Bazm-e-Niswan, working in consonance with women in the area and the local community, has produced trilingual textbooks and modern teaching methods for children, and work and training centers for women.

All three experiments indicate ways in which women leaders working with their constituents can use development activity to advantage. Their success, however, demonstrates that specific well-directed efforts are required before the existing economic structure can be so used, and that without such an effort women will not be automatically benefitted. The success of these three organizations also indicates the readiness of women at lower socio-economic levels to participate and cooperate with women from different social strata in activities which benefit them economically either directly or indirectly. It is important to realize, however, that their participation and cooperation are based on specific social or economic problems, and the success of the new women leaders and organizations lies in their ability to alleviate these problems. This could lead to greater consolidation and unity within women's organizations and to a greater commitment to feminist ideology and goals, which is the purpose of women's movements. In underdeveloped countries, however, where basic survival is the main concern, women's organizations have had to subjugate feminist goals to economic ones. That such organizations can create a sense of unity and strength among women members in a survival economy is important, especially if they can also provide an organizational means of survival.

The goals of economic survival and an effective women's movement are strongly linked. It appears from the three examples discussed here that there is growing understanding of this fact among Indian women. It remains, however, to be incorporated into the ideology of the women's movement in order to be fully effective.

The Side Effects of Development

The infrastructure for aiding women and economically depressed classes exists at many different levels in both rural and urban India. Those who are well-organized or represented, however, are best able to take advantage of the system. In the case of both these disadvantaged sections of the population certain social attitudes prevail which prevent them from improving their economic status. For example, in case of women, the view persists that they do not require special consideration since men in the family or community are being helped, and conversely women take jobs away from men, who have families to support. Similar patterns of prejudice and traditional beliefs operate at all levels.[7] The agencies for women aided by government, including the All-India Women's Conference, work within the traditional framework of limited participation, which has made them increasingly ineffective. The lack of articulation of a formal Indian feminist ideology has meant that there has been no challenge to that tradition. Challenge, if any, has come from a government-appointed committee to collect data on women in all spheres, and that too in connection with the International Women's Year of the United Nations. The Committee on the Status of Women in India presented a comprehensive report on women, reexamined all available data, and for the first time viewed the problem in its entirety. The report revealed that previously unrelated statistics were, in fact, inexorable trends. This has had immense impact, since it questioned the complacency of government and women's organizations and their dependence on legislative attempts to improve the status of women. It also provided the evidence, formerly lacking in India, of the adverse effects of development on women, particularly in the rural and unorganized sectors of the economy. Improvements particularly in the urban areas and in the organized sectors appear marginal and cosmetic, while women's overall situation has worsened over the last sixty years in relative and absolute terms demographically, economically, and politically.

The persistence of certain social factors, supported both ideologically and organizationally, can be considered instrumental in women's demographic, political, and economic setbacks. Despite regional and religious differences in Indian society, overriding customs and traditions are followed by most communities and undermine the legislative or other gains which women may make. The continuation of customs and traditions which perpetuate certain attitudes towards women is reinforced by the desire of different communities to maintain their identity, in reaction to wide-ranging changes in other spheres. Women have therefore been subject to contradictory signals from their communities. While education and even employment are encouraged in the urban areas, other social changes, such as self-determination in marriage, independence in economic matters, and separation from family without marriage, are still unacceptable. The organization of community life, kinship, family, marriage, and descent all emphasize the importance of marriage and motherhood. These conflicts in ideology, organization, and effects of economic development, therefore, continue to compartmentalize women. The new compartments, while widening their options, have proved equally confining.

The selection of marriage partners is extremely important in India, since kinship and descent are necessary to maintain caste hierarchies and community boundaries. Traditionally, of course, the selection of marriage partners was always made by the family in consultation with the village and community elders. For almost a century efforts have been in progress to provide legal support for intercaste and interreligious marriages but semi-arranged or arranged marriages continue to be the norm. Educated young men and women, even in urban areas, continue to leave the choice to parents. The Committee's report, and two studies on women conducted ten years apart in 1959 and 1969, confirm this.[8] The only notable difference is that in urban areas there is some incidence of intercaste and interreligious marriages, and arranged marriages now require the active assent of both parties. Socialization of men and women is an important factor in marriage selection; so too is community consciousness, which was traditionally important and continues to be important, as identity for political and economic advantage becomes a factor in modern representational structures.[9]

One of the manifestations of this continuing process is the increasing incidence of dowry payments. The desire to marry within the endogamous group means that options for a marriage partner are limited and that within this field those with more suitable qualifications are in a better bargaining position. Education and wealth do not appear to have had a liberalizing effect on the practice. Dowry payment is practiced by higher caste and class groups, and in fact, is regarded as a status symbol and is being adopted by groups that traditionally did not follow the custom.[10] This has further devalued women and has, despite education and legislative rights, increased their liability to the family. It has also led to a rash of bride burnings in north India, a way of getting more than one dowry for the same bridegroom. This has led to protests by women's groups but almost no convictions of offenders. The Dowry Prohibition Act passed in 1961 remains a dead letter, with almost no cases reported under the act. The Committee on the Status of Women felt that rousing the social conscience was the only way in which dowry payment could be curbed, as legislative action had obviously failed.[11]

The persistence of traditional attitudes has also resulted in an adverse male-female ratio and an increasing gap in male-female life expectancy. While as in other societies more boys are born in India than girls, unlike other societies the survival

Life Expectancy at Birth (in years)

Decade	Male	Female	Difference
1921-31	26.9	26.6	0.3
1931-41	32.1	31.4	0.7
1941-51	32.4	31.7	0.7
1951-61	41.9	40.6	1.3
1961-71	47.1	45.6	1.5

SOURCE: *Towards Equality: Report of the Committee on the Status of Women in India* (New Delhi: Government of India, 1974), Table 9, p. 16.

rate for girls in India is lower. Life expectancy is lower for girls than it is for boys, from the base year of 1921-31 when it was almost the same.[12] The table on the preceding page illustrates the widening gap in life expectancy.

There are regional variations, and urban-rural differentials. Mortality rates for women are higher from birth to 30-45 years, indicating neglect in the earlier years and inadequate maternity care. In rural India in 1969 there were 20 deaths per thousand women and 18 deaths per thousand for males.[13] This differential is born out by the growing difference in male-female ratio (females per thousand males). The following table indicates this trend, steady over the century.

Male Female Ratio

Year	Total Population	Male Population	Female Population	Sex Ratio
1901	238	121	117	972
1911	252	128	124	964
1921	251	128	123	955
1931	279	143	136	950
1941	319	164	155	945
1951	361	186	175	946
1961	439	226	213	941
1971	548	284	264	930

SOURCE: *Towards Equality*, Table 1, p. 10.

In most western countries the sex ratio is more favorable to women. Cultural factors deeply rooted in Indian society are responsible for this adverse trend, which affects women's ability to take advantage of improved health care facilities and education.

Women's health and related factors are affected by cultural norms which prescribe age at marriage, importance of fertility and sex of childern, patterns of family organization, and community pressures to conform to certain social conventions. Cultural factors dictate the age at which women should be married, and since this is early in their child-bearing period it leads to frequent pregnancies which take their toll. The absence of adequate medical facilities increases the burden on women, for government health facilities have only limited maternity accommodation for women and make few other provisions for their hospitalization. The socialization process, which emphasizes self-effacement and subservience for women also affects their ablility to seek medical help. Similarly, cultural factors affect women nutritionally, since it is customary for men in the family to be fed first and for women to eat whatever is left over.[14] In poorer families, malnutrition from an early age adversely and permanently damages women's health, but hospital records show that fewer women than men are treated for malnutrition. Regional differences, dependent on social attitudes towards women and the low literacy rate for women, are important factors in women's utilization of medical facilities.[15]

Social attitudes are once again important in the literacy and education of women particularly as compared to men, even though there has been some marginal improvement in the enrollment of girls. Enrollment for girls of school-going age has increased from 25% to 35% in the post-independence period. In classes 1-4 in the age group 6-11, 66% are enrolled. The drop-out rate, however, is high: of 100 girls enrolled in Class 1 only 30 reach Class V. By Class VI-VIII, the attendance drops to 22% of the total number of girls in the age group 11-14.[16] Simple enrollment figures too are deceptive, since they do not reflect actual attendance.

Literacy levels are even more dismal for women, at 18.7% for females, 39.5% for males, and 29% for the whole population. Due to the growth in population, illiteracy levels for both males and females have been increasing since independence, but the rate of growth for females is much higher. While male illiteracy has risen from 139.9 million in 1950-51 to 172.0 million in 1971-72, female illiteracy has risen from 161.9 million to 215.3 million[17] in the same period. Even among female literates, 40% have no formal education; the Committee refers to them as semi-literates. Only 7.8% are matriculates, and 1.4 are graduates.[18] Illiteracy therefore constitutes a major barrier to any improvement in women's status.

Social attitudes are also responsible for the declining participation of women in the labor force. Women's participation in agriculture and service industries was always under-enumerated as was their dependence on their own labor for livelihood. With structural changes in the Indian economy, their employment in almost all sectors has been steadily declining. This decline can be attributed to the reorganization of Indian agriculture, which led owners of small holdings to lose their land due to increasing indebtedness. This affected women and led to a decline in the number of women cultivators and an increase in the number of women laborers.[19] The increase from 12.6 million women laborers in 1951 to 15.7 million in 1971 is indicative of the lack of alternative employment opportunities, without specific training facilities to make such alternatives viable. The following table indicates the decline in female employment. It uses successive census data from 1911 to 1971 to establish this trend. Due to a change in census definition of a worker in 1961 the data for that year is skewed; in the 1971 census this definition was dropped and the trend established earlier continues. The decline in female employment, therefore, can be regarded as a continuous process.[20]

Distribution of Women Workers
(in Million)

Year	Agriculture	Industry	Service	Total	Female Population	Female workers as % of Total Labour Force
1911	30.9	6.1	4.8	41.8	33.7	34.4
1921	30.3	5.4	4.4	40.1	33.7	34.0
1931	27.2	5.1	5.3	37.6	27.6	31.2
1951	31.1	4.6	4.9	40.5	23.0	29.0
1961	47.3	6.4	5.2	59.4	28.0	31.5
1971	25.1	3.3	2.9	31.3	11.9	17.4

SOURCE: *Towards Equality*, Table 1, p. 153.

Many household industries in which women participated, such as hand weaving, rice pounding, and tobacco processing, have given way to factory production from which women are excluded, since they have not been trained to use machinery or the new processes.[21]

In the organized sector, that is, all public and private establishments of ten employees or more, women have improved their position from 1.37 million in 1962 to 2.14 million in 1973, an increase of 56.2%. The overall increase in employment in this sector was 49.6% over this period. Women's share of employment in this sector remains small, however, at 10% in the government industrial sector and 20% in the private industrial sector.[22]

The bulk of the expansion in women's employment has been in government service and the professions, and not in industry where it has been declining. The impact of labor laws to protect women workers, equalization of wages between men and women, and structural changes in industry are some of the reasons advanced for this decline. The Committee, however, felt that since expenditure on maternity benefits has been negligible and wage differentials continue to be freely practiced despite laws to the contrary the decline could only be due to discrimination against women. This would also explain the non-availability of training opportunities for women.[23]

In the services and professions, the Committee felt that certain jobs were already identified with women. In the professions, they were mainly teachers and doctors, and held certain clerical jobs which were considered low prestige and hence suitable for women. Women's dependence on government employment in education, health, and social services would make them vulnerable to cuts in government spending, unless they could be provided opportunities for diversifying into the production sector.[24]

This overall lack of women's representation in the economy is borne out by the lack of representation at the political level.[25] While their participation in the political process as voters has been increasing, their success in winning nominations and elections has been declining, both at the state and national levels. In the present political climate, where political office represents not only access to the power structure, but a forum where different communities can display their unity and power and make demands on behalf of their community, it is difficult for women to separate their women constituents from their community regional interests. The struggle for power regionally or and nationally between different communities has made securing nominations and elections expensive and difficult, quite apart from the difficulties that beset women candidates in a restrictive social milieu.

The lack of a vibrant women's movement has meant that women leaders are not created by the movement and therefore do not find it incumbent on them to support women's issues or to represent their interests. In addition, women leaders are generally drawn from political families and are not always in touch with the economic and social realities of the general run of women. In the period before independence and until the passage of the Hindu Code Bill, women leaders were active, motivated by their legislative goals. Subsequently those in the legislatures have identified with community or regional interests. The newly emerging women leaders have identified specific regional problems and have organized women to deal with them, but they have not evolved the ideological basis for a new Indian women's movement. There is, therefore, neither the commitment nor the structure to promote feminist ideals free of community or regional interests. While there is no doubt that such an ideological commitment is in the offing, from the data available on Indian women, time appears to be an important factor if the social, political, and economic trends are to be reversed.

Conclusions

The national movement in India certainly provided the emerging women's movement with momentum and established the link between independence and legislative equality for women. This objective was fulfilled both in the constitution and with the passage of the Hindu Code Bill in 1956. Without links to the national movement, the women's movement would have found it difficult to achieve their objectives, nor could their leaders have attained national status and recognition. The difficulties were to come later, and lay with the failure of the leaders to create a wide-based movement in which women from all strata could participate. The failure also lay in the acceptance of western feminist ideology of the time, without relating it to realities in India. It took a generational change to realize that the problems of women in India could not find ready solutions from western examples. The solutions, like the problems, had to be specifically Indian.

It also took time for women to realize that legislative changes did not always translate into reality, that they had to be prepared to use the laws and take advantage of opportunities provided, and that this could not be done unless there was an ideological and structural change in the composition of the women's movement. The present women leaders seem aware of the need to make such a change, but their efforts remain nebulous and without clear ideological guidelines. Such efforts remain essentially piecemeal and individual, not operational at the national level, and thus cannot infuse new life into the dormant women's movement.

Indian development has many admirable economic goals. The attainment of those goals is complicated by the social structure which remains resistant to change as far as women are concerned, and by the increasing communal (these include regional, caste, and religious) rivalries. These rivalries have resulted from the modernization process necessitating political, social, and economic adjustments of communities. The effect on women has been two-fold. First, the lingering traditionality of the social structures continues to limit their participation in the economic and political spheres. Secondly, structural changes, while secularizing and increasing interaction between communities, also increase the importance of identity. This identification with community in the modern context is not for traditional ritualistic reasons but due to the importance of numerical strength in representative government. This criterion remains important in determining the community's economic performance. The need to maintain a distinct separate identity requires the usage of traditional and ritualistic links, not for a return to traditional forms but for secular gains. This is implemented, however, not through the revival of male traditional customs, which would be inconvenient, but through female traditionality. For women there are contradictory signals particularly in urban areas. While women's greater participation is urged and encouraged in education and employment, they are required to maintain community cohesiveness through marriage and rituals. They are in fact pawns, used by the community and society, neither of which consider the interests of women themselves. This is, of course, due to the absence of a cohesive women's movement.

Without an ideology specific to the conditions and issues confronting Indian women the movement such as it is has neither the focus nor the determination to deal with these conflicting pressures. The result is women's worsening political, economic, and demographic situation. Women leaders, particularly those in politics, are not representative of their natural constituents but creations of political parties for their own ends. Their loyalties and interests are therefore not served by highlighting women's problems. Nor are they encouraged by political parties to do so. It is quite clear that neither development nor the compendium of social, political, and economic changes benefit women when no attention is paid to their specific requirements. Their overall position worsens, even though there are pockets of progress.

There also seems to be no correlation between the women's movement *per se* and an improvement in their achieved status, since in the Indian case it is clear that even while the women's movement was operational, only legal rights were considered important. Other aspects of women's status continued to be neglected and deteriorated even as their legal rights improved. Nor does there appear to be a correlation between particular religions[26] or castes in which women's status across the country can be said to be superior to others. The correlation, therefore, appears to be with social attitudes and customs which vary regionally, and with economic strata, which implies education and greater opportunities that can overcome social restrictions to some extent. An active women's movement with clear objectives and goals, related to specific cultural and economic conditions, can help Indian women achieve greater political and economic participation and greater social independence. Due to the colonial past, the Indian women's movement took its cue from western feminists, and the achievement of legal rights remains an important part of Indian women's transition to a better status.

To complete this transition requires restructuring to suit specifically Indian needs and Indian conditions. There are signs of such a restructuring, although it is as yet unclear whether it will develop soon enough to reverse some of the more disturbing trends in women's socio-economic condition.[27]

NOTES

[1] Leonore Manderson has made this point about the Malay women's movement in "The Shaping of the Kaum Ibu (Women's Section) of the United Malays National Organization," in Wellesley Editorial Committee, *Women and National Development, the Complexities of Change* (Chicago: University of Chicago Press, 1977), pp. 210-28.

[2] All books on this subject follow the lead provided by Esther Boserup, *Women's Role in Economic Development* (London: George Allen and Unwin, 1970), and support her original study which indicated the negative effects of modernization and economic development on women. Three out of a growing number of works on this subject are Irene Tinker, Michele Bo Bramsen, and Mayra Buvinic, eds., *Women and World Development* (New York: Praeger, for the Overseas Development Council, 1976); wellesley Committee, *Women and National Development*; and June Nash and Helen T. Safa, eds., *Sex and Class in Latin America* (New York: Praeger, 1976).

[3] Peggy R. Sanday, "Towards a Theory of the Status of Women," *American Anthropologist* LXXV 6, (December, 1973), p. 1682.

[4] Janet Z. Geile and Audrey C. Smock, eds., *Women: Roles and Status in Eight Countries* (New York: John Wiley, 1977), p. 4.

[5] *Towards Equality: Report of the Committee on the Status of Women in India* (New Delhi: Government of India, 1974), p. 41.

[6] This was true of the women in the Gandhi, Nehru, Tyabji, and Ali brothers' families, and of Sarojini Naidu, Begum Ikramullah, Begum Shahanwaz and most other women leaders.

[7] M.S. Gore, *Urbanization and Family Change* (Bombay: Popular Prakashan, 1968), p. 68.

[8] Promilla Kapur, *The Changing Status of Working Women in India* (New Delhi: Vikas, 1974).

[9] The reaction of communities to wide-ranging changes, part of a country's development, is mixed. While economic and political changes are of necessity adopted, the desire to maintain continuity in community and to limit social changes, as a reaction to the pressures of modernization, has been noted by social scientists in the case of both developing and developed societies. Daniel P. Moynihan and Nathan Glazer, eds. *Ethnicity: Theory and Experience* (Cambridge, Mass: Harvard University Press, 1975); Cynthia Enloe, *Ethnic Conflict and Political*

Development (Boston: Little, Brown, 1974); Abner Cohen, *Customs and Politics in Urban Africa* (Berkeley and Los Angeles: University of California Press, 1969).

[10] *Towards Equality*, pp. 54, 70
[11] *Ibid.*, p. 115.
[12] *Ibid.*, p. 11.
[13] *Ibid.*, p. 20.
[14] *Ibid.*, p. 58.
[15] *Ibid.*, pp. 318, 321.
[16] *Ibid.*, p. 240.
[17] *Ibid.*, pp. 30, 265.
[18] *Ibid.*, p. 31.
[19] *Ibid.*, p. 163.

[20] This employment data is based on different censuses, and thus is not entirely acceptable to purists since over time there have been certain changes in the definition of a worker. But these changes are marginal, and do not detract from the overwhelming evidence of the reverses that women have suffered as a result of the modernization of the Indian economy.

[21] *Towards Equality*, p. 153
[22] *Ibid.*, p. 185.
[23] *Ibid.*, pp 191-93.
[24] *Ibid.*, p. 204.
[25] *Ibid.*, p. 292.

[26] Perdita Huston, by conducting a series of interviews with women in many different developing countries, has made the point that religious or cultural differences did not affect women's status; they were most affected by their economic strata. *Third World Women Speak Out* (New York: Praeger, 1979).

[27] Some of these ideas have been discussed by the author in "Indian Women Give Development a New Dimension," unpub. paper presented at a Conference on Women, Family Planning, Health, and Development, organized by the Center for Population Activities, Washington, D.C., January 31, 1978; and in "Whither the Indian Women's Movement?" *Economic and Political Weekly* XII, 44 (November 16, 1977), pp. 1948-1951.

9

Two Faces of Protest: Alternative Forms of Women's Mobilization in West Bengal and Maharashtra

AMRITA BASU

The extent and form of women's participation in political protest is indicative of characteristics of a movement as a whole. The larger the mass base of a movement, the greater women's participation and the more successful the movement, for the democratic character of a movement is an essential component of its success. Movements which are both radical and democratic have recorded the greatest success in organizing women. Mass education at the grass roots level through democratic structures has encouraged the large-scale participation of women; the cultural and political radicalism of such movements has permitted the questioning of women's sex-linked roles.

Within the Indian context, West Bengal and Maharashtra illustrate two alternative patterns of political protest. While in West Bengal the Communist parties have mobilized women, in Maharashtra there are no state-wide movements of women or the rural poor. Mass democratic movements have mobilized women by avoiding reliance on political parties and by creating alternatives to formal structures and modes of participation. Such movements have occurred in isolated pockets of the state, linked by common methods and approaches but not organization and leadership. In the Shramik Sangathana movement in Dhulia district, Maharashtra, women's participation has been unusually high, and in CPI (M)-led rural movements in Midnapur and Bankura districts, West Bengal, women's participation has been generally low.[1]

Women's participation has varied not only because of differences in political strategy, but also due to social and economic differences between the two states. The nature of women's participation in protest movements is largely shaped by the Bengali and Maharashtrian contexts, regardless of specific features of Dhulia, Midnapur, and Bankura districts. The most important contextual influences on women's mobilization are, firstly, varying levels of women's participation in the labor force, particularly as agricultural labor. Differences between a capitalist* and a pre-capitalist situation, and between tribals and non-tribals further define the extent and nature of women's participation in protest.

In Maharashtra, women's employment has been significant, agricultural labor has become proletarianized, and commercialization has challenged pre-capitalist values. Women's political participation has thus been qualitatively and quantitatively higher than in West Bengal, where rates of women's participation in the work force are low, and labor relations and culture remain predominantly pre-capitalist.

To counteract the tendency to regard West Bengal and Maharashtra as two polarized, ideal types, atypical cases will also be discussed: a mass democratic movement in West Bengal, and a CPI (M)-led movement among women in Maharashtra. The greater strength of CPI(M)-led movements, and weakness of mass democratic movements, in West Bengal compared to Maharashtra, suggest that socio-economic conditions and political organization and ideology mutually define the character of protest. The established Communist parties have impeded grassroots protest in West Bengal, which in part has occurred in Maharashtra because of the very absence of a strong Communist Party. The higher levels of women's participation in mass democratic movements than in centralized, party-led movements

---

*Capitalist refers, in this context, to commodity production, wage labor, commercialized agriculture, and mechanization.

in both states shows the importance of political strategy in determining the extent of women's participation.

The first section of this paper will examine the extent and form of women's participation as an outcome of differing political strategies by studying women's participation in movements organized by the Communist parties historically, first in Bengal and then in Maharashtra. In Bengal, party-directed, institutionalized movements increasingly replaced spontaneous forms of women's militancy after independence. In Maharashtra, in contrast, the most dynamic movements have been non-party tribal movements; the Shramik Sangathana in Maharashtra is a case in point. The second part of this paper will show that political protest is structurally confined because of the diversity of women's roles in the spheres of production, culture, and the family.

In both West Bengal and Maharashtra there have been traditions of women's politicization: from social reform movements concerned with improving the position of women, to women's participation in the nationalist movement and in movements since independence. In contrast to states like Assam, Jammu & Kashmir, Rajasthan and U. P., the states of West Bengal and Maharashtra are more advanced in terms of women's formal participation, like voting, and informal participation, like protest.[2]

In certain respects, West Bengal represents a state which is highly politically developed, with vigorous Communist Party activity, but economically underdeveloped, with low levels of women's participation in the labor force. Maharashtra, by contrast, is undeveloped in the extent of Communist Party movements and economically advanced.

The low level of women's participation in protest in West Bengal is paradoxical, given its cultural and historical background. West Bengal experienced one of the longest traditions of political radicalism in India, through the activities of the early terrorist movements, the CPI, the CPI(M), and the CPI (ML), culminating in a Left Front government in power at the present.[3] Secondly, a *zamindari* system in West Bengal created a situation more conducive to class polarization and conflict than the *ryotwari* system in Maharashtra, where exploitation among small and marginal peasants is both less visible and less direct. Thirdly, through the impact of leftist movements, and a possible factor in their success, caste barriers in Bengal are considerably weaker than in Maharashtra. The elite culture in Bengal was more radical than the elite culture in Maharashtra, and in fact caste exclusivism was a major barrier to the spread of the Maharashtrian Communist movement.[4] Thus the earlier cultural radicalism of the Brahmo Samaj and the later economic radicalism of the Communists created a more likely basis for political protest in Bengal than in Maharashtra.

Similarly, the oppression of Bengali women has not been as brutal as in many other parts of India, where young brides are burnt for an insufficient dowry and where scheduled caste and tribal women are raped. Yet, women's participation in political struggles, and particularly their expression of their own grievances and demands as women, has been surprisingly limited in West Bengal. The oppression of women and atrocities against scheduled castes have been considerably greater in Maharashtra than in West Bengal. Maharashtrian women and scheduled castes have also protested this injustice to a larger extent.[5]

PART I: WOMEN AND POLITICAL MOBILIZATION

A. Women's Participation in CPI (M) Movements

1. West Bengal

Women have been most active in political struggles during periods of crisis, frequent in Bengal. They have shown exceptional militance during wars, famines, periods of communal crisis, and scarcities. A women's movement could have developed during such periods, but instead, women's participation has been limited to acts of individual heroism and personal sacrifice. The Communist parties have not sustained the organization of women around their own interests and demands.

Bengali women, particularly in Midnapur, played an active role in the most militant phases of the nationalist movement, as in the civil disobedience movement of 1930 and the Quit India movement in 1942. Matungini Hazra, who was killed during the nationalist movement in Midnapur, is still revered as a martyred symbol of women's courage.

The Communist Party worked through the All-India Women's Conference during the first phase of the nationalist movement. After World War II, although Congress and the Communist Party continued to cooperate on certain issues, they differed on questions ranging from the membership for the AIWC, to organizing on a limited versus mass basis. In 1942, with the legalization of the Communist Party, the Mahila Atma Raksha Samiti (MARS) or Women's Self-Defense League was formed as a mass front of the Communist Party, working amongst 43,000 women, over half of whom were party members.[6] MARS was particularly active during the famine period in organizing large-scale hunger strikes for food, movements against black marketeers and hoarders, demanding proper supplies and controlled prices, and the opening of ration shops in the slum areas.[7] MARS also started literacy classes and political study groups. It trained women in self-defense and public debate and began to raise issues concerning women's subordination. In the rural areas, members of MARS were generally middle peasants, sometimes rich peasants, rarely poor peasants or agricultural laborers.[8]

The Tebhaga movement (1946-50) led by the Kisan Sabha of the Communist Party, was perhaps the only movement in West Bengal in which women's participation surpassed that of men as the movement intensified and men were arrested. *Adhi nai, Tebhaga chai* ("We want two-thirds not one-half of the crop") was the main demand of sharecroppers. The Tebhaga movement was the most active in Twenty-Four Parganas and North Bengal. Women participated at all levels of the Tebhaga struggle: in the forcible harvesting of crops, in meetings, demonstrations, and delegations. Women were trained as guerillas in Twenty-Four Parganas when the movement led to armed struggle.[9] However, women were rarely members of the elected or nominated committees in the villages.

The radicalism of Communist Party leadership of the movement, and the jarring of mechanisms of social control in a period of exceptional upheaval, led to the unsurpassed participation of women. Tremendous repression called for women's active mobilization and inadvertently brought them out in defense of their homes and families. Women were able to call the attention of party leaders to sexual oppression and wife-beating, once the initial demands of the movement were met. Scheduled caste and tribal women were the most active participants. Even Muslim women participated, and there was unusual unity between Hindus and Muslims during a period of communal strife elsewhere.[10]

The experience of World War II, the Tebhaga movement, and continued police repression often led women to organize actively. Leftists were imprisoned without trial because of the passage of the Preventive Detention Act six months after independence. Women were particularly adamant in demanding their release. In April 1949, four Communist women were killed in Calcutta and many peasant women were killed in the districts during this period of repression.[11] Women's organizations became more closely tied to the Communist Party after the period when they had been working illegally and underground (1949-51).

Women were mobilized around the anti-price rise and food movements in the 1950s. In 1959, MARS was reconstituted under the name of the Paschim Bangla Mahila Samiti, currently the most important constituent of the National Federation of Indian Women. Yet after independence, women's participation subsided considerably. As an active participant in women's organizations lamented, a women's movement had failed to emerge in the 1950s.[12] The militancy of women declined as the Communist women's organizations became primarily concerned with securing legislative gains for women. The pressure exerted by women's organizations was at least partially responsible for the creation of the National Social Welfare Board, the Labour Appellate Tribunal in favor of equal wages, and the introduction of social legislation concerning women in Parliament.[13]

A political organizational report of the CPI(M) Central Committee of December 1968 admitted that in West Bengal, the party had been unable to activate working class or peasant women. The report stated that leaders had not shown sufficient interest in building women's organizations.[14] A recent survey of women's political participation in West Bengal claims that among the major reasons for the low levels of women's political awareness are disillusionment with political parties and their feeling that there is a lack of leadership.[15]

The CPI (M) still does not have a national level women's

STATE OF WEST BENGAL, INDIA

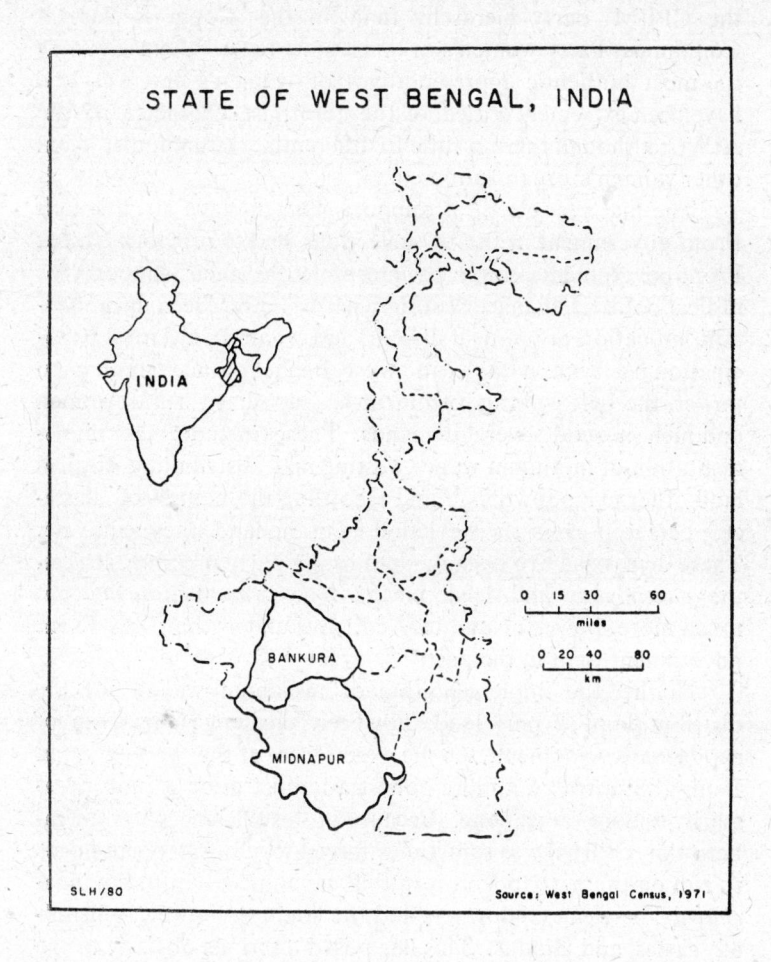

Source: West Bengal Census, 1971

organization, although CPI (M) women's organizations exist in seven states, the largest and most active in West Bengal and Kerala. The CPI (M) formed the Paschim Bangla Ganatantrik Mahila Samiti in West Bengal after the CPI and CPI(M) women's organizations split in 1970. Fewer women occupy positions in the CPI(M) party hierarchy than in the Congress Party.[16] Communist Party women's organizations regard themselves as the most authentic representatives of women's interests and have been extremely critical of the reformist character of the AIWC, although there is little to differentiate Communist from other women's organizations.[17]

The massive electoral support women gave to the Left Front government in the 1977 elections, and to previous United Front governments, might be interpreted as their support for radical political change. Voting itself has often been an important indication of political dissent, and women's electoral participation has been notable in West Bengal. Since coming to power, the Left Front government has mobilized rural women and men around several demands. These include: the implementation of minimum wages, vesting and distributing surplus land of large landowners,[18] and recording the names of sharecroppers to prevent their eviction from the land they cultivate. These demands have been made through party pressure, strikes, the *panchayats*, and legal means. The *gram panchayats* are much more powerful and less corrupt under the Left Front government than in the past.[19]

Neither the implementation of minimum wages nor the distribution of surplus land, however, challenge the logic of capitalist development. As the experience of the *panchayats* in Bankura illustrates, a more honest administration is not necessarily a more radical one. Because of insufficient party members, the CPI(M) was sometimes forced to allow large landlords to run on the party ticket, resulting in conflicts within the *panchayats*, between landowners and the landless, between scheduled castes and Hindus. This has posed a serious obstacle to the *panchayats*' effective implementation of land redistribution.[20] The party has softened exploitation by inspiring greater self-confidence in the rural poor and fear in landlords. Women and the rural poor have thus benefitted from a more sympathetic and supportive institutional framework than under any previous

Congress government. Yet much of the CPI (M)'s popularity results not from its proclaimed radicalism, but from its deliberate cultivation of a welfarist approach.

Today, the Paschim Bangla Ganatantrik Mahila Samiti has a memberhip of 250,000 women.[21] It has almost become a recreational activity for wives and daughters of party members, or a training ground for women who are still insufficiently qualified to become party members. The lack of trained cadre and the low level of political consciousness of *mahila samiti* leaders in part explains their orientation toward social services and relief work, rather than political organizing among women. The urban middle class membership of *mahila samitis* has further led them to reinforce women's housewife roles; sewing and embroidery centers in the rural areas are of little consequence to female agricultural laborers.[22]

Women's attendance at Communist Party meetings is considerable. Women's articulation of their own problems and needs, however, has been negligible, because male-dominated political parties have initiated organizing. Women have often been mobilized solely for purposes of increasing party strength through their passive support. A women's demonstration in a tribal area of Bankura district illustrates this.

The *mahila samiti* organized women to *gherao* the Block Development Office and the *panchayat*, in Bankura in the summer of 1979. Over a thousand women demonstrated before the office of the *sarpanch* of the *panchayat*, who was also the most active CPI(M) leader in the area. The *mahila samiti* made the following demands: that the block should be declared a drought-stricken area so that funds could be released by the Central and State governments for relief and employment, for equal wages, government provision of interest-free loans to small farmers, and free schools in the villages. The chairperson of the *mahila samiti* stated: "We do not want to create any trouble. We realize that the Left Front government has been trying to help us. But we are going to encircle this office and remain here until all our demands are met." She then went inside the office to negotiate with the *sarpanch* while the women waited outside. Half an hour later they emerged and informed the women that the negotiations had been successful.

The *gherao* was a prelude to a series of speeches by party

members, who claimed that the Congress Party was attempting to undermine their organization. The speakers criticized Congress for campaigning at a time of drought and scarcity, unlike the CPI(M) which was only concerned with the well-being of the people. "Rich, middle, and poor unite when it comes to the drought. We are all equally affected."[23] The entire issue of the drought was clearly secondary to the approaching elections. The *gherao* itself was a staged drama in which the actors were party members, and the mass of women the audience, with no direct role to play. The ostensibly agitational nature of the *gherao* had little meaning where the demands amounted to a plea for more charity from Central and State governments. The demystification of what appears to be a large-scale upsurge of political discontent often reveals the party's manipulation of dissatisfaction for electoral purposes. The CPI (M)'s approach to organizing women is indicative of a more critical failure in its approach to political mobilization, its centralized party control and insensitivity to local level demands.

2. *Maharashtra*

The CPI (M)'s peasant and women's organizations have traditionally been weak in Maharashtra because of the party's neglect to organize agricultural laborers, its lack of state-wide organization, and its rivalry with other leftist parties. While the CPI (M) in Bengal was fighting for the reduction of rent, for land to the tiller, and the ending of feudal intermediary tenures, no such objectives were defined in Maharashtra. The All-India *Kisan Sabha* of the CPI (M), founded in 1936, remained weak throughout the next decade. In 1943 the membership of the AIKS was only 9,996 in Maharashtra, compared to 83,160 in Bengal.[24]

The biggest movement the CPI(M) undertook in Maharashtra, was amongst the Worli tribes in Thana district in 1945. The main demands around which the CPI(M) organized were the abolition of forced labor, *veth begar*, and the *palemor* system of moneylending, the implementation of minimum wages, and the distribution of land to the tiller through granting ownership rights to tenants and fallow forest land for cultivation.

Godavari Parulekar, a young middle-class woman who joined the Communist Party on her husband's initiative, became the leader of the movement. Although she was not specifically concerned with organizing women, women played a strong supportive role in the underground activities of the party. The party's emphasis on production-related issues, however, deterred the active participation of women. The CPI(M) only superficially raised women's isses like curtailing drinking and marriage expenses until recently, when it found other organizations successfully dealing with them. The CPI(M) continues to function in Thana, but electorally and organizationally it has only a fraction of its former strength. There is growing dissatisfaction with the party's tendency to make ideological and political compromises.

In 1974 the Maharashtra Rajya Shramik Mahila Samiti collaborated with the Samajvadi Mahila Sabha in Bombay against inflation, and organized the most impressive CPI(M) women's movement in Maharashtra. Initially the NFIW, the CPI women's wing, called for mobilization on a limited basis. Mrinal Gore of the Socialist Party, and Ahilya Ranganeker of the CPI(M), decided to expand the base of the movement from middle-class to slum and working-class women. They formed the Joint Action Committee for Resistance Against Price Rise in September 1973. The Committee's main demands were that the government take over wholesale trade in essential commodities and ensure their distribution at reasonable prices. It also wanted the manufacture of cotton cloth and pharmaceuticals to be nationalized, black marketeers rigorously punished, and a network of ration shops started, supervised by local vigilance committees.[25]

The noteworthy aspect of the anti-price rise movement is that it overcame narrow party differences and mobilized thousands of women through innovative forms of struggle. When the CPI (M) movement was oppositional in nature, and its leadership sensitive to women's participation, it partially overcame barriers in the way of organizing women. The anti-inflation movement lost momentum with the Emergency and the subsequent merging of the Socialist Party with the Janata.

The extent of women's participation in CPI (M)-led movements varies between West Bengal and Maharashtra because of differences in leadership and the strength of the party in each state. The similarities in women's participation in CPI (M) movements in the two states, however, are much more striking. Women's organizations have been subordinate and ancilliary to the party, and the level of women's political consciousness and participation very limited in both cases.

Aside from the CPI (M), the Lal Nishan Party has been organizing sugar factory workers in Kolhapur, Satara, and Ahmednagar districts.[26] The LNP was formed in Maharashtra in 1942 when it broke away from the Communist Party. Female agricultural laborers have participated in the strikes organized by the LNP, but because the party decided to concentrate on economic demands, it has not raised women's issues. The CPI (ML), in Nanded district, the CPI in Nanded, Nagar and Bombay, and the CPI (M) in Thana and Nagar, have also been active on a limited scale.

Non-party village-level movements in tribal areas have been the most significant and dynamic movements in contemporary Maharashtra. The most notable of these movements are the Bhumi Sena and Kashtakari Sangathana in Thana district, and the Shramik Sangathana in Dhulia district. Although these movements are distinguished from one another in their leadership, organization and maturity, their general approach and methods differ fundamentally from the established parties of the Left. Each of these movements has a loose organizational structure in which there is no hierachical chain of command, but each of the activists live and work among the tribals rather than directing them as alien leaders. *Tarun mandals*, youth organizations in the villages, have encouraged the fullest participation of tribals in the movements. Political education is emphasized through *shibirs*, training camps that teach methods of struggle. The activists have assisted tribals in fighting against social and cultural oppression, and internal as well as class-based forms of exploitation. The democratic nature of these organizations has encouraged women spontaneously to raise issues which concern them. Women's participation in such non-party movements, both in West Bengal and Maharashtra, will be examined in the following section.

B. Women's Participation in Non-Party Mass Democratic Movements

1. West Bengal

The CPI (M) took over direction and control of several strikes independently organized by local laborers in Bankura district, and softened their initial militance.[27] But another kind of movement, in tribal villages in Jhargram, Midnapur, encouraged high levels of women's participation, though such movements are sporadic, isolated, and atypical of movements in West Bengal.

The site of one such movement, Damodarpur village, is inhabited by the Lodhas, perhaps the most exploited and neglected tribals in West Bengal. The Lodhas were branded criminal tribes by the British, since some of their practices were deemed barbaric, because they had not yet taken to agricultural cultivation, and because the forests, with which the Lodhas had close emotional and economic ties, became government property. The Lodhas' criminal reputation was perpetuated by their Mahato landlords who encouraged them to engage in petty theft. Police repression against Lodhas was so great that they spent most nights hiding in the jungles, fearing the frequent raids on their homes. It was only prior to the last elections that the CPI (M) attempted to improve the condition of the Lodhas.

Approximately five years ago a development organization, largely financed by foreign funds, began working in Damodarpur. It was headed by a man from Calcutta, but staffed by people of the area.[28] Unlike most socio-economic development organizations, it felt it should assist the Lodhas in organizing themselves, with education in agitational methods taking priority over economic development programs, so that women and men are given the confidence and opportunity to express their own grievances and demands. The development organization arranged political study groups and literacy classes, revived dances, songs and other festivities of the Lodhas. It also decided to transform a traditional political institution, the village committee, known in Bengali as *solo anna*, into a forum where direct democracy could be practiced.

DISTRICTS OF BANKURA AND MIDNAPUR, INDIA

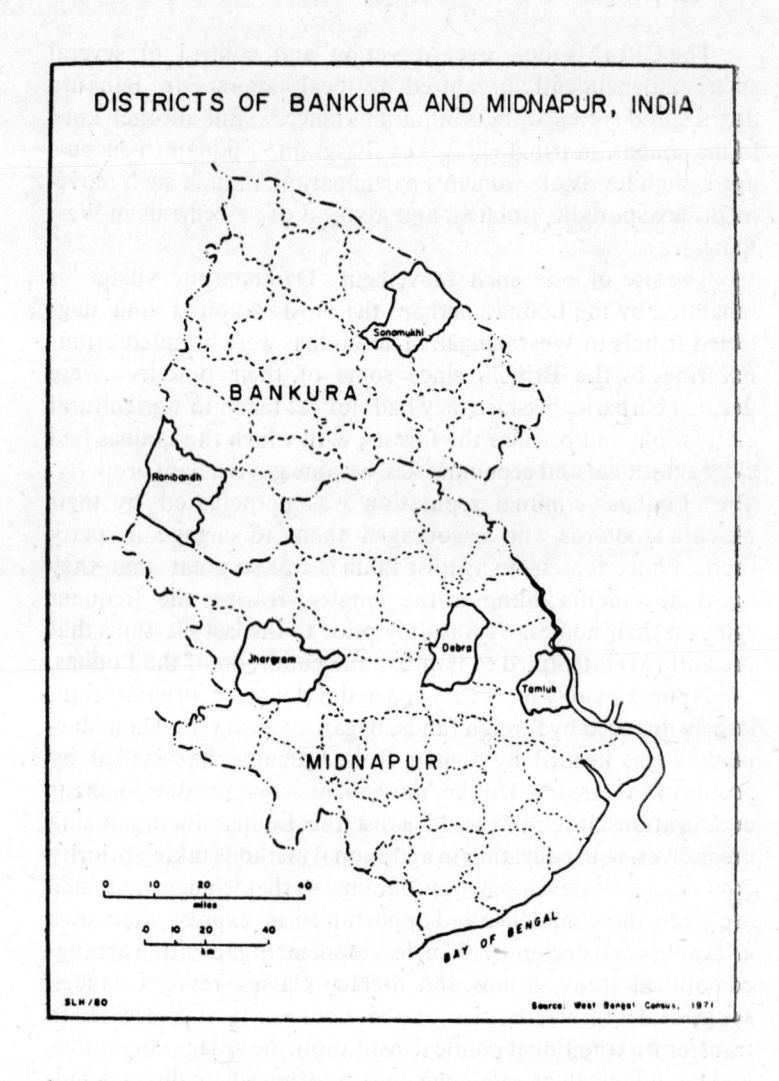

Source: West Bengal Census, 1971

As often happens, the committee was dominated by the largest and most influential landlord in the village. Gradually, however, as the Lodhas began to attend the meetings of the committee regularly, they became increasingly assertive and aware of their numerical strength. Within a few months, the Mahato landlords were forced out of the committee. The dominant landlord who had been ousted, decided to run for the *gram panchayat* elections on the Congress ticket, so as to counteract the growing strength of the village committee. A young boy named Hitesh, the most educated Lodha in the village, campaigned against him on the CPI(M) ticket and won. The backing of the parallel CPI(M) dominated *panchayat* strengthened the informal village committee of the Lodhas.

The *gram panchayat* and the village committee sometimes dealt with the same issues. The village committee, however, encouraged the Lodhas actively to implement programs themselves. In recovering their land from Mahato landlords, in recording share-croppers, and in strikes for higher wages, men and women were able to identify their achievements as a result of their own struggles.

On other issues, the village committee acted independently of the *gram panchayat*. The village committee petitioned the government for schools, housing, electricity, roads and a community forest. It attempted to abolish the moneylending system by reviving a Bengali tradition of *anradhan*, whereby each of the villagers would contribute a handful of rice to a community grain bank. Three hundred pounds of rice were collected the first time this was tried, which the villagers borrowed in the lean season at nominal rates of interest. Damodarpur village formerly had the highest crime rate in the *taluka*. The village committee stopped the Lodhas from stealing through strict vigilance. It also stopped the prostitution of women, a practice rampant in the past.

Perhaps the most remarkable feature was women's participation. Women quite spontaneously demanded that a women's committee should be formed, that women should attend the general committee meetings every night so that they could check on the decisions made by men, and that separate literacy classes should be held for women. Women also demanded that there should be a greater sharing of housework responsibilities and that they be allowed to control the family income.

Women distinguished themselves from men in their commitment and integrity. For instance, during a strike in the harvesting season of 1977, a few of the men accepted bribes from the landlords and agreed to resume work. When the women found out, they made them return the money and stop working. Another example was women's response to a tribal hostel which was going to be built near the village by the government. A few children were eligible to live in the hostel and receive free education, clothing, and books. When the village committee met to discuss the proposal, women opposed it adamantly. They argued that this kind of a program would alienate their children from the community by conferring special privileges on them. Upon their insistence, a mass petition was sent to the Tribal Commissioner, objecting that the scheme had been imposed on them without their consultation or approval, and would result in further isolating the Lodhas.

Movements like the one in Damodarpur raise fundamental dilemmas. Women were able to make demands more successfully through the creation of local democratic structures than in movements initiated from above. Yet in the absence of direction and structure, such a movement is unable to sustain itself and women's participation remains confined to a strongly supportive role. The development organization provided material and psychological resources in the early stages, and because of a conscious policy of not functioning as a relief-charity agency, was able to encourage initiative from within the Lodha community. Yet the movement has remained hampered by its origins. Fundamental change is not feasible in one village in isolation. There are also tendencies to regard the development organization as a rich benefactor and to resent it, as any other employer, out of feelings of dependence.

A related problem is the lack of a clear political and class perspective, a tendency which sometimes results in regarding an improved standard of living, through better health, education, and sanitation facilities, as an end in itself. The lack of class perspective has also resulted in slight but noticeable divisions between Mahato and Lodha agricultural laborers. The village committee decided, for example, that the Lodhas should be given priority over Mahato landless laborers in the distribution of land which they had acquired from Mahato landlords. In the absence of a viable organizational alternative, people may tend to view change complacently as a product of development efforts, or become dependent on the CPI(M).

2. *Maharashtra*: *The Shramik Sangathana in Dhulia District*

Bhil tribals, mainly landless laborers, form the majority of the population and Gujars the dominant class in Dhulia district. Gujars migrated to Dhulia in the 1830s and settled there as cultivators. The growing demand for cotton from the region fostered the commercialization of agriculture. The Gujars appropriated tribal land through direct coercion, legal occupation of leased-out land, and a few legal transfers, leading to extensive land alienation. Landlessness kept increasing, despite legislation to the contrary. Today rich peasants form approximately 10-20% of the population, owning 70-80% of the best land. The rest of the land is divided into small plots among the peasants; 50-60% of the population is landless.[29]

The rich peasants used their control over district cooperatives and the state machinery to bring in capital, equipment, and expertise for agricultural transformation. Through the introduction of new varieties of sugar cane, wheat, and grass, of mechanization in the form of pumps, threshers, tractors, and power tillers, and the vast expansion of irrigated land since the 1960s, the old feudal landlords began to transform themselves into commercially-oriented rich peasants. The value of land increased five times between 1968-73.[30] The result has been the increasing impoverishment of the *adivasis*, the disintegration of the class of middle peasants, and the transformation of landlord-tenant into capital-wage labor relations.

The Bhil tribals waged a continuous struggle against their increasing impoverishment. Bhils not only battled exploitation by Gujar landlords but equally attempted to change their own community by fighting against various forms of cultural and social exploitation. One of the earliest movements in the area (1936-39) was led by Gulab Mahraj, a laborer and spiritual leader. Gulab Mahraj attempted to improve the conditions of the *adivasis* through social reform. After his death, his brother, Ramdas Mahraj, continued his religious reforms and combined

STATE OF MAHARASHTRA, INDIA

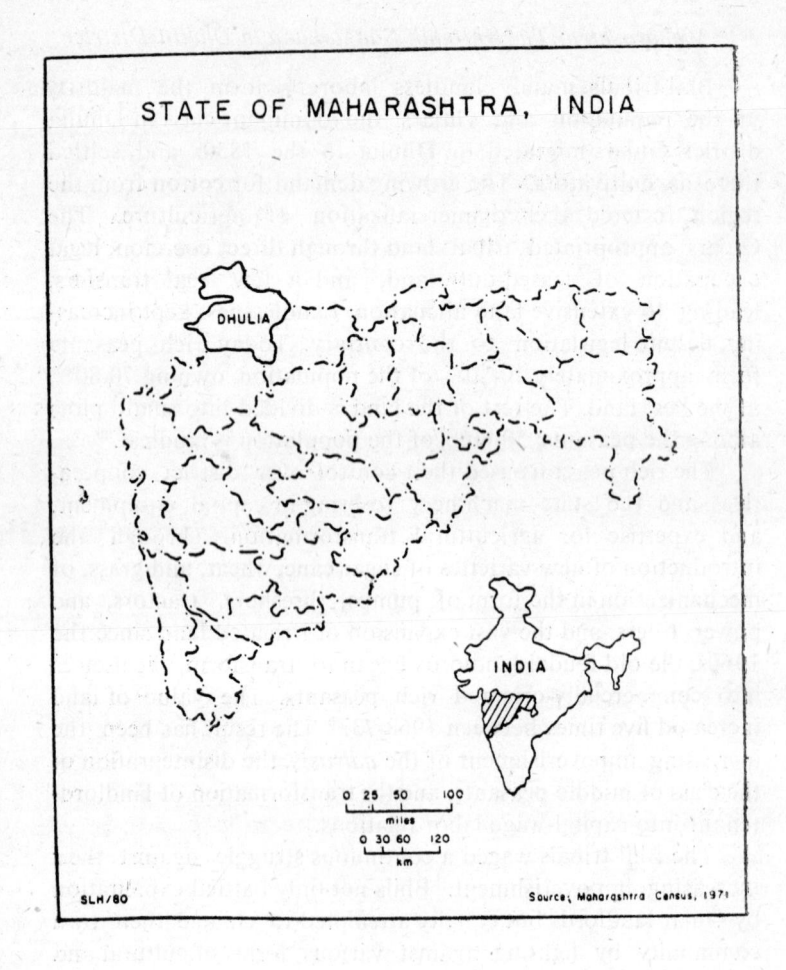

Source: Maharashtra Census, 1971

this with nationalist activities, which resulted in his expulsion from the area. When he later returned to continue his work, it was suppressed. Sri Dada Saheb Sounarkar, a social reformer, started political agitational work among the tribals after Ramdas Mahraj. The movement died out when Sounarkar joined the Congress party.[31]

In the second phase, the Sarvodaya Sangh, a Gandhian organization, began running kindergartens, schools, ashrams, and health centers, and demanding the restoration of tribal land. Ambersingh Suratvanti, a young Bhil from the area, radicalized the Sarvodaya and became one of the most important leaders of the movement. Ambersingh "Mahraj" a term of respect Ambersingh earned for being a renowned *bhajan* singer, formed the Bhil Adivasi Seva Mandal in 1971, which took up cases of injustice towards *adivasis*.

In November 1971, Ambersingh Mahraj asked the Sarvodaya Sangh to send a study team with volunteers to Shahada. Six young activists who came to Shahada formed the nucleus of the Shramik Sangathana, which was formed on June 5, 1971 because the Sarvodaya organization was not sufficiently mass-based.

The present-day movement originated from the Patilwadi incident, which attracted public attention to Dhulia district. The government had given Vishram Hari Patil, a large landowner, 500 acres of land to develop a seed farm. On May 2, 1971, a few hundred *adivasis* approached Patil's sons asking for loans of twelve kilos of grain each. The police surrounded them at a village near Patilwadi as they were returning home. The Gujar landlords asked the police to open fire on the *adivasis*. When the police refused, the landlords started shooting. The Bhils retaliated with bows and arrows. Nine Gujar landlords were acquitted in the case against them. Seventeen Bhils were sentenced in another case booked in the Sessions Court. The activists filed an appeal in the High Court, but six years later when it was settled in favor of the *adivasis*, they had nearly completed their imprisonment.[32]

Five thousand *adivasis* attended a Land Liberation Rally, the Bhu Mukti Andolan, held in Shahada on January 30, 1972.[33] This Conference determined to occupy land belonging to tribals to build up pressure on the government for employment, to

DISTRICT OF DHULIA, INDIA

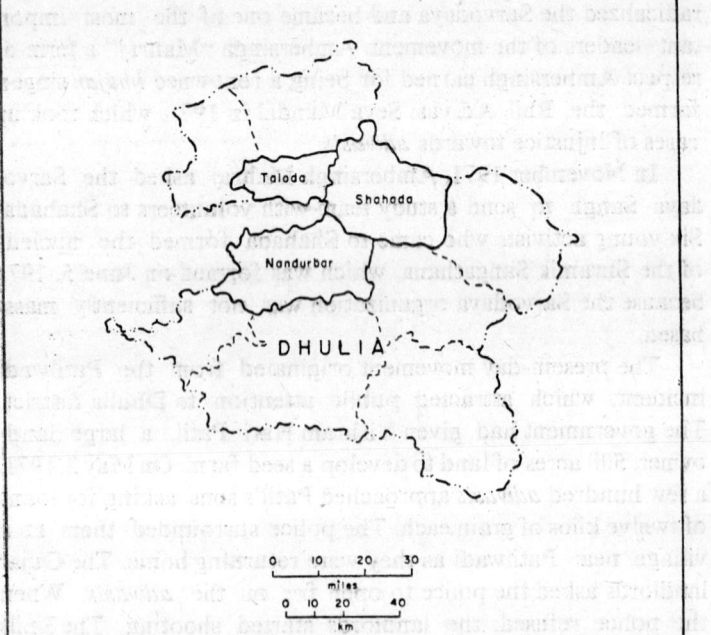

Taloda
Shahada
Nandurbar
DHULIA

0 10 20 30
miles
0 10 20 40
km

SLH/80   Source: Maharashtra Census, 1971

force the government to cancel retroactively *adivasi* land transfers and debts, and to enforce minimum wages. Within a period of about three months, tribals forcibly harvested and took over four thousand acres of land illegally held by landlords. Also at that rally, Govind Rao Shinde, a Sarvodaya leader, decided to form the Gram Swarajya Samiti, or Village Self-Government Association.[34]

In addition, the Shramik Sangathana actively boycotted the 1972 Legislative Assembly elections, in order to draw attention to a number of incidents of harassment of the *adivasis* and to press the Government to pass legislation for the restoration of tribal land and the fixation of minimum wages. Their attempt was successful and voting fell from the usual 55-60% to 33%.[35]

The major subsequent struggle was for increasing the wages of *saldars*, annual contract laborers.[36] On May Day 1972, eight thousand laborers and *saldars* attended a meeting to demand an increase in wages, a weekly holiday, and the proper maintenance of the records. Initially, the rich peasants refused to concede any of the demands. The *saldars* then went on strike and were joined by day laborers and small peasants in seventy villages. The annual pay of *saldars* was increased by Rs. 150-200 and for daily laborers by Rs. 2-3 for men and Rs. 1-2 for women.[37]

The activists simultaneously launched a major struggle in the hill areas of Shahada for the abolition of the *begari* system of compulsory labor for the forest department and for the acquisition of waste land for cultivation. The forest department declared this illegal and arrested a few hundred people. A few months later two hundred people were arrested at a major open *dharna*.[38] The Shramik Sangathana and the Gram Swarajya Samiti together forced the government to grant them more relief after the 1973 famine than it gave to any other part of Maharashtra by organizing mass rallies and demonstrations.[39] They took out a huge *morcha* on July 30 in which seventy-eight people were arrested, and conducted a *gherao* to demand relief work on August 22, 1973.[40]

With the declaration of the Emergency, the harassment of activists lessened their agitational activities. The twenty-point program was "implemented" through active struggle, such as relieving debt by regaining mortgaged goods from landlords, thereby demonstrating the ineffectiveness of the government program. A major new development after the formation of the Janata government was the split between the Gram Swarajya Samiti and the Shramik Sangathana, on June 23, 1977. The immediate reason for the split was that while the Gram Swarajya Samiti supported the Janata party, the Shramik Sangathana did not, for it felt that Congress and Janata represented the same class interests. They further differed in ideology and methods. The Sarvodayists gave priority to constructive activities and claimed that the Shramik Sangathana was creating strife and destroying the unity of the villages.

The Shramik Sangathana has emerged since the split as the more radical and active of the two groups. The Shramik Sangathana increasingly believes in the necessity of class struggle and considers mass participation and support over a wide geographic area essential.[41] It utilizes all methods of struggle which involve mass participation—*gheraos*, *dharnas*, *morchas* and *satyagrahas*. The Gram Swarajya Samiti, in contrast, has developed a welfare approach by taking grants from the government and development agencies, hiring salaried workers, and emphasizing the need for compromise and negotiation.

When the young activists first began working they lacked a clear theoretical perspective, but they felt dissatisfied with the existing Communist parties. Gradually, their concrete experience confirmed that perspective. The Shramik Sangathana's approach to various issues, like their stress on organizing against casteism and for left unity, and among the landless and tribals, reveals the difference between their approach and that of the Communist parties, and suggests why they have been so successful in facilitating women's participation.

C. Issues Affecting Political Mobilization

1. *Left Unity*

In contrast to the CPI(M) in West Bengal which has become involved in interparty clashes, even within the Left Front government,[42] the Shramik Sangathana has increasingly stressed the need for left unity. From early on the Shramik Sangathana believed that caste inequality should not be subordinated to class conflict, and attempted to draw together leftist groups to eradicate caste feelings. The Samata Sammelan, or the equality march against casteism, was jointly organized by the Shramik Sangathana and several leftist parties, and involved 3000 people from 300 villages.[43]

The Shramik Sangathana felt that the elections were an opportunity to unite small, independent leftist groups and to provide an alternative to the established parties of the Left in Parliament. It felt it was wrong to dismiss bourgeois democracy as meaningless; furthermore, electoral participation could provide an important form of political education. The Shramik Sangathana nominated two candidates in the 1977 Legislative Assembly elections and one candidate in the 1980 Parliamentary elections. In both cases, Shramik Sangathana candidates lost. Bhuribai, a tribal woman who had been nominated in both elections, has been active in the Shramik Sangathana for several years. Bhuribai has become increasingly articulate and forceful in encouraging women to struggle against their subordination.

The Shramik Sangathana was not trying to acquire power through electoral means as an end in itself, as their electoral slogans demonstrate. "Elections are only a tool; the united movement of the toilers is our politics." "We will not make any bargains with you—to develop the area in exchange for your vote." They made no pretenses at representing the interests of all classes, but only those of the landless and poor peasants.

The Shramik Sangathana has been cautious about participating in the elections, however, for it believes that in certain situations, electoral participation can lead to ideological compromise. Although the Shramik Sangathana is strongest at the village level, it has not participated in the *gram panchayat* elections for it feels that it can be more effective as a pressure group when it is not forced into dependence on government officialdom.

2. *Class Allies and Enemies*

The Shramik Sangathana's premise that the fundamental antagonism of class interests is between the emerging rural proleteriat and rich peasants contrasts with the CPI(M)'s premise that conflict exists between the rural poor as a whole and feudal landlords. In part the difference is theoretical, in part a result of objective differences, for Dhulia has experienced more capitalist development than either Midnapur or Bankura.

Capitalist agricultural development has facilitated the Shramik Sangathana's movement, which has been most successful in Shahada, Taloda, and Nandurbar *talukas*, where capitalist development has proceeded furthest. Tribals' "freedom" from bondage, debt, and even land ownership, coupled with the continuation of landlord oppression, has often sparked protest.

CPI(M) leaders in Bankura have suggested that feudalism is one of the major barriers to rural mobilization. The Communist parties' view of feudalism as the main enemy, and thus their willingness to ally with so-called progressive forces, has disregarded the rapid changes in class relations in the Indian countryside. The CPI(M) has often relied on the middle peasantry, ostensibly because of the progressive character of middle peasants compared to landlords. It tends to contradict even this defective political line by compromising with feudal landlords and neglecting the demands of agricultural laborers; this permits the interests of the middle peasantry to dominate.

The Shramik Sangathana has isolated middle peasants, for it feels that middle peasants generally side with rich peasants over demands like higher prices for agricultural produce, the cheap supply of inputs, and low wages. In the initial stages of the movement, small peasants were at the forefront of the movement, for they were more independent and less subject to victimization than agricultural laborers.[44] In the later stages, however, the landless became the main force behind the movement. The Shramik Sangathana has given priority to wage demands because of the conservatizing effects of property ownership, unlike the CPI(M) which has not questioned the political consequences of land redistribution.

3. *Women's Participation*

In the early stages of the Shahada movement, women's participation in wage, and particularly land demands was limited, although when women participated they showed great militance, and they were very active during the famine in 1973.

Shramik Sangathana activists had no clear perspective on the role women could play in the movement, but as they believed in the right to self-determination, they felt it was undemocratic for women to be excluded.

Ambersingh Mahraj showed particular sensitivity to women's oppression, which was in fact the impetus to his own politicization. The women of Ambersingh's village challenged him, as the most educated person in the village, to do something about the fact that an *adivasi* woman had been raped. Ambersingh felt humiliated at his past inactivity and committed himself to eradicating such injustice. As a tribal himself, Ambersingh was more sensitive to issues of social oppression than an outside leader could have been.

Tribals have sometimes shown the same sensitivity to women's oppression in Bengal. Hitesh encouraged men and women in Damodarpur to fight oppressive attitudes to women. He chastized the men by telling them, "we recreate the treatment we have received from Mahato landlords with our women."[45]

The Shramik Sangathana held a training camp for women in March, 1973 for the first time. Men initially resisted the idea of a three-day *shibir* for women and complained that women would neglect their household responsibilities. But after the activists reasoned with them, one hundred and fifty women of different castes and communities from thirty villages attended the camp.[46] The women formulated the program for the meeting themselves, deciding that one woman from each village should recount the problems she faced. The major grievances expressed were men's excessive drinking and wife-beating. The women spontaneously went into a village, broke all the liquor vessels, and demanded that the *police patil* should explain why he had condoned drinking.

After the first camp, Ambersingh laid down some guidelines for follow-up action, which suggested that women should: (1) not be afraid or ashamed, (2) discuss their experiences with women from other villages, (3) form a women's committee to deal with matters affecting them directly, (4) stop men's drinking and gambling, (5) work with youth committees in matters relating to wages, land, etc., (6) attend night schools and become literate. Women received the program very enthusiastically.[47]

The campaign against drinking was a great success. Women realized that drinking was not an isolated problem but related to other social issues. When drinking recurs, women form bands which roam the villages and break liquor vessels. Thus women spontaneously raised issues relating to their social, cultural, and sexual oppression. Confronting these issues unleashed their energy to participate in other struggles.

The issue of men's drinking was also a major grievance among women in Damodarpur, who felt it was a drain on family resources and led to wife-beating. One day, three of the most respected men in the village got drunk and beat their wives. The women tied the men to a tree and beat them with their *chappals* in the presence of the whole village. The women then decided that if the men were found drinking, they would be fined one rupee and the money would be kept by the women. The fine would be increased and the men put under social boycott if the drinking persisted. In Damodarpur, however where the movement is weaker and younger than in Dhulia, there has not yet been a progression from concern with sexual oppression to attempts to eradicate class-based exploitation.

Women's participation in the movement in Dhulia developed its own methods of struggle without formal organization, and raised new issues concerning women. The activists encouraged this spontaneous upsurge rather than channelling it into rigid modes of expression and thwarting its instinctive character. The activists held a second *shibir* in December, 1973 which was attended by women from Poona and Bombay, and a three-day camp shortly thereafter. Separate women's *shibirs* are now regularly organized. As the activists' and the women's consciousness of sexual oppression grew, in the later phases of the Shahada movement, they mutually decided on issues around which women could organize. Two incidents illustrate this.

The first incident took place in a village in Nandurbar *taluka* in August, 1978. A landlord in the village had the habit of throwing his garbage in front of an *adivasi* woman's house. When she complained one day he became enraged at her "impudence," grabbed her and dragged her twenty feet by the hair. He tore off her blouse, threw her on the ground, sat on her stomach and beat her severely.

WOMEN'S MOBILIZATION IN WEST BENGAL & MAHARASHTRA 243

The Shramik Sangathana activists sent the woman to the police to register a case against the landlord. The police told her that although the case was non-cognizable, they would investigate it, but never did. The activists decided to take the woman to the surrounding villages so that other women would be incited to take action. When the woman and the activists reported the incident, women responded immediately. They decided on a date to take a *morcha* to the landlord's house.

Two hundred to three hundred women from about twelve villages, and one hundred to a hundred and fifty men, whom the Shramik Sangathana persuaded to remain in the background, collected on the appointed day. They appealed to the *sarpanch* and the *police patil*, who did nothing. The women surrounded the landlord's house, forced him to come out, and demanded that he recount the incident. They allowed him ten minutes to justify his actions, in the form of a public trial. When he could not, the women garlanded his neck with their *chappals*, blackened his face, and sat him on a donkey. They then paraded the landlord through the villages where the women beat him and abused him. The police arrested sixteen villagers that night. The activists were released on bail but told to report to the police station daily like criminals. Two hundred women came forward and told the police they were prepared to be arrested, and one thousand people offered to pay the bail. The cases were eventually dropped.

The second incident followed soon after. A demonstration had been staged by a women's organization in Poona against a Marathi film which portrayed women, particularly tribal women, in a degrading manner. A few activists of the Shramik Sangathana described the film to a gathering of about one thousand women. They marched to the theatre where the film was being shown and read out the following statement:

> This demonstration is to protest against the increasingly pornographic and degrading treatment of women in Marathi and Hindi films. It pretends to be art but its purpose is purely commercial. Women, particularly rural women, are portrayed in a distorted manner. The female body is senselessly displayed in every film. No rural woman in reality bears any resemblance to the one depicted. But in

portraying her in this manner, the producer and actresses have insulted us. If the film is not immediately withdrawn from Nandurbar, we will launch a *satyagraha* to stop it.[48]

The demonstrators clashed with the police, but the film was withdrawn.

On certain issues like landlord rape, women have shown particular militance. Many incidents of rape went unnoticed prior to 1972, for tribals were afraid to file cases against rich peasants. In some villages, the wives of *saldars* had to sleep with the landlords in order to get employment. This has stopped completely, and women react violently if there is a suggestion of sexual exploitation.

Women's participation in mass democratic movements shows certain distinctive characteristics, common to Damodarpur and Dhulia. Women have shown great courage in fighting police repression to protect their homes and families. Women are able to sustain struggles for longer periods of time, show less susceptibility to corruption than men, and are best able to express themselves through spontaneous and innovative forms of action.

Women's greater endurance, lesser susceptibility to corruption, and greater distrust of charity, may stem from the fact that women have been less touched by political parties and have withstood greater hardship than men. Women have been at the forefront of *gheraos*, demonstrations, and strikes. Yet their sustained participation and leadership has been deterred by their housework responsibilities. In the youth committees in Dhulia and in the village committee in Damodarpur, women's participation lags far behind that of men. Nor have the women's committees which exist become as powerful as the youth committees.

The most active women in Dhulia have been older, either with adult children, or divorced or widowed. A few women have complained that after marriage they are unable to remain active in the Shramik Sangathana. Marriage severs a woman's ties with her own community, when she goes to live in alien surroundings and is completely dependent on her in-laws and husband. The fragmentation of class and sexual solidarities, which migration similarly entails for men, is the inevitable result.[49]

The shortage of full-time female activists has also deterred women's participation, a problem the activists are keenly aware of themselves. The Gram Swarajya Samiti has a woman activist, the wife of the late Ambersingh Mahraj, but she has not organized among or for women. Consequently, women's issues have not received adequate attention. The inadequacy of female activists is a problem which is not confined to Dhulia or Damodarpur, but exists in almost all rural political movements in India.

PART II: SOCIO-ECONOMIC FACTORS AFFECTING WOMEN'S POLITICAL PARTICIPATION

Thus far, the extent and form of women's participation in political protest has been analyzed solely as a result of differences between Communist Party and mass democratic movements. Clearly, political strategy cannot be formulated in a vacuum, but must contend with differing socio-economic conditions. In the second part, the most significant deterrents or stimuli to women's politicization in the socio-economic sphere will be analyzed.

A. The Economic Sphere: The Extent and Form of Women's Labor Force Participation

Women's economic participation is an essential prerequisite to their political awareness and participation, at an individual, village, and state level. Women have thus been involved in protest where concentrations of female agricultural laborers are greatest, in Maharashtra rather than Bengal, and in villages in Jhargram and in Dhulia.

Employment under debilitating, exploitative conditions is by no means a liberating experience in itself. Yet for women to break out of the isolation of housework and childcare, they must participate in the larger economy. Women's household roles lead to much greater seclusion than unemployment does among men. Women's militancy is much more probable when women experience class exploitation, through discrimination in wages, conditions of work, and unemployment, coupled with sexual exploitation. As both producers and organizers of consumption for the family, female agricultural laborers suffer most the brunt of economic crisis. Men are able to find escapes more easily, whereas unemployment, rising prices, and the non-availability of food are hardships women are forced to confront at home. In fact, often women's militance has not directly confronted the work situation, but rather their role as mediators of consumption. Women have been more concerned with larger forms of class exploitation, such as the deterioration of economic conditions, than more narrowly production-based issues.

Women of the lower classes are accorded far greater equality, independence, and mobility through their economic contribution than women of the upper classes. Rich peasant women are secluded within their homes and restricted from participation in the public arena, for paid work is neither socially sanctioned nor economically necessary. In West Bengal, where middle peasant women have been more active than agricultural laborers, movements have tended to be reformist, neither challenging class nor sexual inequality. In the western, southern and central states of India, the proportion of agricultural laborers is much higher, and rates of sharecropping and tenancy lower, than in the northern and eastern states. The former states are precisely the regions where women have participated most in political protest.[50]

In Maharashtra, there has been a longer tradition of women's labor force participation, in part because of the influence of the *ryotwari* system, than in West Bengal. In fact, in western Maharashtra, female agricultural laborer and small peasant labor force participation is often higher than male, for if the family owns a small plot of land, it is customary for the man to cultivate it and the woman to work for wages. While middle peasant women rarely work for wages in West Bengal, in Maharashtra they work more than their husbands in times of need.

In West Bengal, male labor is replacing female labor in agriculture. The demand for female labor arises only if male labor is insufficient, and then only for exclusively female operations.[51] Planting paddy seedlings used to be exclusively women's work, but male laborers have been employed for this work in the past two decades. Husking and threshing machines, pesticides, and rice mills have all reduced women's employment.[52] Today, ploughing, leveling the land, preparing the seed beds, spraying pesticides, and spreading fertilizers are all paid male jobs. Parboiling paddy at home, dehusking with the country husker, drying the paddy, winnowing, and cleaning the agricultural fields are all female unpaid jobs.[53] Important as the fact of women's employment, therefore, is its form. Bengali women perform a variety of unpaid agricultural tasks. The absence of collective organization and the independence associated with a wage reinforces women's belief that the tremendous agricultural labor they perform is only an extension of their housework.

Unemployment rates for women have been highest in the south, slightly less in the north, and lowest in the west.[54] Not only is unemployment more acute for women in West Bengal, but a significant proportion of women who are usually members of the labor force shift to domestic work, and by definition leave the labor force, when labor demand is slack. A large number of rural women who are available for employment but do not report availability are classified as housewives.[55] Hence statistics on unemployment grossly underestimate female unemployment.

Socio-cultural and economic factors are integrally related in accounting for women's seclusion or independence, which in turn contributes to the likelihood of women's political passivity or independence. The mutually reinforcing nature of cultural and economic factors suggests why scheduled caste and tribal agricultural laborers have everywhere been more likely to engage in protest than other women.

B. The Socio-Cultural Sphere: Tribal Women and Political Protest

The Bengali value structure emphasizes women's dependency and passivity to a much greater extent than Marathi values. Islamic culture, which stressed female seclusion and modesty, had a greater impact in West Bengal than in

Maharashtra. Yet in both West Bengal and Maharashtra, women are subject to the strict sex models of caste Hindu society.

Tribals in West Bengal and Maharashtra have been able to escape most restricting roles imposed on women. The sex ratio for tribal women at 98.2:100 is better than for all Indian women at 93:100.[56] Mortality rates of girls and suicide rates of women are probably lower among tribals than Hindus. Within the home, though tribal women are primarily responsible for housework and childcare, there is a greater sharing of responsibilities than among Hindus.

The relaxation of strict sexual norms gives tribal women considerable freedom before and after marriage. Marriages are supposed to be arranged but a large number are based on choice. Among tribals, the age of marriage is higher than among Hindus. Tribal women are permitted to divorce and widows to remarry, for marriage is not considered a sacrament as it is among Hindus, but rather a social contract between husband and wife. Bhils pay a bride price upon elopement and return it upon divorce to formalize the negotiation. Physical beauty is not a criterion of a woman's eligibility; the girl should be strong, hard working, and healthy.[57]

The custom of bride price has been interpreted as indicative of women's higher status among tribals than the dowry system among Hindus. Yet the concept of having "purchased" a wife in the hill areas of Shahada, and thereby expecting her to perform certain duties, makes this interpretation questionable. In Dhulia the bride price varies from 125 to 500 rupees, exclusive of marriage expenses. The Shramik Sangathana arranged a mass marriage on May Day in 1978, to eliminate the bride price and the large expenses and liquor consumption marriages usually entail. The idea of group marriages is slowly gaining currency.

Tribal women's authority within the home is not matched by equality in the inheritance of property, in the ritual sphere, or in participation in traditional political administration.[58] Women were traditionally excluded from the village *panch* in Maharashtra and to the *solo anna* in Bengal.[59]

Tribal women have been exploited on a class and sexual basis, but it has not led to the same internalization of subordination as among Hindu women. Tribal men and women share a history of exploitation, and this may be one of the reasons for their greater equality. Women have had to play an active role in protecting men from police and landlord repression. Men in turn, having witnessed brutal atrocities against women, may have developed greater sensitivity to women's oppression. Landlord rape, which has often been a form of class-based oppression, has also frequently been a catalyst to tribal revolt.

The most vibrant and militant political movements in contemporary India have been tribal movements: the Jharkhand movement in the tribal areas of Bengal, Bihar, and Orissa; the CPI (ML) movements in Andhra Pradesh and West Bengal; and the Shramik Sangathana and other tribal movements in Maharashtra. Are these movements likely to remain isolated and atypical?

Certain movements have been more relevant to tribals than to non-tribals, for instance, movements for the restoration of tribal land or the allotment of forest land. On the other hand, there is evidence that the rapidly deteriorating condition of non-tribal agricultural laborers has reinforced the common class basis of exploitation of tribals and non-tribals.[60] Political movements often begin among tribals because they are the most exploited and rebellious of the rural poor.[61] The leaders of a movement must then make the transition from a purely tribal to class-based movement. In Shahada the activists have deliberately involved Hindus in the movement to make this transition. Similarly, the issues around which tribal and caste Hindu women can both be organized must be identified. Tribal women have been more receptive to fighting sexual oppression because of greater sexual exploitation from without, and freedom from within their own community. Caste Hindu women on the other hand have shown greater concern with deteriorating economic conditions, such as rising prices, the provision of better facilities at work, schools, hospitals and low wages. Political organizers must demonstrate the practical link between sexual and class oppression and in so doing, bring together tribal and non-tribal women.

The Communists in West Bengal have been as unsuccessful in organizing among tribals as among women. Their own upper-caste backgrounds and their theoretical stress on the primacy of economic issues have meant that the established Communist parties have neglected to struggle against social and cultural oppression which concern tribals and women most directly.

C. Caste and Class at the Village Level

The particular structuring of castes and classes at the village level is a crucial determinant of political protest. Class conflict is more likely where classes are polarized between rich peasants-landlords and agricultural laborers than in villages with numerous intermediary classes. The overlapping of class and caste distinctions reinforces class polarization. In villages where the dominant economic class is the dominant caste, and the subordinate caste and class is also the same, the likelihood of conflict is much greater.

On the other hand, migration has been an important potential factor in mitigating class conflict. High rates of in-migration mean that employers can substitute migrant labor for the local labor force and pay them lower wages, thus subverting wage movements. Migrant laborers, having come from areas where wages and employment are even more adverse, are vulnerable and isolated in alien surroundings and less likely to become involved in strikes than the local labor force. Similarly, high rates of out-migration thwart the possibility of building stable organizations of agricultural laborers. Conversely, strong organizations of agricultural laborers have curtailed the detrimental effects of migration on wage movements.

Radhamohanpur village in Midnapur illustrates the difficulties of organizing in a village where the majority of the population are small peasants. The entire population of the village is Mahishyo, a caste which has adopted strict norms of seclusion and taboos against manual labor for women. Most women work on their own plots of betel leaf land or exchange labor with relatives or friends. Women's agricultural work is considered an extension of their housework. Partly as a result of the caste-class structure of the area, the CPI (M) is weak and has not organized any protest movements. The prosperity of the area has led to large-scale in-migration so that local laborers can easily be replaced by outside laborers at lower wages. Mahishyos are more concerned with upward social mobility than sudden, drastic change. As work is dispersed on individual plots of land, there are few possibilities of collective organizing.

On the other hand, a highly diversified class structure also deters political protest. In Krishnanagar village in Bankura, a variety of intermediary castes and classes have made it difficult to develop class consciousness and organization. The dominant class in the village has purposely cultivated ties with the well-to-do scheduled castes, in order to break the unity of the majority of scheduled caste agricultural laborers. Scheduled caste agricultural laborers are further internally stratified by rank and economic position. While the majority work as casual laborers, the lower-ranking scheduled castes work as contract labor, which involves long hours of agricultural and domestic work, and ties of dependence to the landlord through the system of advances. The differences between the lower and higher-ranking scheduled caste women are striking. The former, who work mainly as domestic servants, are submissive and frightened, whereas the latter, who are agricultural laborers and fisherwomen, are out-spoken and militant. The CPI(M) has not been successful in overcoming the intricately structured system of class and caste inequalities in Krishnanagar.

Shramik Sangathana movements have been more successful in the plains, where class and caste polarization exist, than in the hill areas of Dhulia. Ratnagiri village in the hilly region of Dhulia exemplifies the difficulties of organizing in a purely tribal village. The village is isolated from the plains and thus there is no experience of confrontation with landlords or rich peasants. Tribals are divided into two groups: the relatively prosperous Pawras and the Bhils, but stratification between the two groups is indistinct.

Fragmentation along caste and class lines is the more typical pattern in Maharashtra as a whole. The *ryotwari* system in Maharashtra prevented the development of intermediaries and vested interests in land, which by and large meant an absence of class polarization. The process of impoverishment of the peasantry was much slower in Maharashtra than in areas of the country under the *zamindari* system. As a result, a large section of owner-cultivator peasants are able to eke out a subsistence from the land they own.[62] Self-employment has weakened the possibilities of organization.

In each of the villages described, Radhamohanpur, Krishnanagar and Ratnagiri, there are major obstacles to class-based organizing. Yet strong political movements have been able to overcome these barriers by organizing contract laborers, preventing migration, and fighting casteism. Structural barriers to class organization cannot be dismissed as insignificant; rather they call for particular attention on the part of political activists.

Conclusions

West Bengal and Maharashtra are both unusual in the extent to which there has been protest involving women. Even where protest has occurred, women's participation has been confined in time, space, and according to the character of political movements. Women have passively supported most political movements, but their active participation, and particularly their expression of their own interests, has been very limited.

The binding ties of family, the burdens of housework, and traditional values have all reinforced the dependency created by the decline in women's role in commodity production. The obstacles to women's politicization are tremendous, and organization and leadership among women are lacking. Middle-class women have started feminist activities recently, but so far these movements have been restricted to the cities and have not attempted mass organizing among rural or urban women. The established national-level women's organizations are even further removed from the problems of poor rural women. Even where political leadership and organization exist, however, they have often discriminated against women. Trade union discrimination, for example, coupled with large-scale unemployment, has deterred women from organizing along trade union lines in the industrial sector.[63]

The nature of women's subordination in part determines the likelihood of their participation in political protest. The sexual oppression of Hindu women can be distinguished from the sexual exploitation of tribal women. Hindu women's oppression is marked by subordination and inequality in the few spheres in which they interact with men, and exclusion from most arenas. Tribal women, by participating in most spheres of social and economic life, are subject to more overt discrimination and sexual exploitation. They experience this as an assault on the greater equality they are accorded by their own community, and are thus prepared to resist. Hindu women generally internalize their subordination, for it is reinforced by the cultural norms and values of their society.

In a patriarchal society, where all women are isolated from the political domain, women have only become politicized by issues which affect them directly. Women have responded most militantly when expectations of justice in their personal lives are violated. Hindu middle- and lower-class women are so defined by their housewife and mother roles that they have been most politicized by issues affecting their position in the family. In both West Bengal and Maharashtra, masses of women have participated in movements against inflation, food shortages, and for relief after famines and droughts. Similarly, peasant women have shown complete fearlessness in resisting police brutality when their homes and families have been endangered.

Tribal women have been outraged at men's drinking because of its association with wife-beating, which violates their pride, strength, and independence. The incidence of drinking may be higher among tribals than Hindus, even when Hindu men drink, their wives are less prepared to stop them. Drinking is also a drain on family resources. Tribal women contribute to and control the family income to a greater extent than Hindu women and are therefore more angered by men's wastefulness. Drinking is also a political problem. Women in Damodarpur and Dhulia feel that men's drinking prevents them from participating in political struggles and for this reason, landlords have often encouraged men to drink.

Women have often responded to innovative forms of protest which utilize symbols drawn from their daily lives. In the anti-price rise movement in Bombay, symbols of women's oppression like the rolling pin and other kitchen utensils, became symbols of women's resistance. Tying men to trees, beating them with *chappals*, and placing a landlord on a donkey vividly illustrate that women are able to express their militance best by defining issues, forms, and symbols of protest themselves.

Women have often been mobilized to widen the mass base of political movements. This has sometimes led women to recognize the importance of their contribution, and instilled in them both a sense of self-confidence, and dissatisfaction at fighting for others' demands. Women's militancy in the Tebhaga movement led them to put forward issues of concern to them as women. Female agricultural laborers in several states like Kerala, Maharashtra, Andhra Pradesh, and Tamil Nadu, became concerned with issues like equal wages, the provision of creches, and emancipation from sole responsibilities for housework and childcare, through their active participation in the unions of agricultural workers in the 1960s.

A large concentration of agricultural laborers and tribals, and the erosion of feudal relations, culture, and ideology through capitalist development have been essential conditions to women's participation in protest. These factors are necessary but not sufficient without a correct political approach. The tremendous objective deterrents to women's participation reveal the importance of political organization, and testify to the achievements of the movements in West Bengal and Maharashtra.

This emphasis on the relationship between women's political participation and alternative political strategies may suggest an overly critical assessment of the CPI (M)'s approach. It would, however, be simplistic to ignore the greater obstacles to organizing in West Bengal than in Maharashtra. Conditions in Dhulia have been highly favorable to protest for several reasons. First, the dominant class in Dhulia is Gujar, a minority caste from outside Maharashtra. Unlike Marathas, Gujars have been unable to use state power to crush political dissent. Nevertheless, rich peasants have used brutal methods to punish and harass Shramik Sangathana activists, under the guise of protecting crops from theft. A scheme for crop-protection societies, proposed by rich peasants in Dhulia district in September, 1973, called for the creation of a para-military force with a capital expenditure of Rs. 4.22 lakhs, and a recurring annual expenditure of 4.74 lakhs. The scheme was only withdrawn because of the questions raised in Parliament, the Legislative Assembly, and the press.[64] The open, democratic quality of the Dhulia movement made possible public outrage at the violation of democratic norms.

Dhulia is also distinctive in the weaker hold of caste feelings, more intensive capitalist development, and greater class polarization than in most other parts of Maharashtra. The Shramik Sangathana stepped into a situation in which protest was almost inevitable because of these favorable conditions. Further, the activists did not deliberately seek out women's participation; it arose quite spontaneously. The relative absence of such conducive factors generally has meant that movements of this kind have been sporadic and isolated.

The CPI(M) to its credit has been able to create more durable organizations of the rural poor, often in the face of greater repression, than most radical democratic movements. Women have played an active role during periods of repression. Thousands of women protested at the downfall of the West Bengal United Front government in 1967. After the central government dislodged the second United Front government in 1970 it unleashed tremendous repression, and the police raped, tortured, and harassed women. Women's groups called for resistance, the withdrawal of police camps,[65] and an investigation into the treatment of political prisoners.

In attempting to maintain both its radicalism and its electoral strength, the CPI (M) is faced with greater dilemmas than the Shramik Sangathana. Yet these dilemmas also result from conscious choices. As the Shramik Sangathana's approach to contesting the elections shows, electoralist strategy does not have to be an end in itself, nor the end to a more radical position.

Political leadership and organizations in both Maharashtra and West Bengal have accentuated underlying tendencies. Shramik Sangathana activists would have been faced with far greater obstacles had they been organizing among a peasantry lacking the propensity to rebellion and protest. Conversely, the CPI (M) reinforced the tendency towards political passivity on the part of the peasantry through its more authoritarian leadership. The CPI (M) has sometimes unconsciously reinforced rather than altered existing conditions, by accepting as theoretical given social structures which are rapidly evolving in practice. For example, while feudalism has unquestionably been an obstacle to political change in West Bengal, it is faulty to regard feudalism as a monolithic, all-determining force.

Further, the CPI (M) has often itself uncritically accepted patriarchal values. This is most conspicuous at the point where patriarchal values are enacted and crystallized: within the home and family. The CPI (M) has not challenged the sexual division of labor, despite the fact that the destruction of partriarchal values would lead to higher levels of women's participation and radicalize the movement as a whole.

Women's participation suggests certain conclusions about a political movement. A critical interpretation of the CPI (M)'s record in organizing women must question its radical character. On the other hand, the Shramik Sangathana's success in encouraging women to challenge sexual inequality is indicative of its radical, democratic character. Mass democratic movements have looked to the CPI (M) for guidance but ultimately learned more from its mistakes. The CPI (M) dismisses these movements as insignificant at best, and regards itself as the most authentic vehicle for radical change in India. Yet the Party's recent greater attentiveness to organizing the landless and women, in fighting casteism and communalism, show that it has been forced to acknowledge discontent at the grass-roots level.

The CPI (M) has failed to bring about radical political change in the day-to-day patterns of class, caste, and sexual inequality. The Shramik Sangathana is most instructive in its continual struggle against such inequalities. Neither the Shramik Sangathana nor the CPI(M) movements are suggestive of an existing or possible future pattern of political mobilization in India. The success of the Shramik Sangathana's approach, however, challenges that of the established Left and confronts it with inescapable questions if it is to provide a viable alternative.

NOTES

This research was made possible by a fellowship from the American Institute of Indian Studies (1979-1980) for doctoral research in India. The field research was conducted in five villages in West Bengal: three in Midnapur district and two in Bankura district, and three villages in Dhulia district, Maharashtra. The names of the villages have been changed in this article.

[1] I was specifically concerned with studying movements organized by the CPI(M) because of its greater strength than the CPI and its more complex relationship to political movements from its position of power in West Bengal. The rural organizing strategies of the CPI and CPI (M) are similar, however, and many of the generalizations about the CPI (M)'s methods and approaches are equally applicable to the CPI.

[2] Pravin Seth, *Political Participation of Women, 1951-79* (New Delhi: Indian Council of Social Science Research, 1979), p. 8.

[3] In the 1977 Legislative Assembly elections, the Left Front Government won 235 seats, and the CPI (M) an absolute majority with 178 seats. In contrast, the Janata won 29 seats and Congress 20 seats. The Left Front government missed winning an absolute majority only in Midnapur, where it won 37 seats, Janata won 17 and the CPI and Congress 2 seats each. Ajit Roy, "Not a Negative Vote," *Economic and Political Weekly* (hereafter *EPW*) XII, 27 (July 2, 1977).

[4] Gail Omvedt, "Non Brahmins and Communists in Bombay," *EPW* VIII, 16 (April 21, 1973), p. 804.

[5] Perhaps in part because of greater caste oppression, more movements against casteism have arisen in Maharashtra than in West Bengal, such as the Non-Brahmin movement in the 1930s and 40s, the Dalit Panthers, and the movement for the renaming of Marathwada University after Dr. Ambedkar.

[6] *People's War*, no. 46 (May 23, 1943), p. 3.

[7] *People's War*, no. 41 (April 18, 1943), p. 8.

[8] Amit K. Gupta, "Protest, Participation and Egalitarian Trends: A Study of Women's Mobilization for Change," unpub. paper presented at the All-India Sociological Conference, University of Jabalpur, M.P., December 28-30, 1978, p. 6.

[9] *Ibid.*, p. 8.

[10] *Ibid.*, p. 5.

[11] Report of the Seminar on Women and Development held on January 28-29, 1979, *Voices of the Oppressed* (Calcutta; Saimudcco, 1979), p. 57.

[12] Hajrah Begum, "Women's Movement in India: A Critical Turning Point," *New Age* III, 4 (July, 1954).

[13] In 1953 the Central Social Welfare Board was formed to promote welfare schemes for women and children in rural and urban areas. Over the past twenty years there has been an increasing shift towards family and child welfare projects, away from women's welfare projects. The number of *mahila mandals*, women's organizations, has steadily declined between the First and the Fifth Plans, from 624 institutions and 1629 centers in the First Plan, to 406 institutions and 1498 centers in the Fifth Plan. There has also been a decline in the funds released for *mahila mandals*, although there was a slight increase after 1975. Research, Statistics and Evaluation Division, *The Central Social Welfare Board 1953-78* (New Delhi: CSWB, 1979).

[14] Bangendu Ganguly, "Profiles of Women in West Bengal," in

Vina Mazumdar, ed., *Symbols of Power: Studies on the Political Status of Women in India, Women in a Changing Society*, Vol. I (Bombay: Allied Publishers, for SNDT Women's University, 1979), p. 334.

[15] Nirmila Bannerjee, "Politicization of Women in West Bengal," in Mazumdar, ed., *Symbols of Power*, pp. 161-162.

[16] In the 1977 West Bengal Legislative Assembly elections, of the 294 seats occupied by Left Front candidates, only four were women. Report of the Seminar on Women and Development, p. 63.

[17] Kanak Mukherjee, one of the most prominent leaders of CPI (M) women's organizations, suggested that International Women's Year was designed by the Congress government to create illusions among the masses, Kanak Mukherjee, *International Women's Year and Ourselves* (Calcutta: Ekshate, 1976), p. 31.

[18] The CPI (M) has attempted to take possession of land held above the legal ceiling through fraudulent registration and in fictitious names, to vest this land in the state and distribute it to landless and land-poor peasants.

[19] The CPI (M) decided for the first time that the *panchayat* elections should be contested on an explicitly political basis. It recorded a fantastic success in electing party members and supporters to a majority of three-tier *panchayats* in West Bengal. The *panchayats* have been entrusted with implementing some of the major programs of the Left Front government.

[20] Such conflicts were apparent in several villages in Shonamukhi block, Bankura, where my field work was conducted.

[21] Report of the Seminar on Women and Development.

[22] *Mahila samiti* programs may be partially shaped by the earmarked funds they receive from the Central Social Welfare Board for such schemes as homes for destitute women, milk centers, and mother and child welfare programs. Meenakshi Apte, "Women and Development in India," *Journal of Social Work* XXXI, 4 (1979), p. 44. Yet there has been no attempt to depart from such sex-linked programs.

[23] This account of the *gherao* is based on observations in the course of field work in Ranibandh, Bankura, in the summer of 1979.

[24] Datta Savle, "Maharashtra," unpub. paper written for the National Institute of Bank Management, Bombay, 1979, p. 88.

[25] P.N. Limaye, "The Politicization of Women in Manarashtra," in Mazumdar, ed., *Symbols of Power*, p. 354.

[26] The Lal Nishan Party has organized among 10,000 village watchmen in thirteen districts. In October, 1974 the LNP organized a big strike at the Rahori Agricultural University in Ahmednagar which was eventually crushed. Savle, "Maharashtra," p. 94.

[27] During my field work, I found in one village in Shonamukhi block, Bankura, that agricultural laborers spontaneously went on strike and were joined by women who were working as maids. The CPI (M) took over the strike after it had continued for a week, and negotiated a compromise which only partially met the initial demands of agricultural laborers. Similarly in Ranibandh, Bankura, agricultural laborers

who pick the leaves used to roll *bidi* cigarettes, mainly women, went on strike to demand a higher price for the bundle of leaves they sold to middlemen. The CPI (M) stepped in after the strike had been on for two months, and scaled down its initial demands.

[28] Information about Damodarpur is based on field work in Jhargram, Midnapur, in the summer of 1979.

[29] P.B., "Organizing the Landless in Shahada," *EPW* VIII, 10 (March 10, 1973), p. 501.

[30] In Shahada *taluka* there were no tractors in 1946. By 1967 there were 50, and by 1971, 300, the largest number in any *taluka* in Maharashtra. The number of oil engines and pumps per 1000 hectares of land increased from about 20 in 1963-64, to 35 in 1966-67, and 50 in 1973 in Shahada. The total area under irrigation has been increasing very rapidly and was 20,000 hectares for Shahada in 1973. *Ibid.*

[31] Vijay Kulkarni, unpub. report on the Shramik Sangathana for the National Labor Institute, New Delhi, 1979.

[32] "The Bhil Movement in Dhulia," *EPW* VII, annual no., 5-7 (February, 1972), p. 72.

[33] P.B., "Organizing the Landless," p. 502.

[34] *Ibid.*

[35] Kulkarni, Report on the Shramik Sangathana.

[36] Before the Shramik Sangathana started organizing in Dhulia, *saldars* worked for 12-16 hours a day performing agricultural work, cleaning stables, carrying water for cattle, and doing domestic work. They were given no relief from work and no weekly holiday. *Saldars* were paid about 100 rupees in 1970, casual laborers in the plans area 2 rupees for men and 1.50 for women.

[37] Mangesh Rage, "Shahada: January 30 to May 1st," *Magova* (June, 1972), p. 3.

[38] P.B., "Organizing the Landless," p. 503. The issue of forest encroachments is dealt with more fully by S.D. Kulkarni, "Encroachment on Forest Land: The Experience in Maharashtra," *EPW* XIV, 45 (November 10, 1979).

[39] Maria Mies, "The Shahada Movement, A Peasant Movement in Maharashtra: Its Development and Perspectives," *Journal of Peasant Studies* III, 4 (July, 1976), p. 478.

[40] A. Manohar, "The Awakening of Shahada's Adivasis," *Times Weekly*, October 7, 1973.

[41] The differences between the Shramik Sangathana and the Gram Swarajya Samiti are spelled out in a bulletin issued by the Shramik Sangathana after the split between the two organizations in 1977, entitled "Our Stand."

[42] "Operation Bargadar," for the recording of sharecroppers led to inter-party clashes within the Left Front government, despite the initial enthusiasm for the program. Asum Mukhopadhyay, "Operation Barga," *EPW* XIV, 37 (September 15, 1979), p. 156.

[43] The Sammata Sammelan was organized to protest atrocities against scheduled castes, *dalits*. The dominant castes unleashed tremen-

dous repression against the *dalits* over the issue of renaming Marathwada University after the famous untouchable leader, Dr. Ambedkar.

Several other issues have also been taken up jointly by leftist organizations, such as the encroachment on forest land in tribal areas of Thana and Dhulia districts. The price-rise agitation was conducted by a joint action committee of leftist groups in Maharashtra in June, 1979. In Shahada it led to an attack by the police and rich peasants on Shramik Sangathana activists. 2000 *adivasis* attended a subsequent judicial inquiry.

[44] Interview with Sharamik Sangathana activists, November, 1979.

[45] Interview with Hitesh in Damodarpur, June, 1979.

[46] Chayyar Datar, "The Relationship Between the Women's Movement and the Class Struggle in Shahada: A Case Study," unpub. paper read at the All-India Conference on Women, Trivandrum, December 27-29, 1975, p. 6.

[47] "A New Profile of the Adivasi Woman," *Maharashtra Times*, January 13, 1974.

[48] Sandeep Pendse, untitled article, *Blitz*, Bombay, 1974, translated from Marathi. The incidents attracted wide press publicity including editorials in three Marathi Newspapers: *Nav Shakti*, *The Free Press Journal*, and *Lok Sahta*, as well as other journals, e.g., "Angry Women Punish An Obnoxious Landlord," *How* I, 6 (November, 1978).

[49] Women's family responsibilities have also meant that literacy levels among the most active women are much lower than among men. Although the activists do not believe that literacy is essential to full-time commitment to the movement, they do feel that illiteracy hampers a high level of political participation.

[50] Gail Omvedt, "Women and Rural Revolt in India," *The Social Scientist* (Trivandrum) VI, 1-2 (August-September, 1977).

[51] Kumaresh Chakravarty and G.C. Tewari, *Regional Variation in Women's Employment: A Case Study of Five Indian Villages in Three Indian States* (New Delhi: Indian Council of Social Science Research, 1978), p. 45.

[52] Report of the National Convention of Working Women, "Fight Unitedly for the Cause of Indian Working Women," Madras, April 4-10, 1979, p. 40.

[53] So far mechanization does not appear to have led to a significant reduction in women's employment in Dhulia. Tractorization may involve some displacement of male labor from ploughing but women still do the weeding and harvesting. Sulabha Brahme and Ashok Upadhyay, *Study of the Economic Conditions of Agricultural Labor in Dhulia District, Maharashtra* (Pune: Shankar Brahme Samajvidnyana Granthlaya, 1975), p. 163.

[54] "Some Employment and Unemployment Characteristics of Rural Women: An Analysis of NSS Data for West Bengal, 1972-73," *EPW* XIII, 12 (March 25, 1978), p. A 35.

[55] Leela Gulati, "Unemployment Among Female Agricultural Laborers," *EPW* XI, 13 (March 21, 1976), p. A 35.

[56] Pratap C. Datta, "Female Population of Tribal India," in *Tribal Women in India* (Calcutta: Indian Anthropological Society, 1978), p. 7.
[57] *Ibid.*, p. 13,
[58] Jyoti Sen, "Status of Women Among Tribals," in *Tribal Women in India*, p. 30.
[59] The traditional village council in both Maharashtra and in West Bengal excluded women and was dominated by elder men in the village. Where the village committee continues to function, women are still largely excluded. In Shahada there is a tension between the old *panch* and the new *tarun mandals*.
[60] Report on the Economic Condition of the Weaker Sections of the Rural Population in Maharashtra, 1970-71, shows that the average annual earning of an agricultural labor household was about Rs. 1253, with a monthly per capita income of Rs. 23, whereas the average yearly expenditure was 1,417 rupees. Indebtedness naturally follows. "Organizing the Adivasis," *EPW* IX, annual no., 6-8 (February 1974), p. 176 b.
[61] S.D. Kulkarni, "Caste and Class in a Tribal Movement," *EPW* XIV, annual no., 7-8 (February 1979), p. 465.
[62] Gail Omvedt, "Working Women: Grapes and Ferment," *Frontier* VIII, 29 (November 29, 1975), p. 13.
[63] At the national convention of the women's wing of the CITU, the CPI (M) trade union, it was reported that the number of women in trade unions has steadily declined since 1961 and women's participation in the CITU is no better than in any other trade union. Report of the National Convention of Working Women, 1979 p. 4.
[64] Sandeep Pendse, untitled article on the Shramik Sangathana, *Magova*, Bombay (June, 1972), pp. 2-3.
[65] A deputation of women from the CPI (M) *mahila samiti* met with Prime Minister Indira Gandhi and presented her with a petition signed by 40,000 women describing the attacks on women and demanding the release of political prisoners. The P.M. denied all allegations. *People's Democracy* VIII, 25 (June 18, 1972).

Glossary

adivasis: aboriginals, original inhabitants or tribals.
anradhan: a community grain bank.
bhajan: religious ballad.
Bhils: the largest group of tribals in Dhulia district and one of the major tribal groups in Maharashtra.
chappals: sandals.
dalits: scheduled castes or "untouchables."
dharna: sit down strike.
gherao: a pressure tactic which takes the form of an encirclement preventing those within the premises from leaving.

gram panchayat: a village level political-administrative body which was revived by the Congress Party for purposes of decentralizing political power. The *panchayat* also functions at the *taluka* and district levels.

Gujar: a caste of cultivators who migrated from Gujarat to Dhulia in the eighteenth century.

Kisan Sabha: the peasant organization of the Communist Party.

Lodhas: a group of scheduled tribes inhabiting Jhargram subdivision, Midnapur district, West Bengal.

lakh: one lakh equals 100,000 rupees or approximately $ 12,500.

Mahatos: formerly scheduled castes from Bihar, the Mahatos have migrated to Midnapur where they have become landowning cultivators.

mahila samiti: women's organization.

Mahishyos: the dominant caste of cultivators in Tamluk subdivision, Midnapur.

Marathas: the dominant caste in Maharashtra.

morcha: a procession, demonstration.

palemor: system of moneylending.

panch: the traditional village council in Dhulia, composed of the eldest and most respected persons in the village. The *panch* continues to be responsible for settling disputes, arranging marriages, and organizing religious festivities.

police patil: a low-ranking government official, entrusted with preserving law and order.

ryotwari: the system of land revenue introduced by the British in Maharashtra whereby the peasant proprietor paid revenue directly to the state.

saldars: formerly bonded laborers, *saldars* in Dhulia district are now annual contract laborers.

sarpanch: the head of the elected *panchayat*.

Sarvodaya: a Gandhian organization, involved primarily in constructive activities and social work, which believes in change through gradual, peaceful means.

satyagraha: a mass demonstration.

shibir: a study group organized over a period of several days, involving intensive political discussion between tribals and the activists.

solo anna: literally, 16 annas make one rupee. Here *solo anna* refers to the sixteen village elders who constitute the traditional village council. The *solo anna* in West Bengal functions in a similar manner to the *panch* in Maharashtra.

taluka: a subdivision of a district, corresponding to a revenue collection area.

tarun mandal: village youth organization.

veth begar: bonded labor.

zamindari: the land tenure system the British created in Bengal, creating intermediaries on the land, responsible for collecting revenue for the state from cultivators.

10
The All Pakistan Women's Association and the 1961 Muslim Family Laws Ordinance

SYLVIA CHIPP—KRAUSHAAR

Members of the All Pakistan Women's Association (APWA), a voluntary social welfare organization founded by Begum Liaquat Ali Khan in the wake of partition, explicitly state that the APWA is not a "political body." In spite of this firm disclaimer, however, one soon discovers that the APWA is, in fact, very much a political body. Since its founding in 1949, the APWA, particularly its Women's Rights and Responsibilities Section, has frequently acted as an interest group to press for passage of laws which its members believed would improve the status of women in Pakistan. The organization claims as its most notable accomplishment the passage of the Muslim Family Laws Ordinance, which was promulgated in 1961 by former President Ayub Khan. In order to understand how the women of APWA were able to influence policy, it is instructive to take a brief look at interest group politics in Pakistan during the fifties and early sixties.

Gabriel Almond and G. Bingham Powell, Jr., in their developmental approach to comparative politics, concern themselves with the "environmental factors which shape the channels and means of access for interest articulation . . . . " As the authors point out, "The channels of access" are most directly dependent upon the "structures of political communication," such as newspapers and radios, available in the society. In addition, the "political culture," that is, values, attitudes, the degree of alienation and hostility, levels of education and awareness, in the society are important considerations. Further, since the "representation of interests on a continuing basis is an expensive procedure," a major influence on the process of interest articulation is "the distribution of resources in the society."[1]

It may not be surprising, then to discover that the interest groups in Pakistan which have been most successful in achieving their demands were those representative of wealthy industrialists and businessmen. The Federation of Pakistan Chambers of Commerce and Industry (FPCCI) represents fourteen chambers of commerce and about fourty-six industries[2] and was quite successful in getting the government to adopt its recommendations. The government-sponsored Pakistan Industrial Credit and Investment Corporation (PICIC) and the Industrial Development Bank of Pakistan (IDBP) have been "vital to the industrial development of Pakistan because their permission is necessary for obtaining foreign exchange and financial assistance to initiate new projects or to modernize existing plants."[3]

These interest groups appeared to dominate the political process in Pakistan, in part, because of their extensive wealth. An added factor was President Ayub's receptiveness to their demands which coincided with his plans for the industrialization of Pakistan. It is interesting to note that the industrial and business groups have become incorporated directly into the political process. For example, in the election of 1964, Muslim League candidates, especially in larger cities, were primarily businessmen and industrialists. Much of Ayub's support in Karachi and other large cities came from industrialists.

As Professor Lawrence Ziring noted in his study of the Ayub Khan period, the coalition governments of the 1950s "reflected the failure of any single party to develop a national following and, to compound the confusion, the political individualists who are so much a part of the Pakistan scene made a shambles of the political process."[4] These conditions led inevitably to martial law in 1958.

When he later set up the Basic Democracies system, Ayub's stated goal was to "restore democracy but of the type the people can understand and work."[5] Basic Democracies ultimately provided democracy in name only, however, in what became a bureaucratic state. The Ayub Government was basically unresponsive to all but a few privileged groups. Widespread strikes and violent mass demonstrations in East and West Pakistan overthrew Ayub and once again brought a martial law regime into power in 1969. The more cohesive and bureaucratized military replaced on both occasions a political system which was unable, and to some extent unwilling, to respond to increasing participation and escalating demands while at the same time maintaining order.

The APWA thus would appear to be one of the handful of privileged interest groups. Ayub was a military man, not a "political animal," and remained aloof from the people. He was never a popular leader, rather, it was the personal and political relationships between Ayub and key APWA leaders that were most significant in securing the Muslim family law reforms. While President Ayub personally supported reform of Muslim family law, he did very little to sell the idea to the general public. This fact meant trouble for the reforms in later years.

The Muslim Family Laws

It is in this context that we go back to 1955 and the beginnings of a dramatic chapter in Pakistan legislative history, the struggle to pass the Muslim Family Laws Ordinance. The news of Prime Minister Mohammed Ali's marriage to his Middle Eastern social secretary in 1955 while still legally married to his first wife crystallized the movement for reform of the marriage laws. An APWA Conference concerning the status of women held on February 22, 1955 passed resolutions calling for such reforms.

There were three basic reasons why the APWA protested the Prime Minister's second marriage. The indignant women pointed out that while Islam demanded "equal treatment for all wives," this condition was not being fulfilled. They further argued that it was "most unbecoming that the Prime Minister of Pakistan should marry a foreigner."[6] The women saw serious implications for the future of society as a result of this marriage; they felt the Prime Minister was setting a bad example. It is interesting to note, however, that the women were cautious about a head-on confrontation with the problem of whether polygyny was actually permitted in Islam.

Princess Abida Sultana, who was representing Pakistan in the United Nations in the 1950s, did not agree with those opposing the Prime Minister's marriage. In a statement to the press, she upheld the Prime Minister's right to take a second wife, contending that women who could not tolerate polygyny for themselves were "free to make this stipulation in 'nikahnama' [the marriage contract] before marriage or even later if they can influence their spouses to agree to do so." In her mind there was "no doubt or question that polygamy [sic]*is definitely allowed in Islam."[7]

Basing her arguments in favor of Polygyny on her belief that a class of "second rate sub-human beings" had been created in the form of illegitimate children and fallen women by men without a sense of responsibility, she posed the following questions: "Is this what our educated women should like to see established in Pakistan and call it Islam?" She saw no justification for "a few educated women to launch an agitation in the name of Islam, or to mislead their less fortunate sisters into believing that this modern rather Western interpretation is the correct interpretation of Islam."[8]

In answer to Princess Abida Sultana's statement, a group of one hundred Karachi women issued the following statement to the press:

> With the existing social and in the majority of cases economic conditions, it is not possible to treat both wives equally. Therefore, the first wife always acquires an inferior status and this is in obvious conflict with the spirit in which polygamy is committed in Islam.[9]

Their statement further denounced Princess Sultana, saying they did not consider her their true representative and that they

---

*Polygyny (which refers specifically to the husband taking more than one wife) is actually what is meant here, rather than polygamy which is a more general term referring to multiple marriages by either sex. The author uses the term polygyny, but the term polygamy is used in most quotes and in the Family Laws Ordinance.

would in the future oppose "any move to make her their representative in any capacity."[10]

Not all protest of the Prime Minister's marriage, however, was limited to statements in the press. Women formed processions, carrying placards with slogans reading "DOWN WITH POLYGAMY," "GO BACK ALIYA SADDY," and "YOU SHOULD MARRY A BACHELOR."[11]

In April 1955, the President of the Karachi Branch of the APWA led one hundred women in forming a League for the Rights of Women. The group set up five committees: Women and Family Law; Responsibility in Family and Community; Education; Political Rights; and Women in Economic Rights and Facilities.

The next month, the League met with the Prime Minister. After a ninety-minute interview he promised he would "shortly set up a high-powered committee to consider the necessary reforms in the present laws regarding marriage, divorce, custody of children and inheritance." He would announce the formation of such a committee on June 1, 1955. The committee "would represent men and women leaders of the country" and "would submit recommendations to Government within six months after it was constituted."[12]

Even after establishment of the Commission on Marriage and Family Laws, other women's groups joined in the opposition to Prime Minister Mohammed Ali's second marriage. The Karachi Business and Professional Women's Club passed a resolution expressing their "sense of humiliation that a career women should have so betrayed her duties to her sex as to be the means of bringing misery and suffering into the heart of another women." They also added a "strong vote of censure against all educated women who betray their sex by being partners to polygamy."[13]

A group of women social workers in Karachi also issued a statement to the press, a call "to stop men from abusing Islamic Laws to suit their selfish ends." The women feared misinterpretation of Islam:

> Polygamy was permitted in Islam, not to set up harems, but to save human beings from sin and immorality. We, however, feel that men now find it convenient to flout those

mandatory Quranic provisions which make it nearly impossible for a man to take a second wife. Our men are thus not only presenting a very bad example before the rest of the world, but they are also exposing Islam to the danger of being thoroughly misunderstood by the foreigners, who are long used to malignant interpretations of certain provisions of Islamic Laws by their thinkers and theologians.[14]

Shortly after the Commission on Marriage and Family Laws met, it issued a questionnaire which was carefully studied by the West Pakistan Provincial Headquarters of the APWA. The Provincial Executive Committee drafted answers to the questionnaire and circulated the proposed answers to all district branches. When the Commission finally issued its controversial report a few months later, the APWA expressed its agreement with the recommendation to raise the legal age for marriage to sixteen for girls and eighteen for boys, to place restrictions on the practice of polygyny, to provide for registration of marriages and divorces, to tighten up divorce procedures, to acknowledge the wife's right to divorce, and to assure adequate maintenance for all wives.[15]

The most controversial of these issues was the restriction on polygyny. The Quran itself, in Surah IV, Verse 3, does not explicitly outlaw polygyny.

> If you fear that you will not act justly towards the orphans, marry such women as seem good to you, two, three, four; but if you fear you will not be equitable, then only one, or what your right hands own; so it is likelier you will not be partial.[16]

The modernist would argue that from the wording of this verse, it would seem that up to four wives are allowed, providing the husband could treat all on an equal basis. It may be possible to provide substantially equal treatment financially, but it is virtually impossible to provide equal love and emotional treatment. Therefore, it is obvious that the Prophet preferred a monogamous society.

Fazlur Rahman, a leading modernist from Pakistan, further argues that there are numerous passages in the Quran which support monogamy. "In 51:49, the Quran states as a general law of creation the 'everything We have created in pairs." This concept is applied to human relationships in family life. "We have made you pairs" (35:11) and, "We have created you in pairs" (88:8). In 4:19, the Quran says,"if you intend to replace one spouse with another..."; this verse, Rahman argues, "clearly assumes that if one wants to have another wife the normal method is to bring her *in the place* of the first wife rather than add her to the latter."[17]

The modernist interpretation of Surah IV, Verse 3 quoted above formed the basis for the Commission's proposal but was not carried to its logical conclusion which would have been to abolish polygyny completely. The Ordinance did not outlaw polygyny; it merely laid down formal procedures, including obtaining the consent of the first wife, for taking a second wife. An Arbitration Council consisting of the chairman and representatives of the existing wife and the husband decide whether the proposed marriage is necessary and just. Reasons considered valid for granting permission for a second marriage included sterility, physical infirmity, physical unfitness for conjugal relations, willful avoidance of a decree for restitution of conjugal rights, or insanity of the wife.

If a second marriage is contracted without the previous permission of the original wife, the husband must pay the entire dower due to the first wife. In addition he may be imprisoned for up to one year and/or pay a fine of up to 5,000 rupees. But the second marriage, in spite of the penalties imposed, is not considered to be invalid.

The commission also recommended reform of divorce laws. The right of divorce for the wife, under limited circumstances, had already been recognized in the Muslim Dissolution of Marriages Act of 1939, passed under British rule. Traditionally, however, the right of divorce had been given only to the husband, who exercized it unilaterally even though the contention that only the husband could exercize the right of divorce is not specifically supported by any statement in the Quran. Certain schools of classical law, such as Hanafi, allowed the wife to exercize the right of divorce if she inserted such a condition in her marriage contract.

The Ordinance contains a similar provision, thus rejecting

the traditional utterance of the triple *talaq* by the husband. Instead, the Ordinance provides that the divorce take place in three installments. Any man who wishes to divorce his wife "as soon as may be after the pronouncement of *talaq* in any form whatsoever" must notify the chairman of the Arbitration Council in writing of his intention of divorce. He must provide his wife with a copy of this notice. The Arbitration Council, which must include representatives of both parties, must be formed within thirty days to consider the request and attempt to bring about a reconciliation between the parties. Failure to comply with these provisions is punishable by imprisonment up to one year and/or by a fine of up to 5,000 rupees. The divorce is not final until ninety days from the day on which notice was given to the chairman.[18]

In addition, the Ordinance provided for the compulsory registration of marriages. The penalty for failure to comply with this provision was a fine or imprisonment or both.

Child marriage was yet another point of controversy. The Commission had recommended that child marriage be prohibited by legislating that no man under eighteen and no woman under sixteen should enter into a contract of marriage, in effect amending the British Child Marriage Restraint Act of 1929. Such legislation would be in "perfect harmony with the Quran and the Sunnah." Proponents of the legislation reasoned that "the Holy Quran makes not only puberty, but a definite state in the development of intelligence as a condition precedent for entrusting property to the orphans." Therefore, the "question of marriage may be decided on the same footing because the entrusting of the life of marrying parties to each other is an affair of greater importance than mere entrusting of property."[19]

Only one from the ranks of the ulama, Maulana Ihtisham ul-Haq, was represented on the Commission. He violently opposed the Commission's final recommendations. In a lengthy minority report, he bitterly condemned.

> ... the effrontery of those who, ignorant of Arabic and Islamic jurisprudence, dared to propose Western innovations in the name of Islam. In Islam the provisions of the Holy Quran and the Sunnah, be they in the form of basic principles or in individual laws, are authoritative and final

for all occasions and for all epochs between the time of revelation and doomsday.[20]

Maulana Ihtisham ul-Haq spoke for many of the more traditional ulama who felt that such new legislation was not necessary. They argued that the position of the woman had deteriorated because she did not realize the "rights that Islam had endowed upon her." She, therefore, did not need new laws, but only to be made conscious of her already existing rights.[21]

Although the modernist claims that woman is man's equal, the ulama point to Surah IV, Verse 34 to support their contention that man is the guardian of woman.

> Men are the managers of the affairs of women for that God has preferred in bounty one of them over another, and for that they have expanded of their property. Righteous women are therefore obedient, guarding the secret for God's guarding. And those you fear may be rebellious admonish; banish them to their couches, and beat them. If they then obey you, look not for any way against them; God is All-high, All-great.[22]

This verse undoubtedly contributed further to the severe criticism to which each of the provisions of the Ordinance was subjected. For instance, it was alleged that restrictions on polygyny would increase extra-marital sexual relationships. In other words, it was far more responsible for the husband to take his paramour as his second wife than to "leave her on the street, unprotected." Likewise, the traditionalist argued that divorce was the exclusive privilege of men, presumably because they, as the "wiser" party would exercize it with more prudence. Further, they objected to bringing divorce, which should be settled in private, to a public tribunal on the grounds that it was a blind following of "Western patterns" which would have a "demoralising effect on family life."[23]

Even the registration of marriages was a point of criticism. While agreeing that such registration was desirable to reduce the chaos which had arisen from nonregistration of marriages, opponents generally argued that instead of penalizing non-compliance, it would be sufficient not to recognize unregistered marriages in certain judicial procedures. As Fazlur Rahman points out, "the criticism of this innocuous provision reveals the intensity of the conservative opposition to the ordinance, without any reference to the criterion of reasonableness."[24]

The proposal to limit child marriage, even though it was an amendment to an earlier law, also met with opposition. Mauluna Abul Ala Maududi, leader of the Jama'at-i-Islami (a politically active religious group), argued that such legislation was "absolutely uncalled for." Since boys and girls reached puberty long before the ages of eighteen and sixteen, fixing these ages as a minimum could therefore be taken to mean "that we are opposed only to the establishment of marital relationships between boys and girls of less than legally prescribed minimum ages, while we would have no objection to their establishing non-marital sex-relationships."[25]

Those who supported the proposed changes argued that the Commission had created "no new rights for women which the Quran and Sunnah had not already granted. . . ."[26] The majority of the Commission members called for a modern interpretation of the Quran and the Sunnah to meet the needs of a changing society of the twentieth century. They held the view that:

> Islamic law, through the centuries, has suffered much distortion and its liberal aspects have been ignored and suppressed. We have to go back to the original spirit of the Quran and the Sunnah and lay special emphasis on those trends in basic Islam that are conducive to healthy adaptations to our present circumstances.[27]

Over two years later, the Commission's report had not been implemented due largely to general political instability and more directly to the intense opposition of the ulama whose political influence was tremendous. On July 4, 1958, which was to become known as "Women's Demands Day," the APWA passed a resolution calling for reforms in family law and implementation of the Commission's report. The APWA also suggested that special Family Courts be established to deal with cases involving divorce, maintenance, and custody of children. Copies of the resolution were sent to the President,

Prime Minister, the Law Minister, the Chief Minister, and the Governor of West Pakistan. Later that year the APWA issued another appeal to implement the Commission report, but their appeals were to no avail. Pressure from the orthodox religious community was too great, and the changes of government too frequent.

The continual fall of governments resulted in the military takeover by General Mohammad Ayub Khan and the establishment of a relatively stable martial law regime which lasted from 1958 to 1962. During this period, Ayub was gradually setting the tone for the creation of a presidential form of government based on a new constitution which he "gave" to the nation in 1962.

It was not until the APWA brought pressure to bear directly upon the martial law ruler himself that the women found a more receptive audience for their demands. Ayub was closer to the modernist point of view, and it was thus less difficult to persuade him that the women of Pakistan wanted the Family Laws Ordinance and would support it. The General promulgated the Muslim Marriage and Family Laws Ordinance in 1961.

The Struggle to Retain the Ordinance on the Books

No sooner had the Ordinance been passed into law than its enemies renewed charges that the provisions to limit polygyny, to raise the legal marriage age of girls to sixteen, and to register all marriages and divorces were "un-Islamic." Begum Anwar G. Ahmed dismissed as untrue charges that the Ordinance "has tampered with the fundamentals of Islamic Law." She continued:

> No change whatever has been effected by the Ordinance in the substantial law as laid down by Islam relating to marriage, divorce, and polygamy. All existing rights of men and women under this law remain unaltered. All that the Ordinance has done is to make procedural provisions for the implementation of the Islamic Laws *as they exist* so that justice is speedily and adequately done.[28]

In 1962 while the Family Laws Ordinance was being examined by the Islamic Council of Ideology, an Ayub-appointed government body charged with judging the consistency of a law with Islam, the APWA was demonstrating in Rawalpindi to show their support for the Ordinance. After first going to the National Assembly and meeting with several ministers, the women went on to the President's House. When President Ayub was advised of their demonstration, he directed his guards to allow the buses and cars to enter the grounds and come straight to his Secretariat. Upon reaching his office, the women assembled in front of the main door. The President came out and talked with the women for about ten minutes.

Although most of the demonstrators were from Rawalpindi several women had come from Lahore and Karachi. These women had worked for two days, canvassing women all over the city, with the result that "a large number of burqa-clad ladies also turned up at the Assembly gate for the demonstration."[29] It was not known exactly how many women participated in this march on the Government houses, but the fact that the public demonstration occurred at all was significant in a country where women did not usually take part in public demonstrations.

Not everyone approved of the women's tactics. In a statement to the press, a group of ulama condemned the women for pressuring the National Assembly on this issue:

> Instead of letting the Assembly decide this purely academic and religious issue after a cool consideration of the whole affair in the light of the teachings of the Holy Quran and Sunnah, a section of our women folk, whose entire life is a standing challenge to even the most fundamental teachings of Islam, have started a campaign to get this issue decided in their favor by force of demonstrations and other such tactics.[30]

A few days later Begum G. A. Khan, a member of the National Assembly and one of the founding members of the APWA, held a public meeting at Rawalpindi Press Club which approximately three hundred women attended. She warned the women to "avoid raising slogans of a negative nature, adding that this is the age of reason, and "we have reasons on our side in our struggle." She also cautioned the women not to neglect their domestic duties so that their "male counterparts do not have anything to complain of," an important consideration in a culture which assigns women a limited role centered around home and family. The women attending this meeting adopted a resolution demanding that the Muslim Family Laws Ordinance should not be repealed "in any case whatsoever." They called upon the members of the National Assembly "who believe in universal democratic values" not to take any steps toward cancelling the Ordinance without first "obtaining the consent of both the Provincial Assemblies of the country." But in case their plea was not accepted, the women resolved that, "the women of Pakistan, being 50% of the population will demand equal representation in all the Legislative Assemblies"[31] Although it was not likely that this latter demand would be met, the Assembly could hardly avoid the conclusion that the women were serious.

The following winter, the APWA, led by the West Pakistan Provincial Executive Committee found it necessary to intensify its campaign to save the Family Laws. The first step was a letter-writing campaign under the direction of Begum K. Inamullah Khan, then Secretary of the Women's Rights and Responsibilities Section of the APWA in Lahore. In a letter to all members of the National Assembly, she appealed for support for the Family Laws:

> You must have read in the newspapers that on Jumat-ul-Weda the Family Laws Ordinance was severely criticized in many Mosques. It was stated that the Ordinance was not acceptable as it is repugnant to the tenets of Islam. Resolutions have been passed to the effect that the Ordinance should be repealed. A bill to this effect is being moved in the next session of the National Assembly to be held at Dacca on the 8th of March.
>
> You being our representative at the National Assembly, we request you to take all steps to safeguard the women's rights, by prevailing upon the other M.N.A.'s to reject moves to repeal the Ordinance and by explaining to the National Assembly that the Ordinance only incorporates the

rights that Islam has given to women and in fact has abolished to some extent the wrongs practiced on women before the Ordinance came into effect. . . .[32]

The next month, the APWA's West Pakistan Executive Committee sent a letter to all District Branches calling for a meeting on March 21, 1963 to protest the growing opposition to the Family Laws. The meeting adopted a resolution viewing with concern "the retrogressive activities of the reactionary elements in our society who are opposed to this law" and appealed to the President and the Government to stand by the progressive enactment. The Resolution further stated that the Family Laws Ordinance could be made more effective "if special Family Courts on the district level could be established without any extra expenditure to the Treasury."[33] Copies of this resolution were sent to the District Branches, with the request that they send them with a covering letter to President Ayub Khan, the National Law Minister, the Governor of West Pakistan, and the Provincial Law Minister.

In spite of the continuing grassroots lobbying efforts of the APWA women, in July 1963 the West Pakistan Provincial Assembly passed a resolution recommending to the National Assembly that it repeal the Family Laws Ordinance. A letter from the APWA's Provincial Headquarters to the District Branches urged the women to meet with their own National Assembly members and their wives, "to try to persuade them to help and support the Family Laws Ordinance in the next session of the Assembly to be held at Rawalpindi. . . ."[34]

At a meeting of the APWA in Lahore a few days later, a resolution was passed against the "ill-conceived and retrograde step hastily taken by the West Pakistan Assembly in passing the resolution for the repeal of the Muslim Family Laws Ordinance." The women accused the Assembly of passing the resolution for the repeal of the Ordinance "without taking into consideration the responsibilities of men towards their mothers, sisters, daughters, wives, and the nation." They called the action taken by the Assembly "unrepresentative" and an attempt to infringe [upon] certain basic rights of the major portion of Pakistan's population." These rights had been "granted to women by Islam, and had been given belated recognition in

Pakistan through the Ordinance." Most of the speeches made at the meeting re-emphasized that the Muslim Family Laws Ordinance was in "complete accord with the Quran and the Sunnah and that a struggle should be launched against the repeal of the legislation." The meeting once again appealed to the President and the National Assembly to "protect the rights of women and children who made great sacrifices in the cause of Pakistan." The meeting was attended by Begum G.A. Khan, member of the National Assembly and three women who were members of the Provincial Assembly. In another resolution, the women expressed "appreciation for the co-operation shown by the Press for the cause of women's rights."[35]

The President and his Law Minister clearly favored the Family Laws. In a meeting with delegates from the APWA, the Minister of Law told them that the APWA and other women's organizations could work for preservation of the Ordinance by holding meetings to explain to the common people the need and benefits of such an ordinance. President Ayub, in his statement to the APWA delegates, reminded those who "denied human rights to women under the pretext of Islam that Islam was a dynamic and progressive religion which stood for peace and justice in every aspect of human life." A religion like Islam, the President contended, "could only help and not hamper removal of social injustices and inequalities." He predicted that "a time would come when the people would also realize the basic justice of the Family Laws Ordinance."[36]

On November 26, 1963 the bill to repeal the Family Laws Ordinance was defeated in the National Assembly after twenty hours of debate. The Provincial APWA then urged the District Branches to send resolutions to the President, the National Law Minister, the Governor of West Pakistan, and members of the National Assembly expressing appreciation for "the realistic and sympathetic approach given by them to the problem."[37]

A month later the Fundamental Rights Bill, the first amendment to the 1962 Constitution, extended somewhat the role of the courts by making all of the constitution's principles of law-making defendable in court but specifically excluded the Muslim Family Laws Ordinance from review. It thus "remains the law of the land and cannot be challenged in any court."[38] This was a significant victory for the APWA and indicated just how strongly President Ayub supported the Ordinance.

The defeat of the bill to repeal the Family Laws Ordinance and its exemption from judicial review did not end attacks on the Ordinance, however. In January 1965, the APWA's West Pakistan Executive Committee organized to meet a new attack on the Ordinance. A bill for amendments to the Family Laws would be introduced at the Dacca Session of the National Assembly that year. Under the presidentship of Begum Zeenat Fida Hassan, the West Pakistan Executive Committee passed a resolution expressing great concern over the intended move by some Ministers in the National Assembly to repeal the Family Laws Ordinance or bring amendments to it. This resolution appealed to the government and the members of the National Assembly who were to draft the bill to "see that no harm is done to the Ordinance which is one of the great reforms in our country...." The resolution again expressed the hope that "enlightened men will consider the matter sympathetically and without any bias and will take into consideration their mothers, sisters, daughters, wives, and the nation. The welfare of a nation depends on happy homes."[39]

The APWA requested that the District Branches pass similar resolutions and forward them to the Parliamentary Secretary for Finance, the National Law Minister, the Speaker of the National Assembly, and the Chairman of the Advisory Council of Islamic Ideology. In addition, the District Branches were urged to make arrangements to mobilize public opinion in favor of the Ordinance. In order to help the women of Karachi to better understand the Family Laws Ordinance, the Karachi Branch of the APWA established a legal aid service for the women of the city. A legal practitioner acted as adviser to the service. Families with marital problems could consult the legal aid service for a fee of Rs. 5 to register their case. If the family was unable to pay, the fee was waived. Upon registration of the case, the other party was asked to present him- or herself, and the parties presented their case before the Legal Secrettary. An attempt was made to reconcile the husband and wife; but if there was no agreement, the case was filed in court against the party deemed to be at fault. This legal aid service had great potential as an educative tool and a means of political mobilization. The women in charge of this service, however, indicated that it was not used as widely as they had hoped. Hence, it did not provide the desired avenue for broadening women's political awareness.

The APWA's Self Image

The role of the APWA concerning the Muslim Family Laws caused considerable disagreement among APWA members even though that organization had been the primary group responsible for seeking the law's passage. Of twenty-three members of the national executive committee who were questioned,* two women felt that the law was, in certain respects, inconsistent with the teachings of their religion. Both felt that it was "better to have three or four wives than to corrupt society. Adultery is the one unpardonable crime in Islam." They noted "a sex problem among men in our country," and pointed out that if adultery could be eliminated, there would be no need for polygyny. Concerning the divorce provisions, another member observed that "a second marriage is better than divorcing the first wife and throwing her out on the street."

Most of the women interviewed, however, thought that the Ordinance was consistent with Islamic Law, maintaining that civil law gave "recognition to old (religious) law." Begum A observed that the Ordinance tried to "create a humane and just partnership or relationship between man and woman." Begum U pointed out that before the Ordinance was passed, "it was convenient to misinterpret Islam."

Not everyone agreed that the Family Laws have succeeded. Miss Q pointed out that the Ordinance "has not helped in the villages at all." But most believed that the Ordinance had made "women feel more secure." Begum K felt that the Ordinance had been "a great deterrent to the rate of men taking more than one wife or arbitrarily divorcing his wife." As Begum G observed, the only real support which the Family Laws received in the Government was from President Ayub. In fact, had it not been for his support, the National Assembly would have voted against its passage, and the numerous attempts to repeal the

*To preserve confidentiality, members are referred to as Begum or Miss A, B, C, etc.

Laws undoubtedly would have succeeded. This appears to be an accurate assessment.

Most members agreed that the APWA must continue to defend the Ordinance from further attempts to repeal or weaken it. The women of Pakistan must be educated to its purpose. As Begum K explained, "Sometimes permission is forcibly taken by the man to marry another woman. This should be prevented." Since the subject is extremely controversial, nothing is likely to be done to close the loopholes in the law. Begum L felt that "at present there is no chance unless the [Ayub] government stays."

The APWA continued its efforts in the name of Islam, to press for passage of new laws to improve the status of Pakistani women, but the uncertain political climate which followed the fall of the Ayub government appeared to muffle the voice of APWA in government circles. The Family Laws Ordinance came under fire once again in 1969 as an integral part of the bitter attack on the Ayub regime which resulted in another period of martial law. Opposition continued even when Zulfiqar Ali Bhutto restored civilian rule. While women's issues did not hold top priority in his administration, the fact that he had publicly advocated compulsory elementary education of girls, as well as for boys, seemed to indicate a sympathetic attitude toward improving the status of Pakistani women. But when General Zia ul-Haq ousted Bhutto in July 1977, and later executed him, he set a more conservative tone which endangers modernist reform efforts.

Conclusions

It is important to emphasize that the APWA was not a militant feminist organization. Pressure group activities took up only a small part of its energies. Its objectives were very practical and were aimed at the gradual improvement of legal, educational, health, economic, social and political conditions of the woman and her children in their community, but entirely within the context of Islamic culture. At no time did the APWA directly attack traditional beliefs and practices. Likewise, the group remained extremely cautious in its encouragement of programs such as family planning. As an interest group, the APWA was an elite attempting to provide a link of communication between the masses and the ruling elite, a function which the APWA may have been ill-equipped to perform. The lack of understanding between the APWA's relatively wealthy and highly educated women and the illiterate mass of Pakistani women reinforced the gap between these two groups each existing in their own separate worlds. APWA members seemed to be embarrassed by their elite status and consequently denied any lack of empathy with their less fortunate sisters.

In the matter of tactics, the APWA used the standard tools of interest groups, while always invoking the name of Islam. Meetings with government officials and members of the legislature were usual tactics, as were letters from all levels of the APWA to try to convince national and provincial legislators of widespread support for a particular bill. The APWA also made extensive use of the press, both to cover its main activities and to air its opinions. The use of occasional processions, especially during the campaign for the Family Laws, dramatized the issues and was intended as a show of strength. There is something undeniably poignant about a large group of burqa-clad women engaging in a public demonstration.

In the slightly more than ten years during which Ayub Khan was in power, the APWA enjoyed a unique position. Begum Liaquat Ali Khan, the organization's Founder Life President, did not hesitate to make use of her personal friendship with President Ayub to make known the demands of the APWA. Ayub did not hesitate to meet those demands whenever he could. The promulgation of the Muslim Family Laws Ordinance is a case in point. In spite of the responsiveness of the former President, however, other factors, including legislative and religious opposition, often delayed action for many years.

That the APWA had not achieved more extensive changes in Pakistan may be due, in part, to the fact that its members were not social rebels in any way. They were highly educated and socially and economically privileged, but they did not reject their religious, social, and cultural heritage as traditionbound and therefore irrelevant to current conditions. They rationalized their public image in terms of a "liberal" Islam.

They clearly desired to work within the established traditions for gradual improvements—not drastic changes in those traditions. Theirs was a liberal interpretation of Islam, but one which was at the same time apologetic and defensive in its departure from the Islam of the ulama. Influenced by a modern education, the APWA women frequently found themselves caught between the more secular political leaders and those political and religious leaders who viewed their environment from a more conservative religious perspective. Many APWA members expressed fear of the overwhelming power and influence which the ulama continue to exert over the majority of Muslims in Pakistan. Therefore, they argued, the APWA must go slow and not "rock the boat" nor contradict the widespread attitude which accepts virtually everything as dependent upon the "Will of God." In the opinion of most of the ulama, the APWA has been tinkering with a perfectly operating machine and will cause it to break down with its "hypocritical use of Islam for its own selfish ends."

Are Islam and modernization contradictory? The APWA women did not seem to think so. They pointed to the tradition of *zakat* or almsgiving, one of the five pillars of Islam, as the basis for social justice in their Islamic state. The five year plans, basic democracies, and community development projects all find their philosophical roots in *zakat*. To most of the APWA ladies, the Islamic prescription for women which made them subordinate to men in a male-oriented society had little or no bearing on the process of modernization. It is significant, however, that the women found it necessary to remind government officials that women should be represented on the Fourth Plan's Planning Commission and that the emphasis on manpower training should include consideration of womanpower.

It is going too far to call the APWA an "agent of change," if by this we mean a group in the vanguard, calling for far-reaching changes in the status of Pakistani women or for secularization of their way of life. As previously noted, the APWA is a group which has been seeking modernization but entirely within the context of Islam. The APWA, however, has not been able to convince the ulama that they are not defying the basic tenets of Islam. The Government and the APWA were seen as corrupting influences even though they both frequently stated the goals of modernization in essentially religious terms and made no attempt to undermine the position of the ulama. Thus, in spite of financial aid and political support from past administrations, the contributions of the APWA to the social, economic, and legal modernization of Pakistan remain limited and touch upon only a small segment of the overall goals of the country.

In view of the recent revival of militant Islam in Pakistan, it would appear that the modernist reforms championed by groups like the APWA are in deep trouble, particularly since the renewed interest and pride in the heritage of Islam is most pronounced among the young. Even if reform such as the Family Laws are not in danger of repeal, they are likely to suffer from less than enthusiastic enforcement.

NOTES

[1] Gabriel A. Almond and G. Bingham Powell, Jr., *Comparative Politics: A Developmental Approach* (Boston: Little, Brown and Company, 1966), pp. 91-92.

[2] Khalid bin Sayeed, *The Political System of Pakistan* (Karachi: Oxford University Press, 1967), pp. 117, 152.

[3] *Ibid.*, pp. 226, 228-230.

[4] Lawrence Ziring, *The Ayub Khan Era: Politics in Pakistan, 1958-1969* (Syracuse: Syracuse University Press, 1971), p. 8.

[5] Quoted in Ziring, *Ayub Khan Era*, p. 10.

[6] "Angry Women Go to PM's House: Resentment Over Second Marriage," *Dawn* (Karachi), April 17, 1955.

[7] "Abida Sultana on Polygamy," *Dawn* (Karachi), April 21, 1955.

[8] *Ibid.*

[9] "League for Rights of Women Formed: Pledge to Fight Polygamy," *Dawn* (Karachi), April 23, 1955.

[10] *Ibid.*

[11] "Demonstration Before PM's House Staged," *Morning News* (Karachi), April 17, 1955. A newly appointed public relations officer to the Prime Minister was abruptly fired from his position when a lengthy satirical poem he had written about Mohammed Ali's impending marriage to Aliya Saddy was revealed a few days after the marriage.

[12] "PM's Assurances to Women's Deputation," *Dawn* (Karachi) May 15, 1955.

[13] "City Dames Condemn Bluebeards: Call for Struggle Against

Polygamy," *Dawn* (Karachi), July 15, 1955.

[14] *Ibid.*

[15] Freeland Abbott, "Pakistan and the Secular State" in Donald E. Smith, ed., *South Asian Politics and Religion* (Princeton; Princeton University Press, 1966), p. 364-365.

[16] Arthur J. Arberry, tr., *The Koran Interpreted* (New York: Macmillan, 1955), p. 100.

[17] Fazlur Rahman, "The Controversy Over the Muslim Family Laws" in Donald E. Smith, ed., *South Asian Politics and Religion* (Princeton: Princeton University Press, 1966), p. 418.

[18] Khalid bin Sayeed in *The Political Systems of Pakistan*, p. 167, makes an interesting observation concerning the relative acceptance of these two provisions. "In some districts . . . it seems that 80-90 percent of the applications for second marriages have been approved by some of the Union Councils" while in a "great majority of divorce cases compromise was reached." However, Qutubuddin Aziz paints a slightly different picture: "Since the enforcement of this law, the percentage of polygamous marriages has fallen so sharply that, on the average, no more than one male adult in a thousand has more than one wife. Sociologists attribute the upward swing in the number of divorces in the past decade to the legal curbs on polygamy." See "Female Lawmaker Sparks Women's Liberation in Pakistan." *The Christian Science Monitor*, June 26. 1972, p. 8.

[19] Khurshid Ahmad, *Marriage Commission Report X-rayed: A Study of the Family Laws of Islam and a Critical Appraisal of the Modernist Attempts to Reform it* (Karachi: Churagh-e-Rah, 1959), p. 57.

[20] *Ibid.*, pp. 42-43.

[21] Md. Mazharuddin Siddiqi, *Women in Islam* (Lahore: Institute of Islamic Culture, 1959), p. 180.

[22] Arberry, *Koran Interpreted* pp. 105-106.

[23] Fazlur Rahman, "Controversy over Muslim Family Laws," p. 423.

[24] *Ibid.*

[25] Khurshid Ahmad., *Marriage Commission Report X-rayed*, p. 8.

[26] *Ibid.*, p. 96.

[27] Md. Iqbal Choudhry and Mushtaq Ahmed Khan, *Pakistan Society: A Sociological Analysis* (Peshawar; Noorsons, 1964), p. 45.

[28] Begum Anwar G. Ahmed, "Family Laws" (Karachi, West Pakistan, 1961, mimeographed), pp. 8-9.

[29] "Family Laws; President Sympathizes with Women: Rally Before N.A. Against Move to Repeal Ordinance." *Pakistan Times* (Lahore) July 5, 1962.

[30] "Repeal of Family Laws Ordinance: Ulema Condemn Women's Rallies," *Pakistan Times* (Lahore), July 7, 1962.

[31] "Women will Fight for Rights to the End: Public Meeting Against Repeal of Family Laws in City," *Pakistan Times* (Lahore), July 7, 1962.

[32] Letter from Begum Inamullah Khan, Secretary Women's Rights

and Responsibilities Section, APWA—West Pakistan to National Assembly Representatives, February, 23, 1963, concerning repeal of Family Laws Ordinance. APWA files.

[33]"APWA Urges Govt. to Stand by Family Laws," *Pakistan Times* (Lahore), May 23, 1964.

[34]Letter from APWA—West Pakistan to District Branches, July 4, 1963, concerning repeal of Family Laws Ordinance. APWA files.

[35]"'P.A. Resolution is Retrograde Step': Women to Launch Struggle to Save Family," *Pakistan Times* (Lahore), July 10, 1963.

[36]APWA Camp Ordinance: Delegates Meet President, Ayub Vindicates Govt Policy: Lady M.N.A.s Discuss Line of Action," *Pakistan Times* (Lahore), July 17, 1963.

[37]Letter from APWA—West Pakistan to District Branches, November 29, 1963, concerning rejection of repeal of Family Laws Ordinance by National Assembly. APWA files.

[38]Freeland Abbott, "Pakistan and the Secular State," p. 366.

[39]Resolution on Family Laws Ordinance passed by Executive Committee of APWA—West Pakistan, Lahore, January 21, 1965. APWA files.

11
Towards Equality? Cause and Consequence of the Political Prominence of Women in India

MARY FAINSOD KATZENSTEIN

Some years ago a cartoon appeared in one of India's English dailies picturing Mrs. Gandhi seated at a table with a number of other politicians. Referring to Mrs. Gandhi's strong-handed leadership, a leadership which belied the earlier expectations of some party bosses that she would rule in name only, the cartoon's caption read, "the only man in a cabinet of old women."

Mrs. Gandhi's Prime Ministership symbolizes the anomaly of women's position in Indian politics. On the one hand, women appear to be prominent at an *elite* level of politics. On the other hand, there persist gross inequalities between male and female in Indian *society as a whole*—testified to by an imbalanced sex ratio, severe differentials in wages and work participation, and a host of other factors.

In the analysis which follows, this anomaly will be examined from three perspectives: (1) by identifying the extent to which women occupy elite positions in Indian politics; (2) by evaluating possible explanations for women's prominence in elite positions;

and (3) by exploring the impact which women's participation in politics has for the social and economic position of women in Indian society at large.

Indian Women as Political Leaders, Prominent not Plentiful

This paper is not alone in suggesting that Indian women occupy an unusual position at an elite level of politics. In a recent essay on women's political participation in India, two Indian scholars commented, "One of the interesting features of Indian political life is the participation of Indian women. In this respect, Indian society is almost certainly less inequitable than the Chinese, Soviet, and the American. Not merely does India have a female Prime Minister. Women have also succeeded in becoming members of the Lok Sabha and Rajya Sabha [the two houses of parliament], they have been Governors and Chief Ministers of States, Ambassadors, members of the Cabinet and Deputy Ministers; and they have held the highest positions in the organizations of the major political parties."[1]

The essay appears in a book entitled, *Electoral Politics in the Indian States: Three Disadvantaged Sectors.*[2] In a discussion of the book at a seminar in one North Indian University recently, a woman participant wanted to know why women would be included in a book on the disadvantaged. This comment reflects the belief, probably quite widely held, that women do not suffer any particular disability in Indian politics. To what factors can this belief be traced? Is the prominence of women in politics due to the visibility of a few women or to the presence of many?

The conspicuous position of a few leading women does distinguish India from many other countries. Mrs. Gandhi, here, plays a foremost role. But there have been other Indian women of international repute as well: Vijayalakshmi Pandit (Nehru's sister), the former Ambassador to Washington, Moscow and High Commissioner in the U. K.; Rajkumari Kaur, President of the International Red Cross; Lakshmi Menon, Deputy Minister of External Affairs and former Chief of the United Nations Section on the Status of Women; Sarojini Naidu, poet and nationalist leader, etc.

During the nationalist movement, women were active organizers and achieved considerable renown within India. Following the paths of earlier leaders like Pandita Ramabai (1858-1882), Ramabai Ranade (1862-1924), Annie Besant and Margaret Cousins (both Irish by origin) were Kamaladevi Chattopadhyaya, Muthulakshmi Reddi, Rani Lakshmibai Rajwade Rustomji Faridoonji, Begum Hamid Ali, Naidu and Kaur mentioned earlier and a large number of other important women activists.[3]

But to what extent is the prominence of these women in public affairs underwritten by the presence of large numbers of women in politics? The answer here depends largely on the point of comparison. In relation to the numbers of men, there is no question that Indian women are severely underrepresented at all levels of political leadership. However, the representation of women political leaders stands up well by comparison to the position of women in political office in the United States, much of Western and Southern Europe, and in many African and Latin American countries as well.

At all levels of political leadership in India men greatly outnumber women. This is the case in elected as well as appointed administrative positions. Between the first national election in 1952 and 1975 there were thirteen women ministers in the union government of whom one became Prime Minister and one attained cabinet rank. Five became Ministers of State and six became Deputy Ministers.[4]

In 1975, prior to the declaration of the Emergency, there were no women in the Cabinet (Mrs. Gandhi excepted). Of twenty Ministers of State, there was only one woman, Sushila T. Rohatgi, Deputy Minister of Finance.[5] Since independence, most women ministers in the union government have been placed in the less prestigious ministries—in tourism and civil aviation, information and broadcasting, education and social welfare, health and family planning—rather than in the more central areas of finance, defense, agriculture, planning, etc. At the state level, there were two women Chief Ministers, Satpathy of Orissa and Kakodkar of Goa.[6]

The election of the Janata party after the Emergency was relaxed brought into parliamentary office a reduced representation of women. It is said, although it has not yet been fully documented, that women have suffered a setback politically under the new government. In the Lok Sabha, the percentage of women has dropped from 4.8% in 1975 to the present 3.6%. More important, although less quantifiable, is the perception among some women working in government office in Delhi that the present government (which many of them voted for) is less receptive to the concerns of women.[7]

Over time, the number of women represented in parliament has fluctuated around 5% as the number of women represented in the state legislatures (see Table 1). A similar situation has prevailed in administrative positions. In 1975 women were at the head of only two of India's overseas missions, Denmark and Ghana-Liberia. A sample survey conducted in 1963 showed that only 6% of all female central government employees earned over Rs. 300[8] (an amount which then denoted a lower to middle-level clerical position). The one striking and optimistic development is represented in figures on recruitment to the highest level civil service jobs of the Indian Administrative Service, Indian Foreign Service, and Indian Police Service. In these elite administrative services, the ratio of women to men recommended for appointment had risen from one female to every 65 males in 1960 to one female to every 7.6 males in 1972.[9]

TABLE 1: POLITICAL PARTICIPATION OF WOMEN IN INDIA

Lok Sabha 1952-1977 Total Representatives				State Legislative Assemblies 1952-72 Total Representatives			
Year	Elected	Number	%	Year	Elected	Number	%
1952	489	14	2.86	1952	3820	61	1.86
1957	494	27	5.47	1957	2906	192	6.61
1962	494	33	6.68	1962	2930	138	4.71
1967	520	30	5.30	1967	3486	99	2.48
1969	—	—	—	1972*	2757	154	5.59
1970	—	—	—	1975	3570	161	4.51
1971	518	21	4.05				
1975	524	25	4.78				
1977	544	20	3.68				

SOURCE: Election Commission of India, *Women in India* Selected Statistics published by the Government of India, Ministry of Education and Social Welfare, Department of Social Welfare, New Delhi, 1975. Figures for 1977 are from the Delhi telephone directory.

*Excludes Orissa, Tamil Nadu, and West Bengal.

This recent pattern of administrative recruitment to the very elite services is, however, an exception to the general numerical underrepresentation of women in political office in India. The perception, then, that women have attained prominent political office in India would seem to derive from a few very visible women political leaders rather than any numerical strength women might claim, at least with respect to their male counterparts.

However, the representation of women in parliamentary office in India compares well with that of many other countries. Looking, for instance, at the representation of women in parliament or the equivalent body it is clear that India ranks at the middle level among other "third world" countries. With Guinea and China the distinct exceptions, the percentage of women in parliamentary bodies—as the sample of countries in Table 2 indicates—ranges from 10% to zero. India, with its 5% representation of women in the Lok Sabha, falls clearly in the middle range.

India's representation of women in parliament compares favorably with that of many industrialized countries as well. The percentage ranges from the high level in Eastern and Northern Europe (Bulgaria's Council of the People in 1975 was 37% female; Sweden's Parliament in 1975 was 21% female) to a low in Southern Europe (the Greek Chamber of Deputies and Italian Parliament were less than 3% female).[10] In the United States, the number of women in the House of Representatives is eighteen of 435 members (4.1%). The U.S. figure, then, is slightly lower than 4.8% of India's lower house. A recent United Nations report[11] indicates that the comparable figures for Britain are 4.3%, Belgium, under 3%, Japan, under 2%.

The impression that Indian women occupy an important place in Indian politics has been created, then, more by the visibility of a few women, Mrs. Gandhi and a number of historical figures, than by the presence of substantial numbers of women leaders. The numbers of women in ministerial positions, in parliament, etc., are certainly not large in any absolute sense. But the figures are not low in comparison with much of the industrialized and the developing world.

Yet the prominence of women in Indian politics—the prominence of even a few—warrants an explanation. Why in

TABLE 2: FEMALE REPRESENTATION IN NATIONAL LEGISLATURES

Country	Political Body	Size of Body	Year	Percentage of Women
Guinea	National Assembly	—	1975	27
China (PRC)[a]	Central Committee	333	1977	10
Mexico	Parliament	238	1975	8
Paraguay	Legislature	90	1975	7
Chile	Chamber of Deputies	135	1969	7
Liberia	Congress	70	1974	7
Nicaragua	Legislature (bicameral)	70	1975	6
INDIA[b]	Lok Sabha (lower house)	524	1975	5
Costa Rica	National Assembly	57	1975	5
Sudan	Parliament	250	1973	5
Syria	Parliament	122	1973	4
Tunisia	Parliament	90	1973	4
Columbia	Congress (bicameral)	310	1975	3
El Salvador	National Assembly	52	1975	3
Argentina	Legislature	291	1975	2
Guatemala	National Assembly	66	1975	2
Egypt	National Assembly	350	1975	2
Brazil	Legislature	430	1975	1
Panama	National Assembly	505	1975	0
Lebanon	Parliament	99	1973	0

SOURCE: Compiled from Appendix B, Kathleen Newland, "Women in Politics: A Global Review," *Worldwatch Paper 3*, December 1975.

[a]The China Figures are from Central Intelligence Agency, Reference Aid, "The Chinese Communist Party Central Committee, Numbers Elected at 11th Party Congress," September 1977.

[b]India figure from Table 1.

a society where the economic structure, culture, and religion strongly denigrate the role of women should even a few women hold positions of importance in the public life of the nation? In the section which follows, we turn to possible explanations for the participation of women in leadership positions in Indian politics.

Women as Political Leaders: Alternative Explanations

There are two broad sets of factors which ought to be considered in trying to account for women's representation or lack of representation in political office in any country. The first set of factors looks to the *social* conditions, to the class structure, and to the religious and cultural life of the country as a basis for explaining the level of women's political involvement. The second set of factors identifies the *political* institutions themselves, the process of political succession, the nature of the party structure, etc. as supporting or opposing the recruitment of women to positions of political leadership.

The role of social factors—two hypotheses. One explanation of women's involvement in politics points to the culture or religion of a given society and hypothesizes a correlation between women's position in politics and the place of women in the cultural or religious tradition of that country. This link might be made for instance in explaining the difference in political involvement of women in Northern (Protestant) and Southern (Catholic) Europe. Before examining some possible problems with this kind of linkage, it will be useful to consider the status of women within Hinduism.

The position of women in Hinduism, Susan Wadley has noted, contains a duality. On the one hand women are seen as fertile, benevolent, and as bestowers of fortune. On the other hand the female is represented as aggressive, malevolent, and destructive.[12] In one popular myth, the female goddess Kali ("the Black One") is sent to destroy a giant. Delighted with her success, Kali performs a savage victory dance and has ultimately to be restrained by her husband, Siva.[13] Although in this form the female attains power, it is the power of the destroyer, not the creator. Another recent study of the position of women in Hindu tradition begins with a caveat about the differing images of women presented in various epics, myths, and periods of religious development. But this study goes on to comment that, in general, "In Hinduism a woman is described by a multitude of derogatory attributes... fickle minded, sensual seducer of men, given to falsehood, trickery, folly and greed..."[14] Within Hinduism, the study notes, a woman must not read the Vedas or perform any sacrifices. Knowledge of shastras is proscribed. A woman is grouped with the *shudra* (low caste) in the possibility for reincarnation. Simply put, there is little in Hinduism that would give respectability to a woman's claims to political power.

This is not to suggest that religious tradition does not help to explain very general patterns of women's political representation. The very low representation of women in politics throughout the world does coincide with an almost universal depreciation of women in most religious traditions. The wider participation of women in politics in Northern as compared to Southern Europe does parallel a difference in the proportion of Catholic and non-Catholic populations; and it is striking, for instance, that women are to be found more frequently in political positions in the Netherlands (40.4% Catholic) than in the neighboring country of Belgium (97% Catholic).[15]

But there are too many exceptions to these easy correlations. Switzerland with almost the same percentage Catholic as the Netherlands is one of the most "backward" with respect to women's representation. There are furthermore important differences in women's representation among the predominantly Catholic Latin American countries. At the very least, any thesis which attempts to draw links between religion and the political status of women must go beyond a textual analysis of what the "scriptures" say about women to a more careful appraisal of what is enunciated by religious teachers in a particular area and what is believed by the populace. Even were that done, however, it is unlikely that we would be closer to an explanation of Mrs. Gandhi or of the prominence of women in Indian politics.

A second alternative explanation of women's involvement in politics looks to the class structure. The explanation hypothesizes that in a society where class divisions run deep, sex differences will be overshadowed. In a highly stratified society, that is, class status will supersede gender.

This would predict in the case of India where class and caste divisions are strong that women would occupy a prominent position in politics. If this thesis were correct, two patterns might be expected: (1) the absence of lower-class women in Indian politics. If the handicap of gender for a woman candidate can be overcome by social status in a highly stratified society, one would expect to find only—or mostly—women from upper class backgrounds in office; (2) a greater prominence of women in more "backward" or traditional "princely" regions where feudal traditions still have some strength rather than in the more modern and less class-stratified areas, such as the states of Punjab and Haryana. Again, if class status can be expected to override the handicap of being a woman candidate, it is most likely to do so in regions where there is still a ruling family—a "lady of the manor" whose hereditary position determines her status in society.

This "class" hypothesis does not in fact appear to be supported by the data. First, a surprisingly large proportion of women in Indian politics come from lower-class backgrounds. Although a recent report on the status of women in India notes that the "majority of the women candidates come from relatively well-to-do families with a sprinkling of members of old princely houses," the same report goes on to note that of the twenty-one women members in the present (1975) Lok Sabha, six are members of the low status Scheduled Castes and Tribes.[16] In the Upper House, of seventeen women, two are from Scheduled Caste and Tribal backgrounds. Even if, as is likely, the women from the Scheduled Castes are elected from seats reserved for Harijan candidates (former untouchables), it still discredits the hypothesis that class deference would be a chief factor overshadowing patriarchal prejudice.

The second "prediction" is also not upheld. At least with respect to State Assembly representation in the 1975 elections, women fared less well in the former princely regions of Rajasthan than in the Punjab or Haryana. In 1975 seven of 184 Assembly representatives in Rajasthan were women compared to six of 104 and five of eighty-one in the Punjab and Haryana, respectively.[17]

The Role of Political Factors: Three Explanations. Since neither of the "social" explanations goes far towards accounting for a woman Prime Minister or the prominence of women in Indian politics, it is desirable to examine alternative hypotheses. Three possible arguments all relating to the history or character of political institutions in India should be considered.

The first argument cites the importance of war or crises, in the Indian case the nationalist movement, as a factor propelling women into politics. The notion that wartime pushes women into leadership positions is often discussed. It is frequently noted, for instance, that suffrage in many countries followed one of the two World Wars; that Switzerland, the only European country where the population was not mobilized for war, has been one of the last to extend suffrage; and that women's representation in political positions throughout the world was very high immediately following 1945.

In India, the nationalist movement certainly mobilized women into politics. Gandhi, the father of the nationalist movement, strongly encouraged the involvement of women; Indira Gandhi, like a large number of her generation, had experiences as a youth in the resistance campaigns against the British. In order to know if the numbers of women now in positions of political leadership were themselves involved in the nationalist movement, or if they came from families which were, extensive biographical data, not readily available, would be needed. Without such data, however, we must rely on more indirect indicators. If the nationalist movement were the primary force responsible for mobilizing women into politics, one would expect, for instance, a gradual decrease in the numbers of female politicians and a progressively rising age of female office holders. As Table I demonstrates, the lowest percentage of females represented in both the Lok Sabha and State Assemblies was in the first election following Indian independence in 1952. One study, however, which attempted to assess the role of the nationalist movement noted that while the average age of female legislators has increased over time (from 48.6 to 54 years between 1952 and 1972), the age of male legislators has similarly increased.[18] The data is thus ambiguous and indicates no more than that the nationalist movement was not the only force propelling women into politics.

A second political hypothesis explaining the prominence of women in Indian politics might look to the presumed lack of "institutionalized" politics. This argument would draw attention to the fact that the four women recently holding the offices of heads of state were all from developing countries. In many developing societies, it has been argued, a regularized, stable process whereby succession of political leaders is assured is not entirely established; hence there would be a greater probability that kinship factors would enter into the succession process. In a situation where kinship is important, it is not unlikely that a daughter, widow, or sister might succeed to office.

The four most recent women heads of state include Mrs. Gandhi (the daughter of Jawaharlal Nehru), Mrs. Bandaranaike of Sri Lanka (the widow of former Prime Minister Bandaranaike), and until recently both Mrs. Peron, also the widow of a head of state, and Elizabeth Domitien of the Central African Republic. Domitien took office on January 1, 1975, in effectively the number two position. Until that time there was no office of Prime Minister but the office was created, as Keesings recounts, by Marshall Bedel-Bokassa, President of the Central African Republic and Keeper of the Seal. Keesings described Domitien as formerly a vice-president of the MESAN party "who had played an active role in politics for several years accompanying the President on many of his travels abroad."[19]

The lack of institutionalized politics may help to account for women's accession to positions of importance in many other countries—countries as disparate as the U.S. and China. In the United States, Emmy E. Werner writes, "Of the women who served in Congress between 1916 and 1963, about one-half have had relatives in Congress, slightly over one-third had husbands who were Congressmen before them."[20] The Kennedy extended kin and Mrs. Humphrey's appointment to the Senate seat of her late husband also point to the role of family connections in American politics. By contrast, Western European (French, German, British) politics since World War II, it could be argued, is of a far more routinized nature; in any of these three countries, it would seem most unlikely that the highest office in the nation could fall to a widow or female relative.

A third political explanation cites the importance of individual political parties in selecting women as candidates for office. In India this argument suggests that the Congress party, partly because of Mahatma Gandhi's concern with women's political involvement, has endeavored to bring women into positions of leadership. This explanation has some validity. It is true that women have been involved at leadership levels of parties other than the Congress. Both the Jan Sangh and Swatantra parties (interestingly, parties of the "right") have had women in central organizing positions. However, the Congress party is largely responsible for the prominence of women in

Indian politics. In 1975, the working committee, the highest body in the Congress Party, contained three women out of a total of twenty-one and two of four general secretaries were women. The Communist Party of India (CPI) had four members of 110 on its national council; and the Communist Party of India (Marxist) had one female member of thirty-one on its central committee.[21] As one very systematic study of Indian elections demonstrates, moreover, "Were it not for the Congress Party... female participation in the electoral contests would have been more than halved at the Assembly level in 1967 whereas the total candidates fielded would have been reduced by only a fifth."[22] While the Congress Party's commitment to the election of women has fallen far short of its promises, the party was nevertheless largely responsible for the presence of women in positions of leadership.

The Mrs. Gandhi anomaly, or the prominence of women in Indian politics, can be traced then, to a combination of primarily political factors. The mobilizing impact of the nationalist movement, the commitment of the Congress Party to women's activism which grew out of Gandhi's own ideology and the needs of the nationalist struggle, and the greater emphasis which the succession problem in developing countries places on the role of kinship all combine to promote opportunities for women to move into positions of leadership. These political factors help to account for the position of women in Indian politics, a position of greater prominence than would be expected from the low status of women in Indian society at large.

Politics and the Socioeconomic Status of Women

What impact does the political representation of women in elite positions have on the status of women in Indian society? Because the information at hand is not sufficiently specific to indicate whether women leaders have themselves been responsible for legislative reforms, it is necessary to rephrase the question to consider more broadly the impact which politics has had on women's role.

If the written law were sufficient measure of advancement towards social equity, India's record in the area of sex role equality would be impressive. In terms of legislative action,

India has taken far-reaching steps to counter social injustices. It could be argued, for instance, that in comparison to the U.S. Bill of Rights and subsequent Constitutional Amendments, the Indian Constitution affords women essentially more of, and certainly more explicitly, the rights afforded men.[23] Since the adoption of the Constitution in 1950, the legislature has passed a Maternity Benefit Act (1961), a Dowry Prohibition Act (1961), it has legalized abortion (1971), legislated equal pay (1975), liberalized divorce (1976), etc.[24] Through administrative fiat, the government has abolished rules requiring women in elite civil service positions to resign on marriage. The Congress Party has passed repeated resolutions stipulating targets of 15% in the recruitment of women candidates for electoral office.[25]

What is the outcome of this legislation? Primarily, it has helped create an awareness of sex inequalities. This is reflected in the numbers of books and articles which are now being written by Indian scholars on women in India. Chapters or sections of reports on social change in India now often include a piece on women's role. The *Times of India Yearbook*, a standard reference work, now includes along with its count of the numbers of Scheduled Castes and Tribes in political office at the state and union level a tally of the number of women representatives. Reports have proliferated including a superb piece of documentation entitled *Towards Equality* commissioned in the early 1970s by the Government of India.

Yet have concrete changes grown out of these legislative activities and out of the generally heightened awareness of sex role inequalities? The answer in the Indian case is not dissimilar to that in the United States. Progressive legislation has been diluted by failures in implementation. Whether due to economic constraints or ideological rigidities, the social and economic status of women as a class has remained basically unchanged. Legislation in India as in the United States has deeply affected the lives of individual women. But these individual changes have not collectively amounted to an improvement in the income or occupational position of women as a group.

The ineffectiveness of efforts at reform has been closely documented. Efforts at eradicating the oppressive practice of dowry have met with little success. The report on dowry in *Towards Equality* notes that, "we are compelled to record our findings that the Dowry Prohibition Act of 1961 passed with the ostensible purpose of curbing this evil, if not of eradicating it, has signally failed to achieve its purpose. In spite of the rapid growth of this practice, there are practically no cases reported under the Act. During its tours of all the States, the Committee was informed of only one case that was pending before the court in Kerala, in which the father had filed the complaint only because of the ill-treatment meted out to his daughter."[26]

The study team which investigated women's property rights also concluded that efforts to accord women equal rights of inheritance continued to meet strong resistance. ("68.16% of those surveyed expressed their opinion against girls having some share with their brothers in parental property.")[27] In the area of work force participation, the study notes an overall decline in workers to total female population and in their percentage of the total labor force since 1921.[28] There appears, moreover, to be little change in the occupational differentiation. Two visible developments reported by the Committee include a growing concentration of women in teaching and medicine and a recognition of certain low prestige jobs in the clerical services as particularly suitable for women.[29] Female-male wage differentials in agriculture and industry persist.[30] The Maternity Benefits Act, one highly progressive piece of legislation, is in fact hardly operative. Benefits under this act in factories, for instance, have declined from just under $ 1,00,000 to about $ 78,000 between 1961 and 1969.[31]

But the data which most powerfully documents the ineffectiveness of reform is demographic. The sex ratio, often an indicator of the social and economic desirability of female children as well as the health and economic status of adult women, is presently at a highly skewed 930 females to 1000 males. It has, as Figure 1 records, become increasingly imbalanced over time.

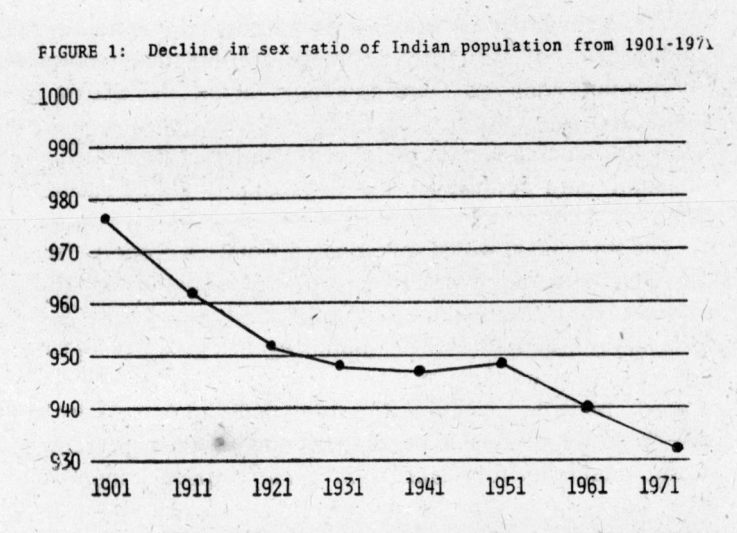

FIGURE 1: Decline in sex ratio of Indian population from 1901-1971

[Line graph showing sex ratio declining from ~977 in 1901 to ~930 in 1971, with data points at 1901, 1911, 1921, 1931, 1941, 1951, 1961, 1971]

Source : "Nutrition, Fertility, and Reproduction," C. Gopalan, National Institute of Nutrition, Hyderabad, p. 14, Table II, as reported in Government of India, Department of Social Welfare, Ministry of Education and Social Welfare, Report of the Committee on the Status of Women in India, *Towards Equality* (New Delhi : Government of India Press, 1974), p. 9.

The ineffectiveness of legislation in changing the overall status of women does not efface the reality that individual women do benefit from specific legislative measures. The 1971 legalization of abortion, the change in marital status rule in civil service recruitment, equal pay legislation, and the liberalization of divorce procedures are all examples of legislation which has benefitted individual women. But the demographic and economic data referred to above give evidence that these changes have not been sufficient to cause a shift in the status of women as a group.

Conclusion

The prominence of women in Indian politics is due more to the visibility of a few women than to the participation of any significant numbers. The prominence of even a few women, however, warrants some explanation. In a society where women are subordinated to men in serious degree, the presence of a woman prime minister or women members of parliament presents something of an anomaly.

The explanation of this anomaly lies primarily in political factors rather than in social configurations. Although it might seem plausible, for instance, to argue that in a highly class-stratified society wealth supersedes sex and that upper-class women might therefore accede more easily to positions of power, this does not appear to be the explanation for the representation of women in elite offices in Indian politics. The access of women to political office in India stems rather from the importance of the nationalist movement and Gandhi's commitment to women's activism, an ideological precept which the post-independence Congress party inherited. The presence of women in office derives also from the pattern of political succession which enhances the role of kinship and thus the possibility for women to inherit office.

The benefit which women as a group derive from the prominence of a few women in leadership positions is insubstantial. There has been an abundance of reformist legislation enacted and awareness of sex inequality seems to have grown, at least within elite circles. The plethora of population, occupational, property and other legislation, moreover, has clearly upgraded the quality of many individual women's lives. But these changes are not indicative of any improvement in the status of women as a whole. If Indira Gandhi and other prominent women have placed India into an atypical category for the study of women *in* politics, an analysis of the impact of politics *on* women brings the study back to a prototypical case of legislative ineffectiveness. In the face of economic constraints and rigidity of traditional custom and attitude, the limits of political reformism are all too clearly revealed.

NOTES

[1] Padma Desai and Jagdish N. Bhagwati, "Women in Indian Elections," in Myron Weiner and John Osgood Field, *Electoral Politics in the Indian States* (Delhi : Manohar Book Service, 1975), p. 165.

[2] *Ibid*. The comment was related to me by an Indian colleague who attended the seminar.

[3] It is impossible to list all the women who played prominent parts in the nationalist movement. The following is a beginning: Women whose activity was not associated with a particular region included Kasturba Gandhi, Kamala Nehru, Begum Attia Habibullah, Nandini Satpathi, Rajendra Kumari Bajpai, Sucheta Kripalani, Tarkeshwari Sinha, Aruna Asaf Ali, Mridula Sarabhai, Man Mohini Sehgal, Lakshmi Devi, Pushpa Gujral, Amar Kaur as well as those mentioned in the text itself. Prominent in Bengal were Besanti Devi, Urmila Devi, Sarla Devi, Lotika Ghosh, and Arunbala Sen; in Punjab, Parvati Devi and Radhe Devi (daughter and wife, respectively, of Lala Lajpat Rai), Bai Zutshi, Smt. Kari Kaur, Atma Devi; in Madras, Muthulakshmi Reddi, Durgabai Deshmukh, Rukmini Lakshmipathi; in Bombay, Kamla devi Chattopadhyaya, Jaishree Raiji, Hansa Mehta, Perin Captain, Maniben Patel, Lilavati Munshi, Usha Mehta; in U.P., Mukund Malaviya, Mandrawati Lakhodpal; in Assum, Kaneck Lata Barua.

[4] Government of India, Department of Social Welfare, Ministry of Education and Social Welfare, *Towards Equality, Report of the Committee on the Status of Women in India* (New Delhi, 1974). This is an extensive documentation of all aspects of women's status. It is an outstanding report.

[5] *Times of India Directory and Yearbook including Who's Who*, 1976 (Bombay: Times of India Press, 1976), p. 673.

[6] *Ibid.*, pp. 674-675.

[7] Comments, not for attribution, were made in the course of interviews the author had with women in Delhi, December 1977. The observation most often made is that because of the rightist element within the Janata, an "obscurantist" view of women has reasserted itself within government circles. While in some sense this is at the level of political "gossip," these observations were too prevalent and uniform to ignore. [Editorial Note: This article was originally published in 1978 during the Janata government.]

[8] *Towards Equality*, p. 209.

[9] *Ibid.*, p. 210.

[10] Kathleen Newland, "Women in Politics: A Global Review," *Worldwatch Paper 3*, December 1975, Appendix B.

[11] See United Nations Publication E/Conf/.66/3, "World Conference of the International Women's Year," pp. 12-13.

[12] Susan S. Wadley, "Women and the Hindu Tradition," in Doranne Jacobson and Susan S. Wadley, *Women in India: Two Perspectives* Delhi: Manohar, 1977), p. 114.

[13] *Ibid.*, p. 117.
[14] *Towards Equality*, p. 40.
[15] Figures on Catholic population from Bruce Russett et al., *World Handbook of Political and Social Indicators* (New Haven: Yale Uuiversity Press, 1967), pp. 249-250.
[16] *Towards Equality*, p. 290.
[17] *Times of India Yearbook*, p. 714.
[18] This study was done by a student at Cornell University, Michael Lombardo, for an undergraduate term paper.
[19] *Keesings Contemporary Archives*, January 20-26, 1975, p. 26932.
[20] Emily E. Werner, "Women in Congress, 1917-1964," *Western Political Quarterly*, March 1964.
[21] *Towards Equality*, p. 295.
[22] Desai and Bhagwati, "Women in Indian Elections," p. 169.
[23] The rights ascribed to Indian women are contained in Article 14, which ensures equality before the law, and Article 15, which empowers the state to make special provision for women and children (a clause which has led to some of the same inequities as protective labor legislation of the 1920s and 1930s in the United States). Article 16(2) forbids discrimination in state employment on grounds of religion, race, caste, sex.
[24] For an account of these legislative acts, see *Towards Equality*. Legislation on equal pay and on divorce is more recent than the report; the divorce legislation was enacted in May 1976. Accounts of the Equal Pay and Divorce legislation are best obtained from newspaper reports.
[25] Target was originally set in 1957.
[26] *Towards Equality*.
[27] *Ibid.*, p. 40.
[28] *Ibid.*, p. 152.
[29] *Ibid.* p. 204.
[30] *Ibid.*
[31] *Ibid.*, pp. 191-192.

Index

Abadi Banu, Begum 11
Abla Abhivardini Samaj 127
Abdullah, Begum 87, 88, 90, 95
Abdullah, Hafiz 173
Abdullah, Sheikh 87, 88, 90, 92, 96, 103
Abolition of *Sati* 109
Adult franchise (*also* adult suffrage) 122, 136
Aftab Ahmed Khan, 103
Aftab Ahmed Khan, Begam 88, 90
'Age of Consent controversy' 80
Age of consent Act 116
'Agnatic theory' 158, 159, 165
Ahmed, Anwar G. 273
Akbar 26
Algerian War of Independence 50
Alice Stone Blackwell 130
Alienation of Land Act 157
Aligarh Girls' College 87, 90, 96, 102
Aligarh Girls' School 87-93, 92, 100
Aligarh movement 97
All Asia's Women's Conference 129
Allen, Lord 134
All India Congress Committee 73, 77
All India Kisan Sabha 226

All India Muslim Ladies Conference (Anjuman-e-Khwatin-e-Islam) 86, 88, 99, 101, 103
All India Sarda Sub-Committee 118, 180
All India Women's Conference (AIWC) 50, 54-63 67, 69-72, 84, 86, 93-102, 104, 118, 121, 123, 130, 135, 137, 201
All Pakistan Women's Association 263, 267, 268, 272-280, 282, 283
Ambarsingh, Maharaj 241
Ameer Ali 95
Amrit Kaur, Rajkumari 73, 118, 119, 123, 136, 137, 140, 149, 287
Amery, Lord 135
Anderson, Sir John 134
Andhra Mahila Sabha 39
Andhra, Movemant 22
Andrews, Charles F. 133, 140
Angelo, Hannah 128
Anjuman-e-Khudan-e-Ka'aba (Society of the servants of the Ka'ba) 12, 89, 90, 91-96, 98-100, 102, 103
Anti-drink campaign 58
Anti-price rise campaign 253
Anti-purdah conference 68
Anti-sati legislation 26

INDEX

Anti-untouchability movement 58
Arbitration council 269 270
Arif, Ghulam Hussain 97
Arif, Sulaiman 97
Arundale, George 126
Ashby, Margery Corbett 237
Ayub Khan, President 263-265 274-281
Azad, Abul Kalam 89

Bandaranaike, Mrs. 296
Basic Democracies System 264
Basavaraju 28, 29
Basu, Aparna 53
Bazm-e-Niswan 204
Begari system 237
Begum of Bhopal 88-90, 100, 102
'Bengal group' 61
Benn, Wegwood 116
Besant, Annie 55, 125-128, 288
Bhagawad-Gita 139
Bhagini Samaj 178, 183
Bhandup incident 187
Bharat Stri Mahamandal 108
Bhil Adivasi Seva Mandal 235
Bhumi Sena and Kashtakari Sangathana in Thana 228
Bhutto, Zulfikar Ali 280
Bilquis, Begum 90
Birla, Rukmini Devi 68
Blavatsky, Helena 125
Blue stocking movement 50
Bokassa, Marshal Bedel 296
Bombay Presidency Women's Conference 180
Bone, James 135
Bose, Subhas Chandra 135, 136
Brahamanical Hinduism 21

Brahmo Samaj 26, 29, 37, 220
Bride price 248
British Committee for Indian Women's Franchise (BCTWF) 122, 136
British rule in Punjab 157
British Unionist Party 165

Captain, Patricia 76
Caxton Hall Conference 116
Central Social Welfare Board 257, 258
Chattopadhyaya, Kamaladevi 60, 74, 128, 288
Chaudhrani, Sarala Devi 106
Chelmsford, Lord 127
Chiang-Kai-Shek 131
Child labour commission 131
Child marriage 49-53, 63-75, 117, 118, 121, 124, 131, 140, 270, 272
Child marriage Restraint Act 63, 116, 270
Child Widowhood 51
Chinese Communist Movement 50
Churchill, (Winston) 139
Civil disobedience 9, 11, 56-59, 62, 102, 116, 134, 183-187, 220
Clan exogamy 154
Clabwalla, Mary 60
Commission on Marriage and family laws 267, 268
Committee on the Status of Women in India 39, 77, 205, 207
Communal Award 60
Communist Parties 217-259, 297

INDEX

Cousin marriage 164
Cousins, James 124, 126
Cousins, Margaret Gillespie 55, 56, 110, 124-129, 137-142, 147, 288
Cripps, Sir Stafford 134

Dass, Bhubananda 119
Dass Amendment Bill 120
Desh mukh Bill 72
Deshmukh, C.D. 71
Deshmukh, C.V. 62
Deshmukh, Durgabai 38
Desh Sevika Sangh 77, 184, 185
Dhulia Movement 233, 254
Din, Malik Muhammad 165, 167, 172
Domitien, Elizabeth 296
Dowry Prohibition Act 208, 298, 299

East India Company 26
Egerton, Sir Robert 152, 157, 159
Emergency 227, 237, 288
Employment opportunities 210

Family Courts 276
Family Planning 280
Faridoonji, Rustomji 288
Fatima, Arru Begum 89, 95
Fawcett, Millicent 112
Federation of Pakisten Chambers of Commerce and Industry (FPCCI) 264
Female, Agricultural Labourers 245, 246, 254
Female Education 38, 51, 55, 56, 63

Female Inheritance 161
Forbes Geraldine 84
Franchise Committee 120, 121
French revolution 62
Fry, Margery 111
Fundamental Rights Bill 277
Fyzee Sisters 89, 91

G.A. Khan, Begum 274, 277
Gandhi-Irwin pact 57
Gandhi, Mrs. (Indira) 135, 286-288, 290, 293, 295-297, 301
Gandhi, Mahatma (M.K.) 10, 13, 52, 53, 55, 58, 60, 67, 69, 70, 73, 96, 116, 130, 132-136, 139, 140, 178, 179, 184, 295, 296, 301
Gauba, K.L. 168
Ghaspure, J.R. 72
Girls' education 27, 33, 35, 36, 40, 91, 182
Goenka, Radhadevi 68
Goer, Hari Singh 63, 71
Gokhle, Avantikabai 178
Gore, Mrinal 227
Government of India Act of 1935 120, 139
Gram Swarajya Samiti 237, 238, 245, 259
Group Marriages 248
Gujars 233
Gujarati Hindu Stree Mandal 178, 180, 183, 184
Gulab Maharaj 233

Halifax, Lord 135
Hammond, Barbara Bradley 111
Harrison, Agatha 108, 118, 128-141

INDEX

Hartog Committee 57
Hartog, Mabel 117
Hazi Musa Khan, Begum 90
Hazra, Matuggiani 220
Hassan, Begum Zeenat Fida 278
Hamid Ali, Begum 61
Heath, Carl 120, 123
Heimsath, Charles 55
Herabai 128
Hindu Code Bill 72-76
Hindu Law Committee 74
Hindu Mahila Samaj 178, 180, 183
Hindu Widow marriage Act 26
Home Rule Bill 125
Home Rule League 55, 56, 125, 128
Home Rule movement 92
House of Commons 138
Hyder, Nazar Sajjad 90

Immoral Traffic Bill 58
'Imported Education' 52
Inamullah Khan, Begum 275
India Conciliation group 120, 133
India League 135
Indian Councils Act 114
Indian Councils Bill 128
Indian National Congress 25, 51, 55, 56, 86, 116, 120, 126, 127, 134, 175
Industrial Development Bank of Pakistan 264
Indo-Muslim Women's Movement 93
Infant marriages 199, 200

Inheritance Laws 7, 156, 164, 166
Intercaste and interreligious marriages 206
International Red Cross 287
International Woman's Suffer-age Alliance 137
Iqbal, Sir Muhammad 161, 164
Irwin, Lord 134
Islamic Council Ideology 276
Ismat 94

Jaijee Raijee 178
Jamait-i-Ulama-i-Hind 173
Janata Government 238
Janata Party 288
Japanese feminist movement 55
Jayakar, M.R. 120
Jha, Manoranjan 65
Jharkhand movement 249
Jinarajadasa, Dorothy 55, 127, 128
Jinnah, Muhammad Ali 63, 68, 167, 173
Joint Action Committee for Resistance Against Price Rise 227
Jones, L.H. Lesile 159
Joshi, M.N. 118
Joshi, M.V. 116
Joshi, N.M. 120
Joshi, Sir Morophant 71
Joshi, V.V. 62, 71, 72
Jumat-ul-Weda 275

Kalra Impartible Estate Bill 172
Karachi Business and Professional Women's Club 267

Karachi resolution 73
Karve, D.K. 127
Khailafat and Smyrna funds 180
Khailafat Movement 8, 99, 103, 105
Khairi, Rushidul 94, 95
Khatun 87, 92
Khediv Jang, Begum 97
Krishna District Social Conference 36
Krishnamurti, J. 126

Labour Commission 132
Lahore High Court 158
Lal Nishan Party 228, 258
Land Alienation Act 158, 159, 165, 166, 171
Land Liberation Rally 235
Land redistribution 224
Lankester, Grace 123
Latif, Baji Rashida 168
Lawrence, Pethick 115
Laxmi, the Rani of Jhansi 175
League for the rights of women 267
League of Nations 136
Left front Government 219, 224, 225, 238, 257
Legal age of marriage 9, 268
Liaquat Ali Khan, Begum, 263, 281
Life, expectancy 207, 208
Linlithgow, Lord 135
Liverpool City Council 138
Liverpool Women's Suffrage Society 112
London School of Economics (LSE) 131
Lothian, Lord 121, 134

MacDonald, Ramsey 134
Madras Anjuman-e-Khawatin-e-Islam 103
Madras Muslim Ladies Association 102
Maharashtra Rajya Shramik Mahila Samiti 227
Maharashtrian Communist movement 220
Mahila Atma Raksha Samiti (MARS) 221, 222
Malaviya, Pandit Madan Mohan 64, 186
Male-female ratio 207, 208
Manchester Guardian 135
Maternity Benefit Act 298, 299
Maya Devi 115
Mayo, Katherine 64, 65, 114, 117
Mazumdar, Vina 53
Mehta, Hansa 74, 186
Mehta, Jamnadas 134
Mehta, Usha 175
Menon, Lakshmi 118, 123, 287
Mies, Maria 52
Migration 250
Minimum age of marriage 116
Missionary education 31
Mitter, D.N. 72
Montagu, Edwin 55, 92, 106
Mortality rates 208
Muhammad Ali 12
Muhammad Ishaq Khan, Begum 90
Muhammad Rafi, Begum 93
Muhammadan Educational Conference 87-90, 96

INDEX

Mukherjee, Ila 70
Mukherjee, Charulata 72
Mukherjee, Kanak 258
Munshi, Lila Wati 185
Muslim girls' education 89
Muslim League 13, 60, 85, 88, 103, 167, 169
Muslim Marriage and Family Law Ordinance 273
Muslim nationalism 71
Muslim Personal Law (Shariat) Application Act 168, 169
Muslim women's education 93

Nafis Dulhan accelato 88, 96-103
'Nafis Dulhan Conference' 99
Naidu, Sarojini 11, 13, 39, 58, 61, 73, 121, 128, 137, 140, 149, 178, 181, 185, 287
National Christian Council of India 131
National Council of Women in India 137
National Girl's School 180
National Social Welfare Board 222
National Trade Union Federation 134
National Union of Societies for Equal Citizenship (NUSEC) 112-115, 129, 137, 138
National Union of Women's Suffrage Societies (NUWSS) 112, 132, 138
Nehru, Jawaharlal 59, 73, 75, 123, 132, 135, 139, 140

Nehru, Kamala 135
Nehru, Motilal 63, 65
Nehru, Rameshwari 74
'New feminism' 113

Omvedt, Gail 52, 53
Open Door Council 149

Pakistan Industrial Credit and Investment Corporation 264
Pakistan movement 85, 103
Paisa Akhbar 162
Palestinian movement 50
Pandit, Vijayalakshmi 73, 287
Pankhurst, Emmeline 112
Pankhurst, Sylvia 115
Partition of Bengal 110
Partition of India 85
Parulekar, Godavari 227
Pashchim Bangla Ganatantrik Mahila Samiti 224, 225
Pashchim Bangala Mahila Samiti 222
Patel, Vallabhbhai 186
Patilwadi incident 235
Paulson, joy 50
Perraon, Mrs. 296
Pickford, Mary 121
Plowden, Sir Meredyth 158
Polak, Henry 119
Political representation of Women 297
Political status of Women 293
Polygamy 95, 96
Power, Beryl 132, 140
Prabhu, Mrs. Kamalabai 186
Prarthana Samaj 29, 37
Pre-emption Act (1906) 157, 171

Prenter, N. Honcock 171
Preventive Detention Act 222
Price, E.L. 65
Privy Council 158
Punjab Anjuman-e-Khawatin 103
Punjab Legislative Council 165
Purdah 8, 50, 53, 63, 66-70, 75, 87, 92, 95, 99-101, 103, 136
Pye, Lucien 20

Qadir, Lady Abdul 59, 67, 70, 72
Quit India movement 220
Quran, 63, 95, 268, 270, 272, 277

Radhakrishnan 59
Rahman, Fazlur 268, 272
Rahmatunnissa, Begum 60, 102
Rajamundry 21
Rajwade, Rani Lakshmibai 72 288
Ramdas Maharaj 233, 235
Ranade, Ramabai 288
Ranganeker, Ahilya 227
Rao, Raghunath 32
Rashtriya Stree Sabha 77, 180, 185, 186
Rathbone, Eleanor 65, 110-129, 134-142, 149
Rathigan, W.H. 159, 160
Rau, Benegal Narsing 72
Rau Committee 72-75
Rau, Dhanvanthi Rana 115
Rau, Kitty Shiva 74
Ray, Renuka 72, 74
Ray, Sarala 123

Reddi, Dr. Muthulakshmi 57, 58, 68-70, 118, 119, 122, 128, 136, 288
Remarriage of Hindu Widows 27
Representation of Women 290
Ripon reforms 29
Risley, Sir Herbert Hope 52
Robertson, Sir Frederik 159
Roe, Sir Charles 158
Rohatgi, Shshila T. 288
Round Table Conferences 57, 73, 134
Royal Commission on Labour 132
Royal Irish Academy of Music 124
Royden, Dr. Maude 131
Roy, Ram Mohun 26, 109, 111
Rustomji, Hilla 60
Ryotwari System in Maharashtra 219, 246, 251

Sakhawat Hussain Memorial School 97
Sakhawat Hussain, Mrs. 97, 98
Salt Satyagraha 184
Sammata Sammelan 239, 259
Sandra, Danforth 50
Sankaracharya 32
Sapru, Tej Bahadur 120, 135, 139
Sarabhai, Mridula 74
Saraswati Mahila Samaj 180, 183, 184
Sarda Act 63, 116, 117, 119
Sarda, Har Bilas 62-66, 71, 116

INDEX

Sarvodaya Sangh 235
Sasson, Sir Victor 132
Sastri, Sivanath 19
Sati 26, 51, 200
Satyagraha Movement 10
Sayyid Mahmud, Begum 88, 88
Sayyid, Mumtaz Ali 96
Self-determination 6, 8
Self-Employment 252
Self-Employed Women's Association 203
Self rule 110, 120
Sen, Hannah 114
Sen, Sushma 136
Servants of India Society 118
Sex Ratio 208
Shafi, Mian Mohammad 93, 96, 103, 158
Shahada Movement 237, 240, 242, 249
Shah Din, Begum 89, 91, 93
Shanghai International Settlement 131
Shah Nawaz, Begum 93, 103, 149
Shareefah, Hamid Ali 118, 123, 136
Shriat 160-162, 164-168
Shriat Bill 173
Sharif Bibi 89, 95
Shenai, Vilasini Devi 74
Sherwani, Habibur Rahman Khan 90, 103
Shramik Sangatha 218, 237-244, 248, 249, 251, 254-256, 259, 260
Shramik Sangathana in Thana 228
Shri Sarada Samaj 180

Simon Commission 57, 115, 117, 119, 121, 128, 129
Sitamma, K. 36
Social and Political Alliance 149
Socialist Party 227
Society of friends 131, 133
Sounakar, Sri Dada Sahib 235
Storrow, Reverend E. 51
Stri-Dharma 54, 126
Subbarayan, Radhabhai 73
Suffrage Movement 92
Sultana, Princess Abida 266
Suratvanti, Amber Singh 237
Swadeshi Movement 9, 179, 181, 185
Swaraj 61, 76
Sylvia 112

Tata Herabal 114, 128
Tata, Lady Mehrbai Dorab 114
Tata, Mathan 128
Tahzib-e-Niswan 89, 95, 96, 99
Tagore, Rabindra Nath 123, 133
Tebhaga Movement 221, 222, 257
'The Latrine Queen' 132
Theosophical Movement 37
Theosophical Society 31, 35, 124, 125, 130
The Secret Doctrine 124
Times, the 113, 122
Third Godavary Social Conference 36
Tilak, B.G. 8, 116
Tilak Swaraj fund 180
Tinker, Hugh 134
Tiwana, Umar Hyat Khan 172
Tupper, C.L. 153-157, 159, 163

Turkish War of Independence 50
Twenty-point programme 237

Unionist Party 166, 168, 169
United Front Government in West Bengal 225, 255
Untouchability 73
United Nations 290
U.S. Bill of Rights 298

Vakil 162
Vallance, Elizabeth 121
Viresalingam 28-32, 36, 37, 39

Wadley, Susan 292
Wallach, William 119
Werner, Emmy E. 296
Whitley, J.H. 132
Whytle, Alexander (Mrs) 133, 146
Widow education 201
Widow immolation (*see* Sati)
Widow Marriage Association 29, 30
Widow marriage campaign in Madras 31
Widow marriage movement 20-23, 35, 36, 51, 73, 83, 84, 86, 87, 199, 201
Wilkinson, Ellen 115
Willingdon, Lord 117
Wintringham, Margaret 122
Women political leaders 288

Women's demand's day 272
Women's education 54, 58, 87-89, 92, 93, 99, 101
Women's employment 202, 211, 218, 247
Women's franchise 139
Women's India Association (WIA) 50, 54-58, 63, 67, 69, 70, 84, 92, 93, 128-130, 184
Women's International League 132
Women's International Suffrage Alliance 113
Women's rights 55, 56, 58, 64, 66, 71, 72, 73, 75, 83, 86, 87, 103, 104, 151, 277
Women's Social and Political Union (WSPU) 112
Women's Suffrage 56, 59
Women's Swadeshi League 78
Women's Year 205
World War I 92, 96
World War II 134

Young India 68
Young Men's Christian Association (YMCA) 132, 139
Yuvarani Saheda of Pithapuram 61

Zakat 282
Zamindari System 219, 251
Zia-ul-Haq, General 280

HQ1743 .E95X

WITHDRAWN
From Bertrand Library